About the author

Frank Navratil BSc. N.D. was born of Czech parents in Vancouver, Canada where he completed a degree in physiology and nutrition. In the 1990's he moved to Sydney, Australia where he studied alternative medicine, iridology and clinical nutrition before practicing as a naturopath, iridologist, and nutritionist. Since 1997, he has lived in Prague, the Czech Republic where he currently runs a natural therapy practice, produces a natural health Internet magazine, and directs the Return to Health International College of Natural Medicine.

Frank has given countless lectures both in Europe and in Australia on the subject of iridology and nutrition. He has also appeared on several television and radio programs to talk about natural means of diagnosing and dealing with disease. His first book, "For Your Eyes Only" has been translated into several languages. He is the author of a number of article series on iris diagnosis and nutrition that have been published in natural medicine and health magazines in Australia and Europe.

He has worked, too, in Ethiopia where he studied the effects of malnutrition and he is presently cooperating with an Ethiopian Aid agency to fund the development of an Education Center for the prevention of disease there.

His practice is based on natural holistic methods that allow the body to heal itself. These include iridology, nutrition, vitamin and mineral treatment, Bowen therapy, and diet and lifestyle changes.

THE EYE FOR AN EYE DIET

Your New Beginning

Frank Navratil, BSc. N.D.

The revolutionary ground-breaking dietary program based on your eye type

10 genetic eye constitutions, 10 nutritional programs

The information contained in this book is for educational purposes only and is not intended for use in the diagnosis of an individual or health condition except by a qualified health practitioner. The health advice and recommendations in this book are based on many years of research and experience by the author. As every person and situation is unique, the author and publisher advise to first consult with a health professional before following any of the recommended diets. The author and publisher are not responsible for any adverse effects claimed from using any of the suggested health advice or procedures in this book.

All Rights Reserved. No part of this publication may be reproduced, stored in a retrieval system, or transmitted in any form by any means: electronic, mechanical, photocopying, recording, or otherwise, without the prior written permission of the copyright owner.

Published by Frank Navratil, BSc. N.D.
Return to Health Books
Kojetická 977
Neratovice
Czech Republic
First Edition
All eye photographs by Frank Navratil, BSc. N.D.
© 2003 by Frank Navratil
ISBN 80-239-0285-7

THE ROAD NOT TAKEN

Two roads diverged in a yellow wood,
And sorry I could not travel both
And be one traveler, long I stood
And looked down one as far as I could
To where it bent in the undergrowth;

Then took the other, as just as fair,
And having perhaps the better claim,
Because it was grassy and wanted wear;
Though as for that, the passing there
Had worn them really about the same,

And both that morning equally lay
In leaves no step had trodden black.
Oh, I kept the first for another day!
Yet knowing how way leads on to way,
I doubted if I should ever come back.

I shall be telling this with a sigh
Somewhere ages and ages hence:
Two roads diverged in a wood, and I –
I took the one less traveled by,
And that has made all the difference.

Robert Frost

Contents

Acknowledgments 6
Preface 7
Introduction 11
- Wake up! Old diets are dead. It is time to implement sound nutritional principles 12
- Shatter your Illusions 13
- It's what you do with what you have that counts! Genotype and Phenotype 14
- Lessons from the old and wise- The Hunza, Eskimos and other cultures 16
- Unlock the secrets that your eyes reveal 18
- Genetic Eye Constitutions – An Introduction 19
- About the Eye for an Eye Diet 20
- The Eye for an Eye Diet Program- 10 (Not so Easy) Steps 21
- Sad Excuses and Job Descriptions 21

Part One: The 10 Essential "Eye for an Eye Diet" Principles to live and (never) die by 23

The First Principle:	You are not normal 24
The Second Principle:	Your health depends on 7 essential processes of life 26
The Third Principle:	Treat the cause not just the symptoms 31
The Fourth Principle:	Holistic health is for the "hole" person 33
The Fifth Principle:	Your eyes are your connection to your nutritional needs 39
The Sixth Principle:	Get addicted to Healthy foods, the greatest drugs around 40
The Seventh Principle:	Make Lifestyle changes; don't shock the body with Crash Diets 42
The Eighth Principle:	Go natural and you can't go wrong 43
The Ninth Principle:	Change with the demands of your body 45
The Tenth Principle:	Get your foot off the brakes! 47

Part Two: "Eye for an Eye Diet" Nutrition – From the Ground Up 49

- **Chapter 1** – The Origin of Living Food 50
- **Chapter 2** – Get into your CELL 53
- **Chapter 3** – The Macronutrients: Carbohydrates, Proteins and Fats 56
- **Chapter 4** – Vitamins: Micronutrients for maintenance of growth and health 65

Chapter 5 – Minerals: Micronutrients for fine-tuning and building a healthy body 74
Chapter 6 – Water: The Fountain of Youth 80
Chapter 7 – Fiber- The essential garbage-disposal nutrient 85
Chapter 8 – Food Group choices: Is the traditional food pyramid valid? 92
Chapter 9 – Factors that affect the nutritional value of foods 98
Chapter 10 – Food contaminants 104
Chapter 11 – What has been added to your food lately? 108
Chapter 12 – Foods that Steal 114
Chapter 13 – Food Addictions 120
Chapter 14 – Foods that Heal 128
Chapter 15 – Contemporary Issues in Human Nutrition 135
Chapter 16 – Nutritional Supplements 142
Chapter 17 – Restricted Diets 151
Chapter 18 – Exercise- The essential nutrient your body cannot live without 156
Chapter 19 – Eye for an Eye Diet Nutritional Advice Summary 162

Part Three: The Eye for an Eye Diet Genetic Action Plan
10 Individual Genetic Eye Constitutions-10 Nutritional Programs 167

Chapter 1 – What are Genetic Eye Constitutions? 168
Chapter 2 – Brown and Blue Eyes 171
Chapter 3 – How to identify your Genetic Eye Constitution 173

Photographs of Individual Genetic Eye Constitutions 177

Chapter 4 – The Ten "Eye for an Eye Diet" Genetic Eye Constitutions 193
Chapter 5 – Specific Nutrition for Genetic Eye Constitutions 203
Chapter 6 – The Eye for an Eye Diet and Suggested Healthy Eating plans by Genetic Eye Constitution 223

Part Four: The Eye for an Eye Diet for Specific Health Problems 229

Chapter 1 – The Eye for an Eye Diet for Weight loss or Gain 230
Chapter 2 – The Eye for an Eye Diet for Diseases of Modern Civilization 237
Chapter 3 – The Eye for an Eye Diet as we Age and Change 275

Conclusion: Your new beginning 287
The Eye for an Eye Diet- Quick Reference Genetic Nutrition Tables 291
Other books, iridology and nutrition education products, courses etc… 301
Index 302

Acknowledgements

As always I would like to thank my mother, Ludmila Navratil, whose lengthy illness and death from cancer several years ago, motivated me to become interested in nutrition, alternative medicine and iridology and share my experience with others.

I would also like to thank all the thousands of my past patients for their belief and support as from them, I have learned a great deal about nutritional therapy in combination with what I have seen in their eyes. The sharing of their health has given me an abundance of research material so that I could write this book.

I would like to thank all the iridologists and nutritionists of the past who have inspired me to continue in this great science and who have permitted me to learn and endeavor to expand upon their pioneering work.

I would like to thank Hanka Kopecká once again for her continued love, patience and understanding while I labored at the time-consuming task of writing my second book.

I would like to thank the late Dr. Bernard Jensen, who has always inspired me to believe that the body can heal itself through nutrition.

Lastly, I would like to thank you, my readers, for coming aboard, for taking a chance and for joining me in the effort to lead a healthy, productive and satisfying life.

Preface

Hello and welcome to my book, The Eye for an Eye Diet. You know I don't know you all or even a small fraction of you for that matter, but I honestly do care about every single one of you because I believe that you all have the ability to achieve the best that life can offer. Your role in life is unique to anyone else in the world and the path you take on the road back to health is very much under your direct control, if you just grab the reins.

As I begin to write this book, the thought of what your expectations may be, crosses my mind. You have obviously purchased this book or somehow it has come into your hands at one moment or one place in time that is unique to each one of you. Something had attracted you to pick this book amongst the hundreds of thousands that exist. Perhaps in it you have seen a glimmer of hope, a chance to learn to take control of your life and your health once again. For giving me that chance I thank each one of you. I will try my very best of what I know and what I have experienced to show you the path back to where I believe each one of us has the ability to reach: the path back to true optimum health.

One of the main reasons that I decided to write this book is that I am, perhaps like you, sick and tired of miracle cures and remedies, get fit quick schemes, and overnight crash weight-loss programs that promise the world with the least amount of effort and time. You know, as attractive as these schemes appear, I sincerely hope that you have learned by now that they just don't work. If you are looking for a way to lose weight or cure your disease overnight, then this book is not for you! Since each one of us is genetically different in physical structure and mental capabilities, each of us reacts to diets and treatments in their own individual way and in their own sweet time, you might say. That is what makes each one of us different and that is what presents the greatest challenge in our health system today.

If however, you are prepared to welcome a new intelligent change or approach to your health problems, and are willing to learn about your individual body's needs, your genetics and apply sound nutritional principles that may take a lot of discipline and work, then you have made the right decision to read this book.

I imagine that each one of you has different expectations from reading this book. Some of you want to lose weight; others have critical health problems such as cancer, diabetes, or other modern civilization problems that plague our society today and for which there is currently no cure by conventional medicine. Perhaps many of you just want to learn a little more about your health and about nutrition that can prevent problems in the future. This is how we all need to think because eventually our bodies will break down, it all depends on our genetic make-up, and we need to compensate for organ weaknesses in our bodies with appropriate nutrition and lifestyle habits so that potential health problems can be overcome. You see your health is your greatest asset and it needs care and maintenance throughout the course of your entire life. Most of us claim that health is the most important gift that we possess but very few take it seriously. Very few of us invest in our health and have the discipline to carry it through. It is usually only when serious health problems appear that we are sometimes prepared to alter our lifestyles or change our diet. We all act like we will live forever but our lifestyle habits usually do not reflect that behavior. Your health, as do the requirements of your body during your life, change. We must be prepared to monitor our health status and adjust to our body's needs as we pass through childhood, adolescence, adulthood, pregnancy, or old age.

Modern medical practices have focused on drug therapy for the host of problems that we suffer from today with the aim of destroying the offending bacteria or agent in our bodies. Yet very few ask the question, why is our body allowing this bacteria or virus to cause infections and diseases? You see if it was not for our sophisticated immune system, we would not be alive as the number of disease producing bacteria around us is always present. It seems much more intelligent and logical therefore, to strengthen this system through natural methods instead of wasting countless millions of dollars inventing new drugs or antibiotics. Yet every day doctors will attempt to convince us that this is the only path to take and unfortunately and often because of fear we succumb to what I call a very primitive system of treatment. This primitive system of treatment has taught us to treat the symptoms of our disease and not the underlying causes. We need to get at the root of our health problems so that we can cure not just treat our diseases.

Many of you at this point may feel quite disappointed with our current health system and discouraged that our health professionals have not come up with adequate medicinal cures for our diseases. Many of us have the tendency to blame our doctors and therapists when our health problems are not taken care of, but at the same time we are not prepared to invest in our own health, to learn about our bodies, or to do the necessary work to return to health. We are lazy, and unwilling to accept that only we are responsible for our own bodies, we cannot place the blame on others. Once we can accept this fact, the road ahead becomes clear. We alone, are masters of our destiny and the power to change lies only within us.

The Eye for an Eye Diet

Where do we start? The first step is to keep an open mind. A closed mind learns nothing. We need to drastically change the way we view our world and to see things with a new perspective. As we know, it is very easy to get caught up in a set way of thinking but it often leads to being unable to welcome new changes. Change is the only way we can learn and change is what this book is all about. As you read, try to place what you may have been taught all your life aside and as difficult as it may be, allow yourself to welcome new ideas. Think about how mankind usually finds it quite difficult to change. We are still killing ourselves in wars, and still battling for money, power and fame instead of cooperating with one another on this planet. Have we really learned anything new? We are still behaving in a primitive way yet we boast about our technical advancements. Have we really learned from our mistakes of the past? Do we really think that we can artificially speed up the healing process in our bodies, that which is set by our genetic make-up, with foreign unnatural drugs? Do we really believe that we can fool our bodies? We cannot fool our bodies we can only fool ourselves. We try to fool our bodies everyday with the host of drugs we take from laxatives for our constipation problems, aspirin for our headaches, anti-cold remedies, antibiotics etc, not to mention the thousands of chemical additives that we throw into our foods. Most of us do not however associate these health problems with our diets or what we consume everyday. Our bodies have become like a chemical processing factory with the amount of artificial substances that we ingest. It is not surprising that we just don't function that well anymore, our organs just can't keep up and that so many health problems like cancer, diabetes, obesity and chronic fatigue are creeping up in our society.

I wrote this book to encourage you to view your health with a new perspective. My many years of study and research in Iridology, the art and science of analysis of health status by reading signs in the human iris have enabled me to accumulate an enormous database of information on human health and human genetics. Using the wonderful science of Iridology or Iris diagnosis as it is commonly called and viewing our eyes can unlock many health secrets to our genetic make-up. We are not born with perfect genes. We inherit weaknesses in our body organs from our parents, grandparents and so on. These weaknesses will eventually end up as some kind of disease at some point in our lives. Analyzing what type of eye constitution you have can unveil what health problems you may encounter. I repeatedly observe tendencies to similar health problems in my patients who have similar genetic eye constitutions and these tendencies can be predicted even from an early age. My work with nutrition and iridology has produced significant health improvements in these patients. What does this mean for you? It means that if you can learn more about what kind of genetic eye constitution you have, you will have much greater power to understand your body and to solve your health problems.

The Eye for an Eye Diet is about learning sound nutritional principles, identifying your genetic eye constitution and targeting specific nutrition to strengthen genetic weaknesses so that health problems can be alleviated or prevented. It respects the fact that what works for one person will not always work the same on the other. In a nutshell, The Eye for an Eye Diet respects that we have individual differences. It is not an overnight miracle cure or a radical crash diet that produces only short-term results but it offers an intelligent method to assist the individual body to heal itself through the natural means of nutrition. If your body is able to heal itself then you will be able to maintain ideal body weight much more easily as well as eliminate potential chronic health problems and diseases not just temporarily, but for a lifetime.

The question often asked is why should we strive to be healthy and fit? Why, when our final outcome is inevitable? That is a good question, which sooner or later we all face at some time in our lives. I call this the motivational barrier, that which applies the brakes and prevents us from reaching our goals. Ask yourself why you want to be healthy? Ask yourself why you have not done anything about it lately? If you know the answers, and are willing to make a change then you are ready to begin the journey. You are already half way there to achieving true and optimum health. Welcome to that journey of understanding how our bodies work and how keeping an eye on our eyes can unlock some of the hidden mysteries to our health.

Welcome to the Eye for an Eye Diet. Achieving health the way nature has always intended.

Frank Navratil BSc. N.D.

THE EYE FOR AN EYE DIET

INTRODUCTION

What does health mean to you? To you it may mean being able to live the life you choose without any obstacles or barriers, to be able to achieve your goals and dreams, or to be the very best that you can be. Without health you are not able to enjoy what life has to offer. A weakened or unhealthy body is prone to disease and deterioration, which means that you age faster, you begin to look older, you become less attractive and you begin to lose the sparkle in your eyes. An unhealthy body affects your mind, your emotions, your motivations and your sense of peace and happiness within you. An unhealthy mind is more prone to psychological disorders, depression, anxiety or neuroses. As you lose motivation and begin to feel down on yourself, you begin to lose yourself, you begin to falter off the path that you initially set on and this again affects your physical health, you gain weight, you stop exercising and eating right and soon you just cannot get off the merry-go-round. Your health or should I say lack of health has now taken control of you instead of you grabbing hold of the reins and taking control. Do you see what I mean? I call this the **empty merry-go-round syndrome**. You keep going around in circles but you don't get ahead any further and keep repeating the same mistakes. It's time to get off the merry-go-round and take charge of your own health.

In order to prepare for what you need to learn about your health and your own body it is important to clarify some misconceptions, to learn a little about what your eyes can reveal about your genetics, to throw away some of those sad excuses and take a general look at what the Eye for an Eye Diet Program can offer.

Wake up! Old diets are dead. It's time to implement sound nutritional principles.

I sincerely hope that those old diets and remedies that we have heard about so much in the past that promise anything from quickly losing mass weight to healing chronic problems in a matter of weeks are long dead. The body just does not work that way. We need to think in terms of long-term not short-term strategies. This approach of course is not as attractive to us because in our day-to-day lives we are used to finding quick cures that make our symptoms go away or fad diets that have immediate results. Often we find that we do lose weight but we gain it back quickly and with this kind of cyclic dieting we end up worse than when we started. If we starve ourselves and eat less, our metabolism learns to slow down and when we get off our crash diet, we find that we gain back all the weight we lost plus more. Further when we crash diet we usually deprive the body of essential nutrients, those same nutrients that are needed to metabolize fats, carbohydrates and proteins. It is true that we do eat too much and consume more calories than we generally need but a sound nutritional program is needed that caters to our genetic make-up to really achieve long-term results. Prescription drugs are another great example of the effect of short-term treatments. Our pain or our symptoms are relieved but they just keep cropping up again and again. What becomes worse however is that the constant suppression of our common ailments can often lead to serious degenerative diseases in the future.

We need to think in terms of lifestyle changes and not just try a diet for a few weeks and then return back to our old unhealthy habits. The Eye for an Eye Diet is about making responsible lifestyle changes and for most people, that is not that easy to do. Through my years of experience with nutrition and disease, I have found that at least 90 percent of all health problems in our modern civilization can be eliminated by sound nutritional practices alone. This means without any medication or drug. When you look at it, we have an extremely powerful method at our disposal to combat and prevent disease!

Shatter your illusions

There are many illusions that we have in regards to our health practices. Some have been passed on through the generations and some have been indoctrinated into our educational institutions. It is time to take a look at those longheld beliefs that we cannot seem to let go of and see things with a new perspective. Ask yourselves if you hold any of these illusions below:

Illusion Number 1: Chemicals and drugs will cure my disease and have no long-term effects on my health.
Illusion Number 2: Crash diets will help me lose and maintain weight.
Illusion Number 3: Lifestyle habits have no influence on my health.
Illusion Number 4: I live in a safe and responsible world that is concerned about my health.
Illusion Number 5: If I feel no symptoms, that means that I am cured.
Illusion Number 6: I can stay healthy and maintain ideal body weight without any work.
Illusion Number 7: Everyone reacts to diet programs the same way.
Illusion Number 8: Overnight miracle cures and diets exist.
Illusion Number 9: The physical health we inherit cannot be influenced or altered.
Illusion Number 10: If everyone would eat the same healthy foods, we would all be without health problems.
Illusion Number 11: Manufacturers of foods are concerned about our long-term state of health.
Illusion Number 12: It is my doctor's or therapist's fault if my disease is not cured.
Illusion Number 13: The most important thing is to find out what diseases that you have.

Illusion Number 14: The long-term aim of dealing with health problems is to kill germs, eradicate bacteria and remove tumors or faulty body organs through operations.

Illusion Number 15: Healthy means being free of major symptoms of diseases with the occasional cold or flu, periodic stomach problems, constipation, sore throat, fatigue or skin problem.

Illusion Number 16: It is possible to achieve optimal health with **only** good nutrition.

Illusion Number 17: Diseases like cancer and diabetes can be inherited.

Illusion Number 18: The bodies I see on television are indicative of what a normal body should look like.

Make sure that you read each of the above illusions carefully. We will come back and discuss them from time to time during the course of this book.

Genotype and Phenotype – It's what you do with what you have that counts!

What influences our health? That is the question of the millennium. There are just so many factors but we can break them down into two major variables: our genotype and phenotype. Our **genotype** or genetic make-up is what is handed down to us through the generations by our parents, grandparents, great grandparents and so on. If you have been one of the rare lucky ones and have been blessed with strong genes then you will begin life with great advantage but the battle is far from over yet. It's what you do with what you have that counts! Your **phenotype** is what you have control over and is developed by influences such as the type of environment you live in, your diet and any physical or emotional events that you experience. So what I'm saying is that you may start your life as a brand new car but if you don't tune it up or change the oil when needed, it won't last much after the warranty! If you are one in the majority who start life with average genes or what I call a used car and you put a bit of work and investment in it, you have a chance to outlast your shiny new self-abusive rival! Do you see what I am getting at?

Our genotype and phenotype together influence our health status. Now it comes down to what we have in our control. When we mention genetics, most of you believe that the genes we inherit are fixed and beyond our control. To a certain degree this may be true but we are constantly evolving and our genes are changing. That means that what we do with what we have during our lives will not only influence our own health but also that of our children and their children and so on. I do not believe that we inherit diseases. We only inherit weak organs or systems in our bodies that predispose us to those diseases. This is a very important concept to understand. I commonly hear statements such as "my mother had diabetes and her mother had diabetes as well and now I have diabetes. It must run in the family." Sure, this lady may have inherited weakness in her pancreas or liver or other systems in the body that led to her diabetes but I do not believe that she inherited the disease. Did she make any diet or lifestyle changes? Nine times out of ten, we tend to carry on the same diet and lifestyle as our parents. We have to learn about our bodies and make a change for the better. It is only in this way that we can break the cycle and improve the next generation. Although we may not be able to change our predispositions to certain ailments, we can certainly influence them in a positive way so that they occur less frequently or even not at all.

Our **phenotype** however is our best chance to improve our chance of survival. In most cases it is entirely under our control. Some may claim that stress caused by others around us cannot be controlled nor our environment that we live in but these are all subjective arguments. If we analyze our individual situations carefully, we soon find that even those factors that we believe cannot be changed are under our control but we often choose not to deal with them. Our phenotype as mentioned are all those influences that affect our health after we are born. As a baby you cannot choose whether you prefer mother's milk to formula but your mother can make that decision which as many studies have shown can dramatically affect the future health status of the child. The environment that we live in greatly affects our health. Diet, which is the main theme of this book, is one of the most important influences on our phenotype. There are many other influences on our phenotype including every physical or psychological event that occurs during our lives.

Some negative influences that can weaken our genetic make-up include malnutrition, excess alcohol, starvation, pollution, drugs, cigarette smoking, depression, stress, radiation, inactivity, obesity and lack of sunlight. Some positive influences that can strengthen our genetic make-up include quality nutrition, living in a clean environment, regular exercise, natural drug-free medicine, fresh air and sunlight, positive thinking, balance and good moral behavior.

It is important to realize that we are not born perfect. Each of our bodies comes with an expiry date. This expiry date depends on our genetic make-up (genotype) and what we do during our lives (phenotype) that will influence our health in a positive or a negative way.

We will soon learn about our genetic make-up and what it will take to influence it in a positive way so that we can achieve the optimum health that we deserve.

Frank Navratil BSc. N.D.

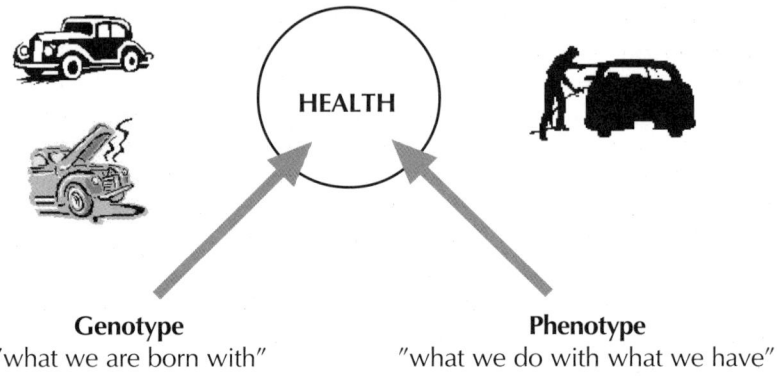

Genotype
"what we are born with"

Phenotype
"what we do with what we have"

Lessons from the old and wise The Hunza, Eskimos and other cultures

Much of what we have learned about nutrition has been through comparisons of different cultural practices around the world. By analyzing the rates of incidence of a variety of diseases, scientists have been able to provide many correlations between diet and disease. This demonstrates how important it is to learn from other cultures and there are a few that are especially worthy to mention.

There are only a few places on Earth where people routinely live to over 120 years of age in good health with virtually no cancer or bone or tooth problems, and where they retain their vitality and strength being able to bear children even in old age. The most famous of these are probably the Hunza of Pakistan. High concentrations of centenarians, or those that live over 100 years old are also found in Abkhazia in the former Soviet Union and in some areas of Bulgaria. Over the years, scientists have endeavored to uncover their secrets of their fountain of youth. Some theories claim that their long lives come from strong genes, others attribute their vitality to natural living, clean water, mountain air and moderate consumption of food.

Studies on Eskimos in Greenland revealed that despite a diet that was over 50 percent fat, they still enjoyed extremely low rates of cardiovascular disease leading to studies on Omega-3 fatty acids from fish and their health benefits for heart disease. Once these Eskimos began to change to a Western diet, rates of heart disease increased to those similar to western cultures. The Japanese, especially those that live near the sea also enjoy low levels of heart disease often attributed to their high fish intake and they enjoy one of the longest life spans in the world.

The rates of other diseases and health conditions are also not the same in all parts of the world. The Bantu of Africa have the lowest rates of osteoporosis of any culture, yet they consume an incredible low amount of calcium daily. Studies have shown that the countries that consume little or no dairy products had the lowest levels of osteoporosis. What does this say about what we have always heard; don't milk products build strong bones? Research is finding the exact opposite. It is important to keep an open mind and remember one of those illusions that we often have, that food manufacturers are concerned about our long-term state of health.

Studies in Eastern Africa have found that problems like obesity, diabetes, appendicitis, diverticulosis, and cancer of the colon barely exist in these countries. What are Western cultures doing wrong since these are the very health conditions that are currently growing at the fastest pace?

What about menopause? Did you know that Asian women report far fewer hot flashes than western women do? Did you know that in India, depression, incontinence, dizziness and other symptoms during menopause are almost unknown? Less than 5% of Chinese women report menopausal symptoms. Mayan women in Mexico report no menopausal symptoms except irregular periods and women in Botswana, Africa report no menopausal symptoms except increased sex drive.

The Czech Republic has one of the highest rates of diabetes and colon cancer in Europe. Could this be attributed to years of communist regime where fruits and vegetables were scarce, meat and dumplings were the staple diet, and wholegrain bread was almost non-existent?

The American population has claimed the highest rates of obesity in the world with almost half the population found to be overweight. This is not surprising, as the number of fast-food outlets and intake of low-nutritious processed foods have increased significantly over the years.

Why are there so many discrepancies? What are the reasons? One cannot help but come to the conclusion that the greatest reasons for these variations are related to diet and nutrition.

In our fast-paced high technology world we have forgotten the basics. We cannot fool Mother Nature no matter how hard we try. Altering her course and living un-naturally has devastating consequences for our society and our health. Maybe those few lucky people who live in the last remaining natural uncivilized environments are our last chance to learn about the secrets of health. Perhaps we will one day learn that in order to live a long and healthy life, such as the Hunza, we must learn to live in association with nature. I have seen many health professionals who have ridiculed the use of natural healing methods such as nutrition and in their own arrogant manner continue to prescribe chemical drugs despite the ill effects felt by their patients. I can't help to think of those lost cultures like the Hunza who never had the opportunity to study at medical school or to learn how to use sophisticated instruments or high technology diagnostic tools, yet are in many ways much further ahead than our modern society is with regards to health. We cannot rely on our medical professionals to take care of us; we need to take responsibility for our own health. Listening to TV commercials that advertise the latest health food craze, or mass advertising campaigns that push the health benefits of certain foods are certainly not an intelligent way to learn the truth about nutrition. They do not have your health in their mind, but unfortunately the almighty buck. I feel the best and most reliable way to learn the truth about nutrition is to learn from different cultures, from experience and from the old and wise.

Unlock the secrets that your eyes reveal

We have often heard the term that the eyes are the windows to the soul. We use our eyes to capture images of the world around us, but we also use them to communicate our emotions, expressions and passions. We can often tell if someone is lying, angry, in love or not well by what we see in the eyes. The eyes are a wonderful tool that we have been given but they are much more amazing than most of us realize. To the average person, a look into the eyes involves usually taking notice of only one characteristic: color. We know what color of eyes that we have as well as those of our loved ones. Have you ever noticed clouds or markings in the iris of your eyes? Have you ever thought that what is seen in the eyes can reveal a wealth of information about your health?

Iridology is the study of signs in the human iris and a method that has been used to diagnose health for well over a hundred years. It is a branch of natural medicine that is used by thousands of health professionals and therapists around the world. I have worked as an iridologist for many years and have had the opportunity to photograph and analyze thousands and thousands of patient's eyes. I have been able to correlate what I have seen in human eyes to what is displayed as health problems, deficiencies in body organs and genetic strengths and weaknesses. If you are interested in having a more detailed look into signs that are commonly seen in the iris and an in-depth look into iridology, please read my book, For Your Eyes Only.

To an iridologist the eyes unlock a map to the entire body. It is possible to analyze the condition of every body organ through the use of the wonderful method of Iridology. Have you ever taken a really close look at the iris of your eyes? Take a look in the mirror or have a look through a magnifying lens at someone's eyes and you will begin to see much more than just eye color. You will see that the iris of the eye is made of threads or fibers that radiate outwards from the pupil. Often there are small holes or breaks in these fibers and often we can see different colored clouds and marks in sections of the iris. You will notice as well that your right eye is not exactly the same as the left eye. That's right. No eye is exactly the same and just like your fingerprint, your eyes are different from any other person.

According to Iridology theory, our nervous system in our body records information about every single event that occurs in our body and this information is transmitted to areas in the iris and results in changes in the appearance of the fibers. This book will teach you the basics so that you can recognize what kind of genetic eye constitution you have in order to find out much more about your own health, possible reasons for your ailments and how to use nutrition to heal and prevent potential problems from occurring.

Remember, "it's what you do with what you have that counts" and by using the wonderful method of Iridology you can learn about what you have in terms of genetic strengths and weaknesses as seen in your eyes so that you can use diet and nutrition to do something about it. That's what is meant by the Iridology-Nutrition connection and forms the basis of the Eye for an Eye Diet.

Genetic Eye Constitutions - An Introduction

We have touched over what is meant by our genotype or our genetic make-up and have recently found out that our eyes reveal information about our health status. What do we mean though by Genetic Eye Constitutions? Even though every eye is different there do exist similarities. We call these similarities Genetic Eye Constitutions. A genetic eye constitution is determined by the color of eyes you have as well as the structure. Almost everyone can be placed into one of these constitutions.

Iridologists over the last one hundred years, especially those in Europe have researched thousands of people with similar types of eyes and found similar dispositions to health problems as well as some aspects of psychological behavior as well. How about that! We can actually look into our eyes and learn about our genetic strengths and weaknesses. For thousands of iridologists around the world, including myself, this is an invaluable method for getting to the root of patient's problems so that a sound nutritional program can be implemented. I have used this method to assist thousands of patients with cancer, diabetes, digestive disorders and others as well as those who have problems with controlling weight.

If we can unlock some of the mysteries of our body through the use of Iridology, our bodies begin to function as they are intended because finally we start giving the body what it needs to overcome those genetic weaknesses and to begin to heal itself. You don't know it yet but soon you will have an unbelievably powerful tool at your disposal, and all you have to do is open your eyes! Just think of all the expensive, painful, and at times unhealthy tests that you have gone through to diagnose your medical problems. The science of Iridology is one of the most gentle and natural forms of diagnosis that I have discovered and it is available for everyone to learn.

How did Genetic Eye Constitutions come about? Well that's a good question. There is a theory that there used to exist only blue-eyed races who came from the cooler climates and brown-eyed races who came from the warmer climates. As a result of interracial mixing, the eye types, or what I call the

Genetic Eye Constitutions became what they are today. Through my extensive studies of human eyes and the human iris in particular, I have found 10 distinct types of Genetic Eye Constitutions. Each of these types has their own set of characteristics. We will later learn how to identify each type by their characteristic colors and structural signs. If we learn what type of Genetic Eye Constitution we have, we will understand much more how our body works and what it requires to be healthy and disease-free.

About the Eye for an Eye Diet

Well, you're probably thinking, finally we're getting to where the action is or at the meat of what the book is all about. Hold on and be patient. I know you want to get going to lose those pounds or to heal those chronic problems but Rome was not built in a day and neither can your body. Remember you can't fool your body you can only fool yourself. Your body has a set way of healing itself and it will heal itself if it receives the right nutrients in the right amounts. We need to follow each step carefully because as I said before this is not a crash diet, so let's not treat it like that. The Eye for an Eye Diet is a lifestyle change. I believe it is an intelligent program that not only opens our eyes to our genetic constitution but also to sound nutritional principles that we can take with us throughout our lives.

In **Part 1** you will learn about the 10 Essential "Eye for an Eye Diet" principles, which are a must for anyone who is really serious about understanding their health. It is intended to make you think about your health with a new perspective and prepare you for the work ahead.

In **Part 2**, "Eye for an Eye Diet" Nutrition will take you from the ground up where you will learn some of the most important concepts in human nutrition and what I believe are many of the forgotten factors that drastically affect the quality of our food and affect our health and well being. You will learn all about food from its origins to where it ends up on your plate. Remember that lack of quality food is the reason for 90 percent of health problems that exist today.

In **Part 3**, The "Eye for an Eye Diet" will teach you how to identify your Genetic Eye Constitution and how to implement a specific nutritional strategy for your genetic type. Eating plans, beneficial foods, herbs and vitamins are suggested for each Genetic Eye Constitution. Color image photographs of eye types are included to assist you in identifying your Genetic Eye Constitution.

Finally in **Part 4**, the "Eye for an Eye Diet" will be applied to specific health problems that plague our civilization today. Included are sound nutritional practices for weight loss or gain, for those so-called untreatable diseases as well as information on how to maintain health as you age. This area will give you additional assistance to get at the root of specific health problems and in combination with supporting your genetic constitution will give you the best chance for activation of your body's healing processes.

The Eye for an Eye Diet Program – 10 (Not so Easy) Steps

I believe that you are now prepared to begin your journey into the "Eye for an Eye Diet". Below are 10- not so easy- steps (Is anything in life that is worth fighting for, ever that easy?) to start you on your way to achieving true optimum health, weight and mental balance. Remember to keep an open mind, as a closed mind learns nothing and don't forget to remind yourself of the reasons why you want to be healthier. You alone have the power to make a change and the strength of this realization will give you the motivation to achieve all the goals in your life that you have always dreamed about.

Step 1: Read Part 1: The Ten Essential "Eye for an Eye Diet" Principles and put them into practice.
Step 2: Read Part 2: "Eye for an Eye Diet" Nutrition – From the ground up
Step 3: In Part 3: Read Chapters 1, 2, and 3 and identify your Genetic Eye Constitution using the color eye photographs.
Step 4: Find the section in Part 3: Chapter 4 that relates to your Genetic Eye Constitution and read.
Step 5: Find the relevant nutritional advice section for your Genetic Eye Constitution in Part 3: Chapter 5 and read.
Step 6: Find the relevant eating plan for your Genetic Eye Constitution in Part 3: Chapter 6 and read.
Step 7: In Part 4: Read Chapter 1 if you are interested in losing or gaining weight.
Step 8: In Part 4: Read Chapter 2 if you are interested in how to apply the Eye for an Eye Diet to diseases of modern civilization.
Step 9: Read Part 4: Chapter 3 for information on applying the Eye for an Eye Diet as you age.
Step 10: Refer back to any of the above sections on a regular basis to keep yourself motivated, inspired and informed.

Read the popular sad excuses below to see if you fit any of the job descriptions.

Sad Excuses and Job Descriptions

Sad Excuse Number 1: *I just don't have the time to follow a health program.*

This is the classic **WORKAHOLIC** who frequently uses work as an excuse for the lack of time during the day. What he or she does not realize is that sooner or later their lifestyle habits will catch up with them. Those donut and coffee breakfasts on the run, those high caloric lunches and late working nights will eventually amount to a lot of sick days, which will not pay dividends in the future. Besides, the extra energy gained in eating right will make up for any additional time in preparation of healthy food.

Sad Excuse Number 2: *Eating healthy is just too expensive.*

I call this individual the **ACCOUNTANT** because he or she measures health in terms of financial expense. Is it really that expensive to eat healthy?

Take a look at how much is spent on over the counter drugs, how many financially productive days are lost due to sick days etc. Take a look at your return on investment and not just what the expenses are.

Sad Excuse Number 3: *Life is short. You are going to die anyway.*

This person is what I call the **FATALIST** who believes that sooner or later an earthquake will hit or a car will run over you and that it is a waste of time to work on your health. Live life! Did you know it is possible to live healthy and enjoy even more the time you have on this earth as well?

Sad Excuse Number 4: *I don't want to know about the health of my body.*

This individual is the **BLINDPERSON** who believes that what he or she doesn't know won't hurt them. This of course is an illusion and not true at all. Turning a blind eye never led to any benefits. The more you open our eyes and the more you learn about your health the more power you have to control your life.

Sad Excuse Number 5: *If I find out something bad about my health, it may really happen as I might bring it on psychosomatically.*

This individual is the **NEUROTIC** person, one that is really just afraid to take their health in their own hands. This person needs to be reassured that just as we do have the power to psychologically influence our health in a negative way, we also have the power to affect it in a positive way. This type of person does not have the confidence to take control of his or her own health.

Sad Excuse Number 6: *I just don't have the willpower to change my eating habits.*

This individual is the **LAZYPERSON.** He or she needs motivation and incentive to work on their health. They need to see the benefits of a healthy diet.

Sad Excuse Number 7: *I don't want to create friction in the family by changing my diet.*

This is the **PACIFIST** who would rather sacrifice their own health and not stir up any waves. Your health is only your responsibility. Don't let others and their bad influences deprive you of the health that you deserve.

Sad Excuse Number 8: *I know lots of people who eat healthy and they are sick all the time.*

This is the **NON-BELIEVER**, who through his experience does not see benefits of a healthy-eating lifestyle. This person needs to be educated and informed about healthy lifestyle choices and their benefits.

Are you guilty of fitting any of the Job Descriptions below?

- Workaholic
- Accountant
- Fatalist
- Blindperson
- Neurotic
- Lazyperson
- Pacifist
- Non-Believer

THE EYE FOR AN EYE DIET

PART 1

The 10 Essential
"Eye for an Eye Diet"
Principles
to live and (never) die by

Frank Navratil BSc. N.D.

The First Principle: You are not normal

Maybe in the past you have tackled a host of diets or health programs and while many others would claim great successes including dramatic weight losses and miraculous health improvements, you have unfortunately been left behind feeling deflated and often disappointed. Perhaps you have started to think that maybe you are not normal because the program did not work for you! I don't blame you for feeling this way because when we look all around us in magazines, on TV and in other media we are constantly bombarded with what the ideal body should look like and you just can't help feeling embarrassed about your body and your health when you see perfection everywhere. Remember this is just one of those illusions. Perfect health does not exist and there is no such thing as normal. I am glad that you feel that you are not normal because none of us actually are really normal.

When we think about it, what is normal anyway? All our lives we have been compared to what is normal. There are normal height -to- weight tables, normal blood tests, normal body temperature and normal behavior. We are constantly being rated against a scale of normality. If we show any variations to this figure, we are considered abnormal or sometimes even crazy. Are we not forgetting one thing though? Are we not forgetting that the one important feature that distinguishes us as human beings from one another is that we are not normal?

I can't help to think of a story that I heard while studying temperature regulation at university. Our professor told us of a situation that occurred way back in history of a man who had a body temperature that was slightly higher than normal. Due to this fact, he spent several years in bed being visited by doctor after doctor who could not figure out what was wrong with him. He felt perfectly fine but lived many years with the thought that he was dying. It was finally revealed that this slightly higher temperature was actually his normal temperature and there was absolutely nothing wrong with him!

Be very careful of normal values. I can't even begin to count the number of patients who have entered my clinic claiming they are unwell despite the fact that every medical test they had undergone showed that everything was normal. However analyzing the eyes through Iridology revealed existing and potential health problems. How many times have you heard that a tumor has been successfully removed and there is no sign of cancer when just a few months later metastasis ensues? My mother, after being diagnosed with ovarian cancer was given only a year to live but she lived over 8 years and that's even with several rounds of radiation and chemotherapy.

Remember as human beings we often make mistakes and although we have tremendous technological capacities our inventions and diagnostic machines are subject to some degree of error. Often we forget in our quest to monitor normal values that the body and its systems interact in an unbelievably complex and dynamic equilibrium to allow us to function optimally.

The important concept to grasp here is that everyone reacts to treatments, diets or medications in different ways. What works for one person, will not necessarily work for the other. We often see examples of this in patients who have been prescribed certain drugs. Two patients who have similar body weight and take the same dosage of the same drug may react differently. One may have no side effects to the drug; the other may have serious stomach problems. It does not matter how many thousands of people were tested using the drug, for each person it is a new experiment. Do you really want to allow drugs to experiment on your body?

We are all different and we are all individuals. We each have a different metabolism; we each have a different liver that cleanses our body and a different capacity of our kidneys to filter our blood. We each handle food differently and at different rates and we are each under a unique set of factors that control how we absorb and digest food, how we burn off calories, how we regenerate our body organs and how we deal with stresses in our lives. We each have different requirements for nutrients and we each recover from injury or operations differently as well as dispose of toxic substances in our body differently. How can anyone say that we are anything but abnormal? I don't care what kind of experts there are in the world but no one can predict what a combination of chemical drugs will do to your individual abnormal body. That's food for thought if you are one of the many who accept drug prescriptions without thinking of the consequences.

As you begin your journey in learning more about your body, you will grow to appreciate how unique you really are. Each of you has something to offer in this world. No one is better than the other, just different. By studying thousands and thousand of eyes over several years, I have never found an identical eye. Just as your fingerprints or tongue print each of your eyes is unique to anyone else's. The science of Iridology respects the fact that we are not normal and that there exist genetic differences, which we call Genetic Eye Constitutions, each with their own set of unique characteristics that make us who we are. Even though there is no other person that is exactly like you are, Genetic Eye Constitutions are something you can all learn about and can assist you with general problems that similar people with similar types of eyes have. It may just be that opportunity to finally discover why your body behaves the way it does and what it really needs in terms of diet and nutrition.

Don't worry. You are not alone. **Principle Number 1: Be proud and respect the fact that you are not normal!**

The Second Principle: Your health depends on 7 essential processes of life

Our body is an amazing miracle of science. If you think of the thousands and thousands of reactions that occur in it every day without you being even aware of what is happening, it can leave you absolutely breathless. We are just starting to uncover the tip of the iceberg when it comes to understanding how the body works. Even if we do not know exactly how each of the specially designed systems in the body all integrate together, one thing is for certain, we cannot live without what I call the seven essential processes of life.

Why do we need to learn about the essential processes of life? If you can grasp the concepts here you will unlock the first door when it comes to learning about what requirements your body has to be able to function in an optimal way. It does not matter whether you are overweight, whether you have cancer or whether you suffer from migraine headaches, it is necessary to know each of the seven essential processes of life to be able to solve those health problems.

The first essential process is **INGESTION**, which simply means what nutrients we add into our body. If you believe that you are what you eat, then all your body functions are dependent on ingestion. Every one of our cells needs nutrients. Nutrients come in the form of food but if we look at things from a wider perspective, nutrients also mean the air we breathe, the energy we receive from the sun, the happiness that life brings us, and the spiritual fulfillment that nourishes our soul. Nutrients come in a variety of forms but what they have in common is that they are needed from our external environment. Our diet and the quality of the food we eat have a dramatic effect on our well-being. We need to ingest food that includes a balance of fats, carbohydrates, proteins, vitamins and minerals every day to stay alive and healthy. The incidence of modern diseases in our civilization is very much correlated to what we eat. The processing of foods and the addition of thousands of artificial colors and preservatives also have an affect on what we ingest and take into our bodies. What about the air we breathe? Are we ingesting adequate oxygen for metabolism? Just take a look at the increase of pollution and smog, smoking and carbon monoxide from cars and you start to realize that many of us live in an oxygen-poor society. Without oxygen we die or our cells become prone to disease. We require energy from the sun for production of Vitamin D as well as energy in the forms of friendship, love, spirituality and nature. We will have a much closer look at nutrients as we progress through this book. Ingestion of the right quality and quantity of nutrients is something we cannot live without. When you are trying to find out why you are sick or why you are overweight or what you need to know to maintain your health, you should always start with looking at what you ingest.

The Eye for an Eye Diet   Part 1

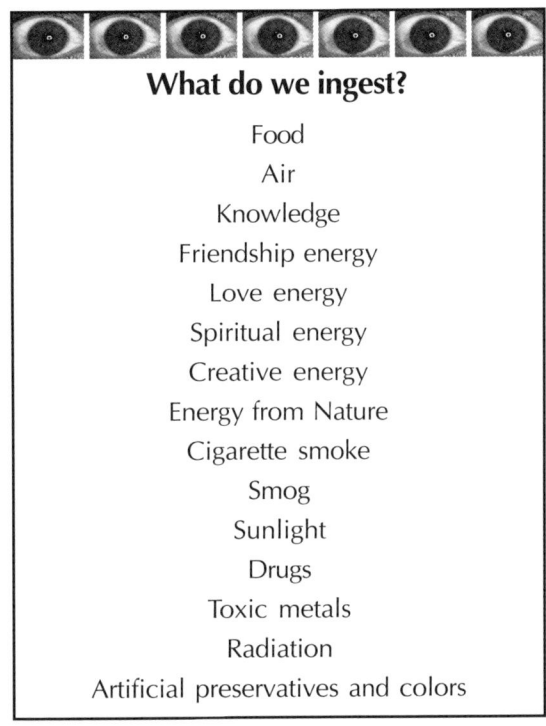

What do we ingest?

Food
Air
Knowledge
Friendship energy
Love energy
Spiritual energy
Creative energy
Energy from Nature
Cigarette smoke
Smog
Sunlight
Drugs
Toxic metals
Radiation
Artificial preservatives and colors

    The next essential process of life is **DIGESTION**. When we talk about digestion, we mean the process that breaks down those nutrients from the foods we ingest into the more basic components we call fats, sugars and amino acids. As we all know this is not as easy as it sounds. Everyday we hear of people having digestive problems or indigestion or they find things difficult to digest. The stomach and the intestines perform digestion. This is where mixtures of hydrochloric acid and a variety of digestive juices, enzymes, beneficial bacteria and bile work together to break down the large pieces of food into smaller units. The ultimate goal is to break the food into small enough particles so that it will allow absorption into the blood. If the environment in our stomachs or our intestines is not optimal then food is not broken down adequately. This can create situations like constipation, diarrhea, indigestion or excess gas. Our pancreas is also involved with digestion because it provides a lot of the enzymes to digest fats, proteins and carbohydrates. The liver produces bile and the gallbladder stores and releases it into the digestive system where it is needed to digest fats. So you can see there are more organs involved in digestion than just the stomach and intestines. All work together to ensure that what you eat has the best possible chance to get absorbed.

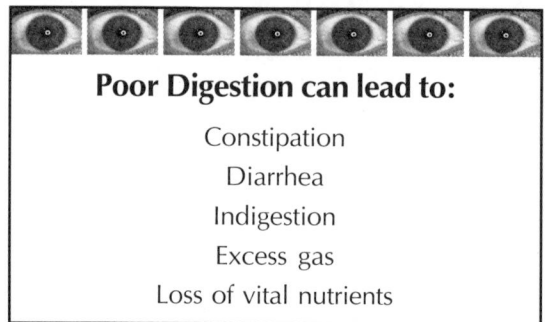

Poor Digestion can lead to:

Constipation

Diarrhea

Indigestion

Excess gas

Loss of vital nutrients

If you guessed the next essential process of life to be **ABSORPTION**, then you are right. The process of absorption is the next step in the transport of food to the cells of our body. We think a lot about digestion but absorption is very much taken for granted. The important idea to grasp here is that without adequate DIGESTION, the particles of food will not be small enough for ABSORPTION and as a result will not get into the blood. When the lining of the intestine starts to wear down due to many factors like poor intestinal micro flora, drugs like antibiotics, or high intakes of milk, white sugar and flour, the quality of absorption decreases. Soon, larger particles that are not completely digested as well as other toxic substances get absorbed into the blood. This is where many health problems like allergies have their roots. Remember we need to absorb fats, amino acids, sugars, vitamins and minerals daily for our survival and if our absorption capabilities are not optimal our bodies will not get what they need.

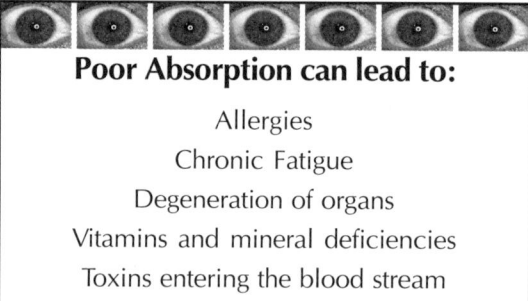

Poor Absorption can lead to:

Allergies

Chronic Fatigue

Degeneration of organs

Vitamins and mineral deficiencies

Toxins entering the blood stream

Once the food particles enter the blood it is the next essential process of life, **CIRCULATION,** that has the responsibility of transporting those absorbed nutrients to their ultimate destination: our cells. Our circulation is made up of our heart, the pump in the system and the vast network of blood vessels that circulate the blood, which contains absorbed nutrients including oxygen to each cell in the body. What do we need to maintain adequate circulation? First of all we have to have an efficient heart and our blood vessel walls need to be strong and flexible to maintain stable blood pressure and to stay clear of fat and cholesterol deposits. Exercise and nutrition is critical for this essential life process. When problems occur in our circulation there can be areas in the body that do not receive enough nutrients, which can lead to degeneration and cell death. This is most evident in heart disease, one of the leading causes of death due to problems of circulation to the heart muscle.

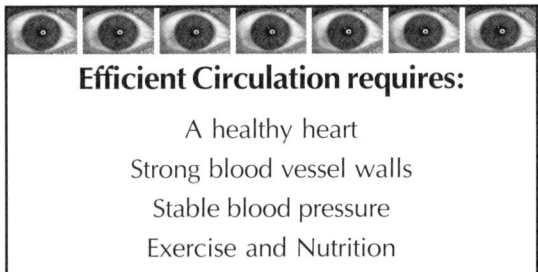

Efficient Circulation requires:

A healthy heart
Strong blood vessel walls
Stable blood pressure
Exercise and Nutrition

The nutrients in the blood may reach the cells through the circulatory system but this does not mean that the cells will utilize them. A very complex system is in place that will allow or not allow nutrients to enter the cell. We refer to this essential life process as the process of **UTILIZATION**. Many factors including our hormonal system control how the cells utilize nutrients and whether they will be allowed to enter our cells. Many drugs take advantage of this and paralyze the natural selective process of utilization to allow entrance into the cells. If the nutrients are in the proper form, the cells will be able to utilize them. If they contain toxins and materials unknown to the cells then the process of utilization will be severely affected. Just remember, we need to get those nutrients into the cells. If nutrients to the cells are inadequate, then just like all biological processes, they will degenerate and die. If enough cells in an organ degenerate, then the whole organ will start malfunctioning. If enough organs begin to malfunction then entire systems will begin to fail and that is the beginning of serious chronic health problems.

Just as each of our living cells require nutrients, each produces wastes that need to be removed from the body from a variety of elimination organs. This essential process of life is **DETOXIFICATION**. Waste products produced through our metabolism and toxic substances that enter our blood stream must constantly be removed from the body through a number of detoxification channels. These include our colon, kidneys, liver, lungs, lymphatic system and skin. If any of these detoxification organs degenerate or become weakened, the ability of the body to eliminate wastes is reduced and the toxic load on the body increases. Increased toxicity can lead to a variety of conditions including headaches, chronic fatigue, skin problems, inflammation, cysts or tumor formation. It is crucial that all our detoxification organs are working well so that the natural processes of the body can operate effectively.

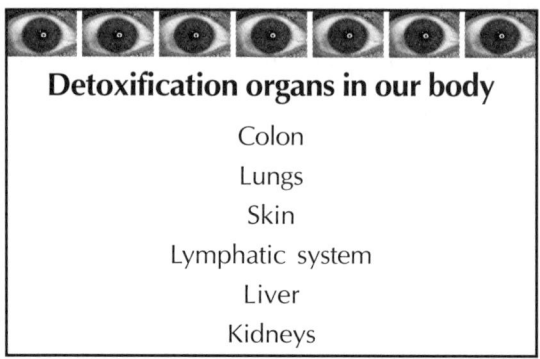

Detoxification organs in our body

Colon

Lungs

Skin

Lymphatic system

Liver

Kidneys

If the cells in our bodies were not able to grow and multiply we would soon be out of action. Even our red blood cells only live 120 days and then have to be replaced. Our skin cells are constantly being renewed as well as every living cell and tissue in our body. Our bones are also living tissue whose cells are constantly being exchanged. This miracle that occurs continuously 24 hours a day without us taking much notice, is the final essential process of **REGENERATION**. Without regeneration we would wear ourselves out very quickly. That is the one aspect that differentiates us from machines. Machines unlike our bodies do not have the living process of regeneration; their components cannot regenerate themselves. The organs in the body can however, but they are dependent on adequate nutrients. The process of regeneration determines how quickly we heal ourselves and how efficiently we exchange old worn-out tissue with healthy new tissue. Through sleep, rest and nutrition, we regenerate and gather the energy for all of our future activities. Our bodies cannot regenerate without adequate ingestion, digestion, absorption, circulation, utilization and detoxification.

Do you understand now how each of these essential processes is vital to our health? There is not one that is more important than the other as a breakdown in one process will affect all the others. Can you see how bad lifestyle habits and ingestion of poor nutrition can lead to disease? We often forget about these 7 essential processes of life when we are searching for a fast-acting drug for our chronic problems or a crash diet to quickly lose weight. Every disease and every health condition is due to a breakdown of one or more of these essential processes. Don't lose sight of them. They will guide you during your quest in learning the secrets to your health.

The Third Principle:
Treat the cause not just the symptoms

Do you know what the greatest crime of the century is in our health care system? No, it has nothing to do with hospital infection rates or malpractice suits against doctors or lack of staff or hospital beds. We are guilty of the greatest crime of all, treating the symptoms of our disease and not the causes. We should all be sentenced to at least a minimum of one-year maximum security without medications, junk food, stressful lifestyles and bad eating habits so that we can come to that realization. Somehow, in the last century or so, we have forgotten what it means to cure a disease by our endless and futile attempts to treat our conditions.

Let's go back again and discuss the difference between "treatment" and "cure." There is a big difference. Often you may have heard yourself say after taking some medication for a migraine headache or constipation that "you are cured." Let me ask you; will that migraine headache or bout of constipation show up again in a few weeks or months? Will that weight problem show up again after that crash diet? Will that blood pressure rise after the medication stops. I can bet it will. This is only a superficial "treatment," not a cure. If you really were cured you would get to the core of the problem not just the surface. We can think of disease as an iceberg and treatments that use medications and chemical drugs only scrape the surface. The core of the problem is much more deeper than we realize.

So why are we spending millions of dollars of research on that fraction that lies above the surface? You know why? Because people want it that way. People want to see results overnight and as we know, the body just does not work that way. People want to lose weight in the shortest time possible with the least amount of work, even though it took them years to get that way. People want to get rid of aches and pains instantly with the pop of a pill. People don't want to ask perhaps what could be causing their migraines, their constipation, their high blood pressure, their obesity, their diabetes or their cancer. Just give us a pill to get rid of it, or operate on us to get it out. Give us the illusion that we are cured! That's what we want and that is the greatest crime for which many of us are guilty. Remember we can fool ourselves but we just can't fool our bodies. If mankind is guilty of one illusion it surely is this one.

There is a price to pay for suppressing our health problems with superficial treatments. Have you ever thought that your asthma or allergies are linked back to suppression of symptoms by drugs back in childhood? Have you ever thought that by treating only the symptoms of your health problem now is like putting fancy gift-wrap over a time bomb that is waiting to explode? Sooner or later these suppressed conditions will surface. They show us as degenerative conditions such as cancers, diabetes, autoimmune diseases, arthritis and many others.

Over the last 200 years, modern medicine has created an endless list of names for all possible existing diseases. Many of these diseases do not have a cure but they surely have a name. When I give seminars on health and nutrition, I often ask people why is it so important to them to know the name of their disease? My patients have often visited a surprising number of doctors in order to find out what they have. We all want to know whether we have cancer so we can do what? Pump our bodies with chemotherapy or radiation? Operate on that malignant tumor to get it out of the body without asking how it got there in the first place? Is this really a long-term solution to our growing health problems? Is this getting to the cause of our problems? I think people should forget about just searching for the name of their disease and start asking questions why something is wrong in their bodies. Health professionals need to think about prevention rather than just finding a nice convenient remedy for a name of a disease. No one wants to ask why the disease started in the first place. Have we all developed into a race that believes we can conquer everything with our modern science and drugs? Is no one out there really interested in learning why we have the problems we have? Well, I know at least you are, otherwise you wouldn't have opened this book.

Enough lecturing. I'm sorry but I can't emphasize the extreme importance of this principle because it really comes down to changing the way we see things. It involves that word change again. We can't change the world overnight. But we can change our own views and perspective on health and this can change others. That is what I am trying to convey to you. The Eye for an Eye Diet I hope will not only give you the strength to change yourself but also to influence others. You know we can go on living our lives with the illusions we have or we can start building a solid foundation based on holistic healing principles. If we believe that our bodies are composed of cells and if each of those interconnected cells receives what they need, then we can build a well-balanced, strong body that will be resistant to any disease or infection that attacks it.

The secret lies in searching for the cause of our health problems and avoiding superficial methods of treatment. I believe that many causes come down to genetic differences and their associated nutritional needs as well as diet and lifestyle habits. The science of Iridology can help uncover some of the causes of your health problems. You will save yourself a lot of time lost in visits to your doctors, and time away from work, as well as gain valuable, healthy years to your lives if you adhere to this third principle. Stop wasting time and get to the root of your health or weight problems! That's what the Eye for an Eye Diet is all about.

The Fourth Principle:
Holistic health is for the "hole" person

A "hole" person is one that is empty or missing something that he or she needs. A jigsaw puzzle with some of the pieces missing. A book with some of the pages torn out. A "hole" person needs to be "whole" or complete. In order to achieve whole health we have to sort out all the pieces and find out what is missing. It's not so easy as just popping a pill because human health is far more complex than that. Human health is the most complex jigsaw puzzle that you have ever come across.

We have in the past moved away from whole health or holistic health as seen in the growing trend to specialization in the medical field. We have our cardiologists, urologists, gynecologists, our skin specialists and neurologists but may have lost our perspective on the idea that each of our cells, each of our organs, and each of our systems in our body, interact together as a whole. It is more than just the sum is always greater than its individual parts. The sum of the body's systems is dependent on each of its systems, organs and cells for its survival. When one organ in the body is deficient, the whole body is affected. Could it be that maybe we have forgotten this basic concept? When we look at the body, we need to look at it as a whole.

What do we mean by "holistic health"? Holistic health means total health and all the factors that affect our health status, including more than just the physical. In order to achieve optimum true holistic health we have to fill in some of those "holes".

Let's take a look at some of the **"holes"** that may be contributing to your health problems.

Poor Nutrition

As nutrition is the main theme of this book as well as what I believe the cause of 90 percent of all health problems, it is not a "hole" to be neglected. When I speak to patients about their diet it is not surprising that they are experiencing the health problems that they have. Remember ingestion is one of the 7 essential processes of life. This includes quality nutritious food as well as natural food supplements that can support our health. We will learn much more about nutrition as a critical contributor to our health in Part 2 of this book.

Lack of Exercise

Most people reach an age where they begin to adopt a sedentary lifestyle. The activity level of our youth fades away and we get bogged down with life's responsibilities such as work and family commitments. The thought

Frank Navratil BSc. N.D.

of having to exercise after a long workday to many is inconceivable. This is however only a modern day problem. Exercise, in the form of going to the gym or participating in aerobics classes has only just come into fashion in recent times. We can thank our scientific and technological advances for our needs to exercise today because before those inventions that made our lives easier, we had to work and sweat. At that time, getting daily exercise was not a problem. Today our elevators and escalators, cars, trains and electrical appliances do the work for us. We don't even need to get out of the car to buy a hamburger anymore!

Exercise is crucial if we want to be free of heart problems, back aches, menstrual difficulties, stress, weight problems as well as almost every single disease imaginable. We just can't achieve whole health if we don't exercise our bodies. If you are planning to start a weight loss program without exercise, forget it. You're wasting your time. There are just so many reasons why exercise is needed. Exercise stimulates our circulation, digestion, absorption, detoxification, and regeneration functions, all of which are essential to the efficient operation of the body.

The Eye for an Eye Diet should be combined with a sound exercise program. Find something you like to do, as the odds are against you lasting very long if you start doing something that does not inspire you. The secret to enduring in your exercise program is finding an activity that is close to your home and doesn't require you to travel far, is enjoyable and has plenty of variety so you don't get bored. It's never too late to start. Studies show that substantial health benefits occur only after 3 months participation in an exercise program. Whether it is fast walking, running, swimming, playing squash, it doesn't matter. The body just has to move and get off the couch and you will see how your organs and systems react favorably. That accumulated build-up of stress will be released, your mind will work much better and you will feel more relaxed and in control of your life. Exercise should be viewed as a lifestyle change, a part of your life not a momentary fad. Put spice into it and all the variety to make it interesting. Climb those stairs, not the elevator and try to think of what our ancestors did before. Remember the first month is going to be the most difficult. This is the time that your body has to react to the changes it is going through. You may feel much more tired than ever before, and will want to quit as that sluggish lymphatic system starts to wake up and dispose of those toxins that have built up, but get through the first month and you're… well almost home free! Try exercising at least 3 to 4 times a week for a minimum of 20 to 30 minutes each time. For a safe simple program to follow see the box below. Remember to consult your physician before starting any exercise program.

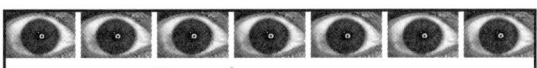

> **Exercise program**
>
> 1. Subtract your age from 220
> 2. Take 70 percent of that number (This will be the minimum pulse rate per minute while you exercise)
> 3. Take 85 percent of the same number. (This will be your maximum pulse rate per minute while you exercise)
> 4. Start exercise and take your pulse after a few minutes
> 5. Maintain your pulse rate between the minimum and maximum numbers for at least 20-30 minutes, 3-4 times a week.

Lack of clean, fresh air

Air contains oxygen and oxygen is one of the life-giving substances that our body needs. Air also contains contaminants due to smog and pollution and that is what we don't need. The decrease in clean, oxygen-rich air that we breathe in contributes to our growing health problems. On top of that, and largely due to stress, we are not breathing properly or deeply enough resulting in low levels of oxygen. Remember, we require oxygen for our metabolism, to burn fats, to produce energy so that all of our 7 essential processes of life can function.

Try to live in areas with little or no pollution and if you can't, get to a park, the mountains or the ocean as often as you can. Many of my patients who have serious degenerative health problems have reported significant improvements when they began to breathe in clean, fresh, unpolluted air.

Lack of Relaxation

Every other person that enters my clinic reports being under severe stress, experiencing problems sleeping or suffering from pressure in the workplace. Ask yourself if you have the Workaholic job description. Ask yourself if you give yourself at least some time everyday to relax and release stress and care for your well-being. Do not underestimate the effect that stress has on your physical health. Periods of stress often precede many cancers that I have seen as well as migraines, hormonal problems, heart problems and digestive disturbances. I think the fact that we are seeing growing problems associated with stress is Mother Nature's way of saying that we are abusing her natural laws. We just can't expect to drive ourselves so hard without suffering from the consequences. When we are under stress, we produce free radicals at a much higher rate. Free radicals are responsible for a host of degenerating conditions. If you are under a lot of pressure or stress and you cannot seem to relax, it's time to slow down and reevaluate what you are doing. Find the "holes" in this list that are missing and do something to fill them in. Lack of relaxation will not allow the body to do its best and will slow down the healing process.

Lack of natural healing methods

As I am a strong advocate of natural medicine and drug-free healing methods, I strongly believe that conventional medicine with its rampant use of antibiotics and other drugs is not the way to go if you are interested in long-term health. We have seen the effects and we should learn from our mistakes. While modern medicine has its merits and often is life saving for acute or emergency situations, I do not feel that long-term drug therapy for chronic conditions such as high blood pressure, migraine headaches, stomach problems or others is a responsible solution for our growing health problems. Remember to search for the cause of health problems, not just the symptoms. With the new resurgence of natural healing methods like nutritional therapy, body therapies, herbals as well as many others, we now have so many alternatives to explore. Beware of risks involved when going for an x-ray too often or taking any chemical drug. Believe that the body can heal itself if given what it requires and give your body the best possible chance for recovery. Just as you would not want to ingest anything but natural foods, use natural healing methods that keep the body clean from contaminants and support the healing process in a natural way. Iridology is a natural diagnostic method that is non-invasive, safe and pain-free.

Lack of time in a natural environment

When was the last time that you spent time in a park, in the mountains or by the ocean?

This kind of therapy should be used by anyone who has any kind of chronic health problem as well as those who want to prevent health problems in the future. Energy from nature around us has powers of healing that we are only starting to understand. The Hunzas and other primitive cultures are known to experience far less of our modern civilization health problems. I know living primitively is virtually impossible for the majority of us but we can learn a great deal from cultures that live in symbiosis with their natural environment. Spending time in the sun is very healthy if it is not in the peak hours between 10a.m and 3 p.m. on summer days. We need the sun to produce Vitamin D and for our skin to breathe it needs to be exposed to the air. Synthetic clothing blocks our skin's ability to breathe and as it is an important detoxification organ it slows its ability to rid the body of toxins and harmful waste products. Several cases of acne and skin diseases like eczema have significantly improved when exposed to fresh air, sun and nature. If you suffer from health conditions including migraines, cancer or depression, get out to nature as soon as you can. Your mind and body will thank you for it. Perhaps you will fill a "hole" that has stayed empty for a long, long time.

Lack of satisfying and challenging work

I believe that as human beings we all have a need for satisfying and challenging work.

Some of us require employment as doctors while others find satisfaction as mothers or housewives. It doesn't matter what you do just as long as you are happy doing it. That's what life's about anyway isn't it? Certainly I hope you are not doing what you are doing just to impress others or just to make money because sooner or later it will catch up with you. I realize that sometimes it is not possible to find the kind of work that will make you happy so maybe you will have to find another way such as a part-time job or a hobby on the side. I have found that many of my clients who do work for the wrong reasons or are unhappy with their working lives will have associated health problems. It is just like any of the other "holes." The longer they stay empty the greater chance that physical and mental health begins to deteriorate.

Lack of balance

What do we mean by balance in our lives? This is not as easy to accomplish as it sounds. I believe that a balanced life is a combination of satisfying work, good friends, family and shared experiences. I see these nutrients as a part of our life-essential process of ingestion. A balanced life is not the life of a workaholic or the life of a lazy person. Equal time needs to be allotted for hobbies, for relaxation, for exercise and recreation, for family, friends and relationships. Any extremes where "holes" begin to show up indicate that our lives are not in balance and we are paving the way to signs of potential health problems.

Lack of positive thinking

It seems a bit cliché when I mention to think positive but we encounter negativity almost every day in our lives. For many people who are very sensitive to energy levels around them, health problems can be experienced when this negativity starts eating away and creating "holes". Everyone says that positive thinking leads to success. I believe that we should accept failures in our lives and learn from our mistakes and find the energy to look forward to the future. We cannot expect that our paths will always be paved with gold but we can try to look at the positive side of things no matter how difficult life can be. When we start thinking negatively our energy levels decrease, we lose motivation and reason to live. Our health is one of the first indicators of the effect of this decreased psychological energy. Our physical bodies are intertwined with our mental processes so positive thinking whether we believe it or not can often determine how quickly we recover from injuries or disease.

Lack of learning and education

I believe that we all have a great capacity and requirement to learn. Most of us though reach a point in our lives where we begin to stagnate. It often shows up as boredom or dissatisfaction in our jobs. We tend to fall into a routine, learn it well but do not move forward. If you are feeling this way, take a chance and make a change. Explore your creativity. Start something completely brand new or take a course and learn what you have always wanted to learn. Exercise your mind with books and live through new experiences. Learning is an adventure and it can take you to places that you have always dreamed about. Do not allow fear to keep you in the safety zone where you know it all too well. Venture out! Life is about taking chances and living through experiences. This is how we learn, and how we move forward. A well-balanced healthy life involves change and learning. I sincerely hope that you learn something of value from this book that will motivate you to make some positive and healthy changes in your life.

Lack of acceptance of ourselves and of others

A healthy holistic lifestyle involves more than just the physical. Often I have seen in practice the effect of emotional blocks on the healing process. For some it is not possible to overcome serious disease unless those emotional barriers are broken down. I believe that life begins when you accept who you are and when you accept those who are around you. We are all different; we each have different roads to take. It's not an easy task but we have to respect our differences. I believe that true health and happiness only will come when we accept who we are and what role we play in this life.

Lack of the sense of spirituality

The final "hole" that many of us can suffer from is a lack of a sense of spirituality in our lives. I am not saying anything about religion but at some point in our lives many of us will have questions about what the meaning of life is for us and we will begin searching for answers or trying to fill a void that becomes apparent. This is a time to explore the spiritual "hole." Holistic health involves the physical, mental as well as spiritual aspects of who we are.

If you want to really find the causes of your health problems, learn to apply holistic health methods to identify and fill any gaps or "holes" that you may have.

The Fifth Principle:
Your eyes are your connection to your nutritional needs

Earlier on we introduced the subject of Iridology as a natural means of gathering information about our health status by what we see in the iris of our eyes. For years I have been using this science with great success to diagnose health problems and to foresee potential health problems. However a natural diagnostic method is only as good as a healing method that goes along with it. My research with many thousands of patients has revealed some very interesting results between what I have seen in the eyes and the use of advanced nutritional methods. These nutritional methods have been used to strengthen genetic weaknesses and to overcome and prevent disease.

You may be interested to know what really started the study of signs in the human eye in our history. Even though records showing a correlation between health and signs in the eye date back several hundreds of years it was not until the early 1800's when Ignatz von Peczely, a doctor in Hungary brought Iridology to world recognition. Legend has it, as a boy he noticed that an owl that had broken its leg had a black stripe in the lower part of the iris and when the leg healed, white lines appeared instead. This made a lasting impression on the young Peczely and later as a homeopathic physician he began to study what he saw in the eyes of human patients. His published work inspired the many great iridologists who have followed his path up to our modern history. Today many health professionals and therapists practice Iridology in several countries around the world.

You can also learn about the basics of your genetic character by what you see in your eyes. By learning about Genetic Eye Constitutions and Iridology in Part 3 of this book, you will find there is a connection to the nutritional needs of your body. I call this the Iridology-Nutrition connection. Your eyes are one of the most sophisticated diagnostic tools that have ever been created. Just think of the different tools modern medicine has at their disposal including x-rays, Cat scans, blood tests, and a host of others. These tools have one common difference. Man has designed them and as we see from time to time, they are subject to some degree of error. As I mentioned before many patients of mine have visited a string of doctors to find out why they have a certain condition and no diagnosis could be made. However, signs in their eyes told a whole different story and often revealed the missing clues to the causes.

According to the science of Iridology, our eyes reveal a whole world of information about our genetics and our health status because they are with us every day, every hour, every minute and every second, recording information from messages in our nervous system. These messages show up in our eyes as color pigments and structural signs in the fibers of the iris itself. When we learn to read the signs in our eyes we can understand what body organs or systems are weak so that we can apply the necessary nutritional program.

Applying nutrition to signs seen through Iridology is a safe and effective natural method to deal with your chronic problems or to prevent them from ever beginning. Iridology can be used to find solutions for your weight problems and what organs need to be worked on to enable the body to work more efficiently so that you achieve long-lasting results.

You may at this point have some doubts how Iridology really can help you with your health problems. Hopefully, Part 3 will clarify any confusion you may have on this topic. If you need more convincing, please read my book, For Your Eyes Only to see the scope that Iridology can unveil about your health. Try to be patient and keep an open mind. I certainly wouldn't spend years of time studying what I see in human eyes and how it relates to health for nothing. I cannot count the numbers of patients that I have helped with this method where modern medicine could not.

Chinese medicine is based on thousands of years of learning to understand the inner workings of the human body from outside the body. Iridology is no different. The study of Iridology is an exciting and growing science in the field of natural medicine. I believe that we have to think differently than we have in the past and need to view old methods in a new light. This is a chance for you to really put something unique into practice. Don't let it go to waste. I believe that Iridology is really the diagnostic method of the future.

Principle Number 5 outlines how important is the Iridology-Nutrition connection and that keeping an "Eye for a Eye" will pay off in achieving the optimum health that you desire.

The Sixth Principle:
Get addicted to healthy foods, the greatest drugs around

Changing eating habits is never the easiest thing to do. Research is beginning to reveal that up to 90 percent of diseases may be due to unhealthy food choices. Our most serious degenerative conditions today including heart disease, cancer, diabetes, arthritis, asthma, skin disease, digestive disorders and osteoporosis, have all been linked to our diet. Just imagine the health problems that can be cured with diet alone! This to many is an amazing revelation but it really is not that surprising considering that what we consume is the essential life process of ingestion which as we have learned affects every other essential life process.

I just can't believe that I constantly run into doctors and health professionals that spend absolutely no time talking to their patients about making healthy food choices. How can this be, when the root cause of so many health problems in our modern civilized world is our diet? One reason is the prescription drug industry, one of the most profitable and socially acceptable forms of drug addiction in our culture. The other is the medical associations who refuse to accept the idea that people have the ability to cure themselves and without medication. There are now so many prescription drugs on the market and many with contraindications and side effects. Do you think that our bodies need anything with possible side effects? Do you think that you should risk having anything like that in your body? These are questions that you will have to answer yourselves. I can only hope that you will look at it intelligently and logically and decide for yourself what is the best natural way for your body to heal itself.

The greatest drugs around are healthy foods. They have natural healing capabilities that even the greatest minds of today cannot begin to understand. While scientists try to extract substances from plants and foods and study their effects on the human body, often the merits of whole complete food are completely forgotten. On one hand food supplements and vitamin tablets are tremendously beneficial for supporting some of our body functions but on the other hand they cannot and will never replace whole food. The basis of a sound diet needs to be pure, natural and healthy whole food.

Where do you start and what do we mean by healthy foods? Remember we are not normal and each one of us has a different genetic background and different nutritional needs. Besides implementing a sound and nutritious diet, as we will learn in Part 2 of this book, we also need to compensate for our genetic weaknesses. We will learn how to read these genetic weaknesses by observing our Genetic Eye Constitutions very shortly. We can then apply specific nutritional strategies for our genetic constitution.

What I mean by healthy food is food in its natural form. Since modern society has really twisted the definition of what is considered natural, we have a big problem. It is becoming more and more difficult to find food that is truly in its natural form. Through advertising campaigns and the media we are influenced to a certain degree about what is healthy for our bodies. Be careful, as this can be misleading. Remember one of the illusions we discussed before. The food companies are out to make money, make no doubt about it, and your long-term health is not on their priority list. You must take responsibility for your own health. You as a consumer of food need to be educated to make the proper food choices.

I think it is almost impossible to find 100 percent healthy food in its natural form other than growing it yourself or purchasing it from organic farms. You can however, choose the best foods in your reach and learn how to select foods that are as close to the natural form as possible. In Part 2, we will look at all the aspects of food from the ground up, as there are just so many factors that affect the food we eat and the nutrition we require.

Food addictions to sugar, salt, coffee and other not-so-healthy products can give us the illusion that we really need them in our diet. Once these products are replaced with healthier choices of foods, your body will not need them as much any more because finally it will be getting the nutrition it really needs.

Changing your diet for the better will not be an easy task but once you do so you will see and feel the benefits. These benefits can make a difference whether you contract disease, whether you continue to suffer from chronic problems, whether you stay overweight or whether you will succumb to serious health conditions in the future. No one wants to end up with those degenerative diseases that we mentioned earlier but statistics show that there is a good chance they will show up if we are not careful of the foods we eat. Applying the Eye for an Eye Diet and compensating for genetic weaknesses will provide on-going support to weakened parts of the body that have been genetically acquired. Changing your diet will influence your destiny or that end of the path where you would most likely end up if you continue on in your old ways. **Make that change now and get addicted to healthy foods.**

The Seventh Principle: Make Lifestyle changes; don't shock the body with Crash Diets

Your body is a very delicate piece of machinery. It relies on a constant balance of resources to produce the energy that is needed to fuel the requirements of each cell, organ and body system. We cannot abuse this delicate balance or homeostasis with the advent of unhealthy and often radical behavior in the form of crash diets.

The body is unbelievably intelligent in its reaction to any kind of stress that it endures. For every action there is an opposite and equal reaction. So for example when you shock the body with periodic crash-starvation diets to lose weight, the body will just learn, adapt and slow down its metabolism so that it burns less calories when you return back to normal. This kind of dieting eventually backfires and you can then put on more weight than you lose.

What I am trying to say is that the answer is not to get on a roller coaster ride of fluctuating diets but to make changes to your lifestyle that will be permanent. If you gorge yourself with fatty foods all year and then think that you can spend just a few weeks burning off that fat and then fall into the same pattern over and over again, you will find no health improvements in the long run.

I have found that significant health improvements come with spending at least four to six months on the Eye for an Eye Diet. This allows for many of the organs to regenerate and heal. Health conditions often improve after this time but the body may still need more time depending on how badly it has been abused in the past with insufficient nutrition. In this case it may take several years to completely regenerate. For that reason, I recommend trying to make some diet and lifestyle changes that will stay with you for your lifetime. Generally, we are all looking for a fast way to achieve results but there is no fast way. This is the only alternative to achieve optimum health. The body has its own way and time for regenerating under the proper conditions of adequate diet and lifestyle. As I have mentioned several times already you can't fool your body, you can only fool yourself. Some of you even despite reading this book will ignore my recommendations and continue to search for those fast-acting miracle cures and diets. This reminds me of the old alchemists who spent all that time trying to make gold when it just was not chemically possible.

Avoid encountering years of disappointment and enduring unhealthy stresses on your body. Start tackling your health or weight problems intelligently and you will achieve results. Diet and Lifestyle changes are the most difficult changes that one can make. That is why most people don't achieve their health goals because most just don't have the patience or understanding of what it really takes. Start thinking differently, don't think of this book as a short-term plan but a life (style) plan. We cannot gain health with our wealth, but through our behavior. Diet and lifestyle changes can produce what modern medicine calls, miracles.

The Eighth Principle:
Go natural and you can't go wrong

There is something to say for a natural way of life. What do we really mean by natural?

Natural comes from nature and getting as close to how nature intended is as far as I am concerned where we should all be striving.

Let's assume the impossible and imagine a world where everything is in its natural form.

Such a world today is virtually unimaginable and unrealistic but one that some uncultured civilizations such as the Hunza people still have today. What would we see in such a world?

For one thing there would be no such thing as processed foods that include artificial additives or colors. Margarines would not exist, as they would be in liquid form as are all vegetable oils that have not been processed. Products would not come with 2-year expiry dates and would have to be eaten fresh daily before they become spoiled. Products would not come frozen, canned, preserved, dried, or wrapped in plastic if they were completely in their natural form. Foods could not be micro waved in such a world or frozen in freezers. There would be no instant soups or instant puddings or just-add-water cake mixes. Fruits would not have to be picked a month before they are ripe and stored for long periods of time before they reach the end consumer but would need to be picked fresh from trees. The same would be with vegetables from the garden. Sugar would have to be eaten in its raw form as well as grains such as rice. There would be no diet cola drinks or artificial sweeteners and no need to really have these products because there would be no chocolate, candy or fast foods and plenty of exercise so ideal weight would be maintained.

In such a world the air in its natural form would not contain toxic gases, dangerous chemicals or carbon monoxide because there would be no smog or exhaust from cars. The drinking water would not come in plastic bottles or have to be filtered. Dishes would not be cleaned with dishwashing liquids or walls and floors with disinfectants or chemical cleaners. Chickens would not be fed antibiotics or cows fed drugs and hormones that increase milk production. Colors and preservatives would not have to be added to meats to make them look fresh.

Imagine this world would not even include any drugs such as antibiotics, aspirins, pain-relievers, antidepressants, laxatives, cold remedies, sleeping pills, and hormone replacement therapy, birth control pills or anti-inflammatory medication. Imagine a world without cars, elevators, escalators, trains, airplanes, and no need for gym memberships, as you would receive all the exercise you need from your normal daily activities. There would not be the sense of stress or urgency telling you that you need a break and have to go on vacation somewhere away from the city because you would already be living in nature. There would not even be synthetic fabrics used in the clothes you would wear.

In such a world if it ever could exist there would be much more time to listen to your intuition and not to advertisements on television, to learn from mistakes and from your elders who have a wealth of experience.

I know that you must be thinking well, it is just not possible to live a life such as this in today's world and you are probably right. We should however learn what we can from the laws that govern nature. While many of the items listed above are near to impossible to attain, many are within our reach. We are paying the price for our unnatural way of life and this is showing up as increasing incidence of cancers and other forms of degenerative health conditions. We all can make some positive diet and lifestyle changes that are closer to the way that nature intended.

People often ask, "What do those civilizations whose residents often live to well over a hundred years have that we don't have? What do you think?

When you are unsure about what direction is best to take, remember the eighth principle, **Go natural and you can't go wrong.**

The Ninth Principle:
Change with the demands of your body

Our bodies go through several transitions in our lives from infancy through to adolescence, adulthood and old age. For women the onset of menstruation, pregnancy and menopause are further examples of life's transitions. As our bodies grow, change and age our nutritional needs also change. If we do not adapt to these changes in nutritional demands, our bodies reach a deficit situation and health problems can arise. It is important to respect these life changes and provide the correct adequate nutrition during these periods in our lives.

It is therefore very important to not only support the genetic weaknesses that we have in our bodies but to also maintain adequate nutrition during what I call "age-related times of stress" and "non age-related times of stress." Those times of stress that are age-related include those growing phases during childhood, hormonal and sexual changes in adolescence, adulthood, menopause, and old age. Those that are not age-related include those stresses that place extra demands on our body during our lifetimes and include: oral contraceptive pill use, hormonal replacement therapy, drugs, smoking, pregnancy, physical and emotional stress, injuries, smog and pollution, obesity, disease, malnutrition, chronic alcohol ingestion and surgical operations. These factors tax the body and place it in a situation where certain nutrients are deficient, meaning that under those conditions above, our bodies are not getting or not producing the correct amount of vitamins, minerals, carbohydrates, fats and proteins to sustain our essential body processes.

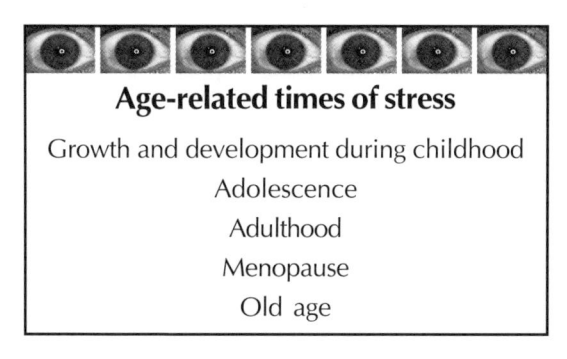

Age-related times of stress

Growth and development during childhood
Adolescence
Adulthood
Menopause
Old age

Non Age-related times of stress

Oral contraceptive pill
Drugs
Smoking
Pregnancy
Physical stress
Emotional stress
Injuries
Surgical operations
Smog and pollution
Obesity
Disease
Malnutrition
Chronic alcohol ingestion

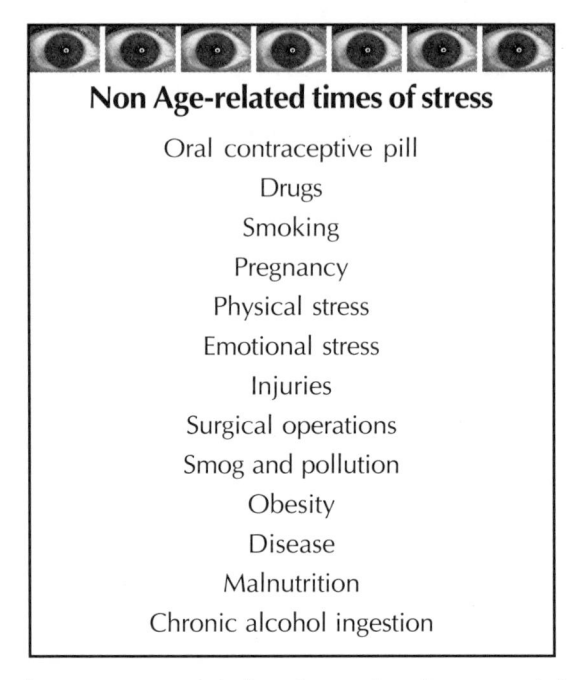

Prolonged stress can result in low immunity, disease and deterioration of body functions.

If we do not receive what we need during these times it is inevitable that we will succumb to disease.

As every person is unique and not normal as we discovered earlier, it is not an easy task to calculate what our requirements are in terms of nutrition. These requirements constantly change as we age, and as we subject the body to a variety of stresses. Keep in mind that we always need to adapt to our changing bodies by compensating with the correct nutrition. In this way they will be unable to reach a deficit situation even as we age.

In a way it's like filling our tanks up before we run low and get close to running out of gas! It's like changing to snow tires in the wintertime or changing the oil more often as our motors age. It's adding antifreeze when it gets cold and going in for a tune-up before a long trip.

We don't know what kind of stresses life will bring us and at times they are unavoidable so we need to adapt and be prepared for the long run. As we come to times in our lives that are subject to stress, we need to be prepared to alter our diets and what we ingest. We need to also reduce those stresses that can be influenced. This will provide the best chance for a healthy and disease-free body for a whole lifetime.

The Tenth Principle:
Get your foot off the brakes!

The last principle is certainly not the least. It is one of the most important principles in the "Eye for an Eye Diet." and often the reason why many fail to achieve their health goals. Have you ever found that you just don't seem to be moving forward in regards to improving your health or reaching an ideal body weight? Well, you are certainly not alone! Achieving optimum health means removing all those obstacles that stand in the way. It means taking your foot off the brakes!

Now, you may say that you have tried absolutely everything under the sun in the last few years and still no results. Some of the factors that may be slowing you down are explained below. Take a look at each one of them and ask yourself if they apply to you.

Are you taking any drugs or have taken any drugs that suppressed your health problems?

If you are taking antibiotics or have taken antibiotics you may have found already that other associated health problems have occurred such as digestive problems, allergies or yeast infections. If you take aspirin, it has been shown in many studies that it actually prolongs the flu. Every birth control pill damages some cells of the liver. Bronchial-dilating drugs for respiratory conditions such as asthma taken over long periods of time will have negative effects. Painkillers, anti-inflammatory drugs, chemical laxatives, and many others only treat the symptoms but do not cure the disease. Further more they only add to our toxic load in the body, which is exactly the opposite of what the body needs to resume its detoxification functions and start to regenerate. In fact every chemical drug that we take into our bodies will slow down our road to optimum and true health. Don't let the immediate effects of drugs fool you into believing that you are cured. You are only suppressing the disease or condition and it may lead to much more serious problems in the future. Taking drugs especially for long-term cases of chronic diseases is one of the greatest brakes that we can apply to the healing process.

Are you suffering from unresolved psychological problems?

There are many cases that I have seen where my patients have received a nutritional program well suited for their needs yet the results were not as expected. Here holistic health plays a large role as unresolved anger, distrust, jealousy, fear and other negative emotions may be at the root of the problem. We cannot neglect the effect that this has on the body's ability to heal itself. Our minds have an incredible power to heal our body. They also have an incredible power to put the brakes on our body as well. Just think how often one spouse dies and the other passes away only a few months later. Is this a coincidence? If you lose the will to live, if you lose the will to look forward to the next day or if you lose your desire to improve your state of health, your body will slow down its healing process. If you suffer from health problems or from being overweight, any suppressed psychological problems need to be resolved. Seek some professional counseling and make some positive changes. The mind and the body must work together as a team if you are to really achieve optimum health.

Have you ever changed some of your bad lifestyle habits?
Most of us know our bad lifestyle habits but few are willing to change them for the better.
Changing the negative aspects of your lifestyle is one of the most difficult things to do but if done can have the most dramatic effect on your health. I hear so many of my patients say that they suffer from intense stress whether from the workplace or in relationships at home. How can a stressed body heal, detoxify or regenerate itself. Many have horrific eating habits and participate in absolutely no exercise due to their extreme lifestyles. Sooner or later this will catch up to them and show up as some sort of health problem as their body's nutritional store is placed into a deficit situation. Many of us stay up much later than we should and as a result cheat our bodies of the sleep that we desperately need to regenerate our tissues, that essential process of life. Bad lifestyle habits are strong brakes that will slow you down on your quest to achieving the health you desire.

Are you having difficulty in motivating yourself?
Look back to some of the sad excuses mentioned earlier on. Motivation is one of the major reasons for failure in achieving health goals. There has to be a reason why we want to be healthy and live a long productive life. Perhaps we are not happy and need to look at all our holistic needs to see if they are being satisfied. I believe that people that are happy with themselves have a balance in their lives, they want to live long and usually are able to find the motivation they need to accomplish their goals. If you are having great difficulty in motivating yourself, try to search for the reasons why and make some changes that will take into consideration all of your holistic needs. This I hope will allow you to finally release the brakes and to get on with improving your life.

Have you ever applied a sound intelligent nutritional program that compensates for your genetic weaknesses as well as for stresses that place extra demands on your body?
If you compensate for your weaknesses that you are born with as well as for stresses that increase demands on your body, you will move forward with your health objectives.
That is what the "Eye for an Eye Diet" is all about. The "Eye for an Eye Diet" is about getting your foot off the brakes, once and for all.

THE EYE FOR AN EYE DIET

PART 2

"Eye for an Eye Diet" Nutrition:
From the Ground Up

Chapter 1

The Origin of Living Food

Our journey into nutrition starts with food at its very first beginnings. Few of us when we unwrap that final beautifully prepared food product ever really think about where it all comes from or where it all begins. Very few of us assess what nutrients we take into our bodies. We need to have some understanding because the quality of what we ingest will have a great effect on all our other essential life processes. Remember we are all a part of the food chain, that transfer of energy from one form to the other. That is how nature has planned it. As humans we are part of an immense ecosystem that is held in delicate balance with our natural environment. We can trace the source of all food back to the sun, our energy supplier, the one that through the process of photosynthesis transfers the solar energy in plants into living food. For their source of energy many animals use living food in the form of plants. I call food that is "living food," the most natural that exists, that which is in its natural form. Unfortunately to the detriment to mankind's health, this living food has lost much of its life through our neglect for nature's laws.

Our food is derived from living organisms, be it plants or animals, which also depend on their sources of food for survival. The quality of our food therefore is dependent on the quality of what our plants and animals ingest.

Our plants require nutrients to grow. They need the energy from the sun to allow for the process of photosynthesis. They require carbon, hydrogen and oxygen, which they receive from carbon dioxide and water as well as major nutrients like phosphates, potassium and nitrates in the soil. If these nutrients are in short supply in the soil, the plant turns out much less nutritious. If we eat plants that are grown in soil that has reduced levels of zinc, iron, iodine or other micronutrients, our diets will be deficient in these nutrients as well. Man's destruction and abuse of soil and irresponsible use of chemical fertilizers and pesticides has led to a reduction in the nutritional value of plant foods.

You may be saying to yourself at this point that this is nice to hear but what can we do about it? This seems to be a subject for environmentalists and those trying to save our planet. That may be right but we need to be aware of the consequences to our health. We should realize that where some food is grown is not necessarily the optimum location. The fact that our soil is in many cases deficient in minerals means that our diets are often deficient despite the fact that we are eating what we believe are natural living foods.

Don't be surprised if you suffer from disease even though you ingest these foods. Your body may still be deficient in valuable nutrients.

The goal of mankind should be to achieve the most natural and purest food sources. This means we need to implement agricultural practices that will protect and not destroy the soil. We need to stop using chemical fertilizers and pesticides. The type of fertilizer used also affects the nutrient value of what is grown. The protein or vitamin content of foods can vary. One carrot or potato grown in one soil is not necessarily equivalent in nutritional value to another carrot or potato grown in another soil somewhere else.

One source of better quality grown food is organically grown produce. Organically grown fruits and vegetables have been found to contain far greater amounts of nutrients than those commercially available. Studies have shown on average that organic crops have a higher nutrient content. Some research has attributed higher incidence of allergies to chemical fertilizers. The world-renowned Gerson cancer institutes rely on food grown organically for their cancer patients and the results have been remarkable. Compared to crops grown with chemical fertilizers and pesticides, organically grown crops generally have a higher vitamin C content, a lower content of carcinogenic nitrates and better protein quality. Even some research on animals fed commercially grown food with chemical fertilizers and pesticides have shown that fertility rates declined over several generations. What are the possible implications for us? Just take a look at the growing incidence of couples having difficulties with conceiving children and the alarming increase of allergies in childhood, not to mention cancer affecting almost one in every three people today.

The use of earthworms has shown to dramatically improve the quality of our soil. The advantages of having earthworms in the soil are that they increase the richness of the soil by adding nitrogen, calcium, magnesium, zinc, and other natural elements. This removes the need for chemical fertilizers that affect the soil in the long run. Earthworms increase the resistance against pests, aerate the soil so it holds more water and clean up dead organic matter by eating it and turning it into premium natural organic manure. Research has proved that vegetables and fruits grown in high concentrated earthworm farms stay fresh for a longer time and are known to improve their quality. So there you have it! Adding earthworms to our soil is a natural way to improve its quality and thus the quality of our plant foods.

I would highly recommend finding food sources that are reliable and that are not grown under commercial chemically fertilized conditions. Today there is a growing awareness of this problem and there is a current rise in organic farming due to demand for better quality food. Organic food usually costs more and doesn't look as attractive but you will increase your intake of nutrients that may be deficient in the food you currently buy in your local supermarket. If you have the rare opportunity to grow your own foods, avoid chemical fertilizers and pesticides. Add earthworms to your soil and let nature do its work.

Our voyage in understanding human health and nutrition has to start with the origins of food. Naturally it is nearly impossible to completely isolate ourselves from food grown under less than desirable conditions, but we need to be aware that what we eat, even if it is considered healthy food may not be enough to protect us from disease and degeneration. If you can understand this concept here you may come to realize that your body may not be getting what it needs and as a result you may not be enjoying the success that you desire in your health objectives. Even though at times you may be shocked at what you hear about our food in this book, it is certainly not the end of the world. I believe there is always a way out of our health problems, we just have to cater the intake of nutrients to our individual body's needs. It really is quite simple when you think about it. Just give the body what it needs. What it needs is "living food" and we get living food best from soil that is free of chemicals, rich in minerals and cultivated under nature's optimum conditions.

Chapter 2

Get into your cell

The cell is the basic unit of life. We cannot neglect mentioning cells when we discuss nutrition because to maintain health we need what our cells need. The cell is the simplest structure in an organism that we can associate with life, yet each is so small that we need a microscope to observe it. Cells grouped together make up tissues, groups of tissues make up organs and groups of organs make up all the systems in the human body. Remember when we discussed holistic health, if our cells are not receiving what they need then the whole body suffers. The nearest total number of cells that can be estimated we have in the human body is somewhere over 60 trillion. We have a variety of different types of cells including skin cells, red blood cells, liver cells, bone cells, muscle cells, nerve cells and many others. While each type of cell is specialized in its function, all cells have a number of common features or minimal requirements to stay alive. It really is quite a miracle that each of our cells receives a constant supply of food and oxygen to maintain its unbelievably vast array of functions in our body.

The cell is where everything happens. The cell is where disease begins, where aging begins, where all our genetic information is kept and where regeneration takes place. If we want to really get to the core of our health problems, this is where it is.

What do cells do? These tiny structures are able to exchange materials with their immediate environment, they are able to produce energy by obtaining nutrients, they can synthesize molecules and many can duplicate themselves. There is still however so much that we don't know about our cells.

Why am I even talking about cells? This isn't a biology course but a nutritional diet program. Well, remember at the beginning I said this is an intelligent diet not a crash diet. If you understand at least some of the basic needs of your cell, you will understand more of what it takes to build and maintain health.

When we look closely at a cell we see that it is filled with a number of granules and surrounded by a very thin barrier called a cell membrane. Like a very thin sheet of plastic, the cell membrane is flexible to an extent and can bend in a variety of shapes. The cell membrane is made up of lipids (fats) and proteins and has the ability to select what materials can enter or pass into and out of the cell. This is one of the essential processes of life called UTILIZATION if you remember back at the beginning of this book. If the cell does not receive what it needs, or if certain drugs or toxins are taken into the circulation, the cell membrane will not be maintained and materials may enter the cells that do not belong there. The cell must also maintain pH or acid / base balance. Our body fluids must maintain the correct acidity for proper functioning of the cells. This concept is very crucial as almost all disease begins with a change in pH of the environment in and around the cell.

Inside the cell we have what is called a nucleus, a large spherical or oval structure usually found in the center of the cell. The nucleus contains genetic information that is carried from parent to offspring and when the cell divides from mother cell to daughter cell. This is what makes us the way we are, the way our metabolism is set and the way our entire body works based on our genetic make-up. Other structures in the cell called organelles have functions that include synthesizing proteins and fatty acids, producing energy for the cell, and breaking down bacteria and damaged cell structures. There are many other structures found in the cell each with specific functions that contribute to cell metabolism. Metabolism refers to all chemical reactions that occur within a cell. As molecules continuously break down, they need to be synthesized. By producing energy the cell is able to utilize this energy to synthesize new molecules that are necessary for maintaining life.

Red blood cells have an average life span of 120 days and need to be continuously replaced. Our skin cells are continuously sloughed off and replaced while nerve cells cannot be replaced. Each of these cells need to bring in nutrients in the proper form and release waste products that have to be carried away by the circulatory system. Muscle cells contract in our muscles to provide movement, nerve cells in our nerves conduct impulses that travel across the network of our nervous system, red blood cells carry oxygen and white blood cells help to fight off the invaders in our bodies.

A normal cell if provided with adequate nutrients and oxygen, is able to undergo all these functions but in some cases that we fully do not understand, cells can mutate and begin to divide beyond control. In these cases we see cancer conditions. I strongly believe that every cell has this capability if it becomes too toxic and loses the ability to remove waste products, which accumulate in the cell and affect its function.

The ability of our bodies to regenerate, to replace worn out cells, to produce energy and rid the body of toxic substances is certainly an incredible miracle. The more we understand about our cells, the more we can appreciate that each of the 7 essential processes of life, including Ingestion, Digestion, Absorption, Circulation, Utilization, Detoxification and Regeneration are interrelated. If nutrients in the form of food and oxygen are to arrive in good shape and number at the cell's doorstep, we need to have all these essential processes working at optimum levels. Only in that way can we maintain health or cure disease.

We may not think about it very often but we neglect our cells by our bad nutritional habits and unhealthy lifestyle choices. As a result cells die or start to function less effectively. We lose brain cells from alcohol or drugs, liver cells are lost from alcohol and every birth control pill you take and heart cells die due to lack of oxygen by heart disease. Cells that line the interior of our digestive systems deteriorate due to antibiotic use and poor eating habits. Muscle and bone cells degenerate when we don't exercise. Overload of toxins in our body results often in skin problems or slow healing of wounds and injuries. These cells lose their ability to regenerate and to replace the old with the new. Our adipose or fat cells get filled up when we overeat.

Little by little this cell loss or decrease in cell function begins to affect the tissue, then the tissue begins to affect the organ, and once the organ is affected the body system involved starts to work at less than optimum conditions. If this persists, sooner or later it will not be able to perform its functions adequately and this leaves room open for disease to occur. We need to start to look back to the cellular level, and allow our cells the best possible chance to do their work. This means supplying adequate nutrition and sufficient oxygen to provide for effective ingestion. This also means optimum gas exchange in our lungs, efficient digestive capabilities and ability to absorb those nutrients into our bloodstream. In this way we stand a chance of getting those substances that our cells need into our bodies. Once in our bloodstreams these nutrients need a barricade-free trip to the cell's doorstep. If no drugs or toxic substances are in the way and the cell membrane is working as it should, and the heart and blood vessels are strong, these nutrients will have the greatest chance to be utilized by the cell for its host of metabolic activities. The waste products produced by the cell then finally need to be removed effectively and cleared by the body through its numerous detoxification channels. Thus the body stays clean, all body functions work at optimum rates because there are no "brakes being applied" and the cells can regenerate, build up their stores of energy for the body so that no disease process can ensue.

The rewards for getting into and understanding our cell and its needs and applying nutritional strategies are many. We will start to look and feel great, we will age naturally and not prematurely, we will maintain our weight, eliminate the possibility of disease and begin to think clearly. In short we will begin to gain control of our health. As we learn more about the cell and the mysteries it conceals we will open many more doors to uncovering the causes of our health problems.

Chapter 3

The Macronutrients: Carbohydrates, Proteins and Fats

In today's society a vast ocean of myths and misinformation concerning nutrition surrounds us and we are so bombarded with advertisements that even our doctors and nutritionists are guilty of being victims of this brainwashing. I find it hard to comprehend but there are so many medical professionals and nutritionists who still believe for example that cow's milk builds strong bones and that infant formula is superior to mother's milk! Those "food pyramids" or food groups that teachers instruct to children all over the world in their health and nutrition classes have been clever marketing tools set up by those enormous food industries that dictate what consumers should buy to be healthy. The realities of health and nutrition are not being taught in schools and most teachers do not have a clue. Just take a look at the food that is being offered in the average school lunchroom or cafeteria. The food and pharmaceutical industries spend billions of dollars on advertising campaigns and fund research designed to convince you that their products are good for you. Remember our list of illusions. The final outcome is that people do not associate their poor health and lack of vitality with the foods they eat or the drugs they take. This could not be further from the truth.

When we first begin our investigation into nutrition we need to look at those nutrients that our bodies require in the largest quantities. These are the macronutrients: carbohydrates, proteins and fats. We have all heard of each of them but do we really know what they do and what we need them all for?

Carbohydrates

Let's start with carbohydrates. When we hear the term "carbohydrates" we usually associate them with "energy". Carbohydrates are the sugars in our diet and as their name implies are molecules consisting of carbon, hydrogen and oxygen. They come in two basic forms: simple and complex. Simple carbohydrates are one, two, or at most three units of sugar linked together in single molecules. An example of a single unit carbohydrate or monosaccharide is glucose while sucrose or commercial sugar is an example of a two-unit carbohydrate molecule or disaccharide. Complex carbohydrates are hundreds or thousands of sugar units linked together in single molecules. Simple sugars are easily identified by their sweet taste while complex carbohydrates, such as potatoes, are pleasant to the taste buds, but not sweet.

There are two groups of complex carbohydrates: high fiber and low fiber. High-fiber, complex carbohydrates are not digestible by human beings because we do not have the enzyme to break them down. Cows however do have that enzyme. That is why they can get calories out of grass and we cannot. The main ingredient in high-fiber, complex carbohydrates is cellulose, which is indigestible by humans.

High-fiber (high-cellulose) vegetable foods are the healthiest choices in terms of nutrition and intake of these foods has been associated with lowered incidence of hypertension, diabetes, cancer, arthritis and other modern diseases. Examples of high-fiber foods are unrefined wholegrains, broccoli and green beans. Examples of low-fiber, complex carbohydrates are bananas, tomatoes, cereals and refined grains, bread, pasta, potatoes and rice.

To the circulatory system it doesn't really matter if the carbohydrate is simple or complex as after the carbohydrate is digested is appears in our blood stream as glucose, which heads to the cells to be used as energy. In order to transform complex carbohydrates into simple sugars such as glucose we need enzymes such as amylase, which are secreted by the salivary glands in our saliva and by our pancreas, which supplies enzymes to the duodenum of the small intestine. Whatever sugar the body does not use gets stored into you guessed it: fat - which leads to you know what: obesity.

Intake of only simple sugars and low-fiber, complex carbohydrates threatens our health when they are consumed in inappropriate amounts. When food from plants is processed into products such as refined sugar or white rice its fiber and/or vitamin content is stripped away. We are often guilty of food processing and a simple example is cutting an orange into two pieces, squeezing the juice out into a glass and throwing away the fiber.

Fiber is important in our diet and even necessary to protect us from some diseases but carbohydrates themselves are not necessary. There exist "essential" fatty acids and "essential" amino acids from protein but there are no known essential carbohydrates.

This is quite interesting because just take a look at the average diet and you find that most of our carbohydrates come from cereals and grains, which are often just processed complex carbohydrates that lack any fiber at all. Our bodies are not designed for this. Most of us just cannot handle such a high load of these carbohydrates.

Yes, we have made some health improvements by lowering our meat intake in recent years but have only replaced it by excessive simple and low-fiber complex carbohydrates. We need to include those carbohydrates with high fiber and that is where we are going wrong. The healthiest source of sugar is from complex carbohydrates present in high-fiber vegetables and sugars in the form of whole fruits. When you eat the whole fruit and not just the juice you receive natural fiber that allows proper absorption of the sugars. If you must drink fruit juice make sure that it is diluted at least 50 percent with water. I have seen so many health problems radically improve when individuals adopted a high-fiber carbohydrate diet.

What are the results when we adopt a high carbohydrate diet that lacks fiber? Our pancreas must work overtime to increase insulin output, and eventually wears itself out leading to insulin resistance and conditions such as atherosclerosis, hypertension, heart disease, digestive problems, hormonal problems, allergy and diabetes start rearing their ugly heads. Our sleep patterns are affected, our concentration and learning capacity is affected as well as our mood and psychological behavior. Those who suffer from asthma, bronchial conditions or emphysema will greatly benefit from stopping the intake of simple sugars and low-fiber complex carbohydrates as mucus is formed by sugar molecules that link together (mucopolysaccharides).

For maximum health and vitality, complex carbohydrates that include lots of fiber should be consumed daily in proper proportion. They contain necessary natural sources of vitamins and minerals as well as a rich source of enzymes when they are in the raw state. However, when carbohydrates are altered or processed they become simply empty calories that have been stripped of their original food value. If much of your diet consists of healthy high fiber complex carbohydrates, you should easily fulfill the recommended daily minimum fiber intake.

The moral of the carbohydrate story is to reduce simple and low-fiber complex carbohydrates and consume more high-fiber complex carbohydrates that contain fiber preferably in their unprocessed, natural raw form.

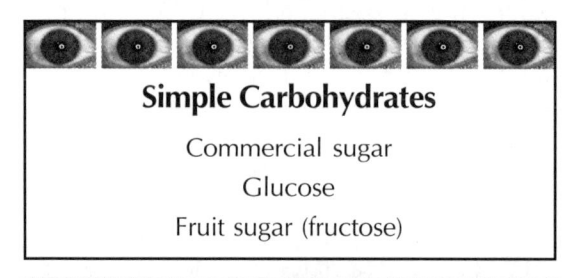

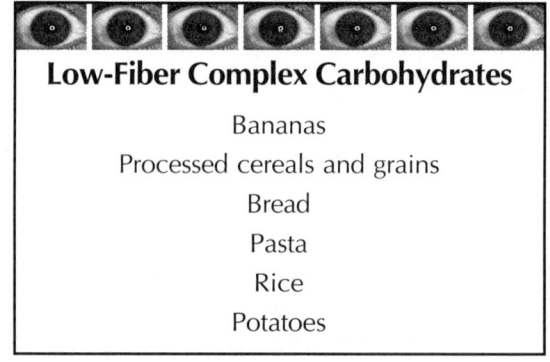

Simple Carbohydrates

Commercial sugar

Glucose

Fruit sugar (fructose)

Low-Fiber Complex Carbohydrates

Bananas

Processed cereals and grains

Bread

Pasta

Rice

Potatoes

> **High-fiber Complex Carbohydrates**
>
> Unrefined grains
>
> Broccoli
>
> Green beans
>
> Vegetables
>
> Nuts
>
> Seeds
>
> Legumes

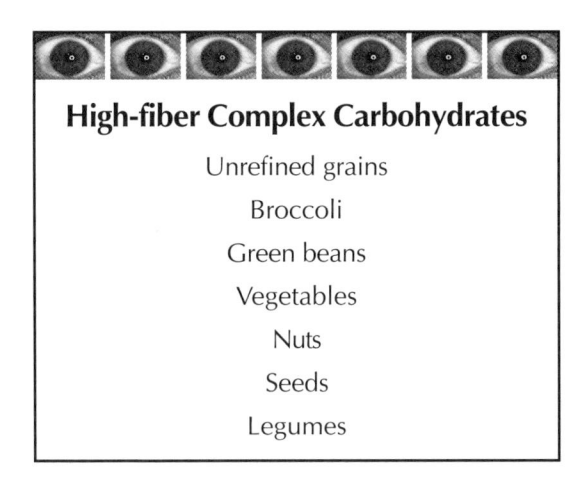

Proteins

Proteins are critical for life. They are large molecules made up of combinations of amino acids of which there are twenty different types. Eight of these amino acids are "essential", which means that they cannot be synthesized and must be consumed from sources outside the body. We need an adequate intake of proteins so that they can be broken down into amino acids, distributed to the cells where they are reassembled back into proteins to then serve a wide range of functions in our body.

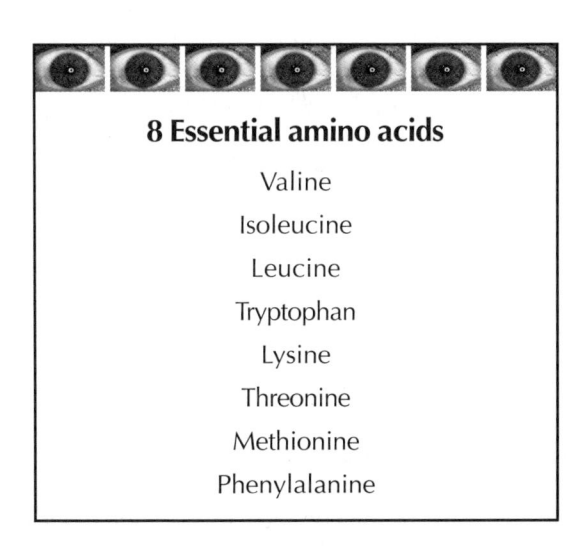

> **8 Essential amino acids**
>
> Valine
>
> Isoleucine
>
> Leucine
>
> Tryptophan
>
> Lysine
>
> Threonine
>
> Methionine
>
> Phenylalanine

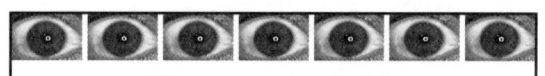

The 20 amino acids

Glycine, Alanine, Cysteine, Serine, Methionine
Threonine, Leucine, Valine, Isoleucine,
Phenylalanine, Tyrosine, Tryptophan,
Histidine, Hydroxyproline, Proline,
Aspartic acid, Glutamic acid, Lysine,
Arginine, Hydroxylysine

We need proteins for building structures, muscle tissue and organs in our body, for enzymes, for hormones, for our immune system, and as an energy source since they can also be converted to glucose. Protein digestion starts in the stomach where the acidic environment and the enzyme pepsin that is secreted by the stomach cells begin to break down the protein. In the small intestine primarily the duodenum, the rest of protein digestion occurs under the influence of enzymes from both the pancreas and the intestinal cells themselves.

If the environment in the stomach and digestive system is not in good order, proteins that we ingest will not be absorbed effectively and critical functions in the body will suffer. As we mentioned there are many systems in the body that depend on essential proteins and all cells must synthesize proteins in order to survive. Furthermore, improper digestion and absorption of proteins have also been linked to the formation of allergies and hormonal problems.

It is important to understand that all proteins are broken down and replaced in the cells with different proteins being replaced at different rates. Some hormones composed of proteins must be replaced every few hours while other proteins such as hemoglobin in the red blood cells must be replaced every 120 days.

Not all amino acids are present in all proteins, which means that there exist low-quality proteins that lack one or more of the essential amino acids and high quality proteins that contain the full complement of amino acids. An example of this can be found in cultures that suffer from protein deficiency such as in some areas of Ethiopia that consume primarily corn, which is deficient in the amino acid lysine. I remember visiting these communities where children with bloated stomachs due to protein deficiency (called kwashiorkor a Ghanian word for "the evil spirit that infects the child.") were being fed only corn and literally being starved of complete protein due to lack of education. It is important to combine proteins so that the full complement of essential amino acids are ingested daily. For instance, although beans and brown rice are both quite rich in protein, each lacks one or more of the essential amino acids. However, when you combine brown rice and beans with each other, you form a complete protein that is a quality substitute for meat. Complete protein can be achieved in a variety of food combinations, some of which are listed. All soybean products including tofu and soymilk are complete proteins. They contain all of the essential amino acids as well as several other nutrients and they can be used as alternatives to a meat diet.

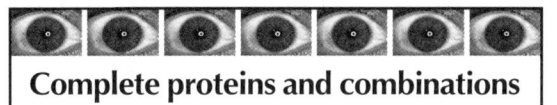

> **Complete proteins and combinations**
>
> Beans with: brown rice, corn, seeds, or nuts
>
> Soybean products
>
> Meat, fish or poultry
>
> Sour milk products, yogurt
>
> Brown rice with: beans, seeds or nuts

Yogurt or soured milk is one of the few complete-protein sources derived from animals that I recommend from the milk products group for frequent use in the diet as long as it does not contain sugar and is obtained from natural sources or preferably made at home. It is produced from milk that is curdled by bacteria, and contains Lactobacillus acidophilus and other beneficial bacteria needed for adequate digestion. Many of our modern diseases can be prevented when yogurt is added to the diet. Several of the long-lived cultures have used soured milk or yogurt in their diets.

The majority of protein we ingest in Western society is from animal protein in the form of meat, milk and eggs. Vegetable sources include soy, legumes, and nuts. It is possible to achieve high quality protein intake through food from vegetable or animal origin or a combination of both. Vegetarians must be careful to combine the appropriate foods to achieve all 8 essential amino acids. Soybeans contain a significant proportion of high quality protein. Meat and milk are considered high quality proteins but they come with the problem of added antibiotics, hormones, pesticides and other additives, which will be discussed in a later chapter. Most people do not have enough high-fiber foods in their diet to move things along quickly in the intestinal tract so excessive animal protein or meat intake leads to putrefaction in the intestinal tract and the production of harmful bacteria. In Western cultures there is not a problem of not enough essential protein but too much protein. The recommended intake of protein has been claimed to be approximately 0.8 grams per kilogram of body weight. Excess protein is defined as more than 1.6 grams per kilogram of body weight. For an average-size man weighing 70 kg this amounts to between 56 and 112 grams. I would recommend that in general about 25 percent of your diet should be protein preferably the majority from plant origin with only occasional fish, poultry and eggs. During growth or pregnancy and lactation, protein intake needs to be increased due to extra demands.

While it is generally recommended for athletes and very physically active people to increase their protein intake as muscle breaks down during exercise, excessive protein can cause problems. With high protein intake there is an increased load on the kidneys, as surplus urea has to be excreted. The high purine content of high-protein intake can lead to gout and kidney stones, as purine breaks down to uric acid, which crystallizes in the kidneys and joints. Arthritis is very common is high meat eaters. A typical western diet of excessive meat, eggs, milk, fish and poultry also throws the body into a negative calcium balance. This lost calcium must come from somewhere in the body, and the largest store of calcium is in the bones. The bones are slowly decalcified and the result can be osteoporosis, one of the most common and serious health problems of elderly people in developed countries.

To cut a long story short, we need to make sure that we are obtaining quality protein in our diet that includes all the amino acids but not in excessive amounts as found in most Western cultures and to increase our protein intake from fish, nuts and plant sources.

Fat

Many of us spend our lives trying to eliminate fat from our diet, and treat fat as if it were a bad word. The truth is however, that if we did not have any fat in our diet we would not be alive. During infancy and childhood, fat is necessary for normal brain development. Throughout life, it is also essential to support growth, for our hormonal system and to provide energy. After about two years of age, the body requires only small amounts of fat, much less than is provided by the average Western diet. Excessive fat intake is a major cause of high blood pressure, coronary heart disease, obesity and colon cancer and is linked to many other disorders as well. To understand how fat intake is related to these health problems, it is important to become familiarized with the different types of fats available and the ways in which these fats act within the body.

While proteins are made up of amino acids the building blocks of fats are fatty acids. There are three main categories of fatty acids: **saturated, polyunsaturated, and mono-unsaturated**. Fats are categorized according to their saturation. The term saturation means the number of hydrogen atoms attached to the fat molecule. When a fat molecule contains the maximum number of hydrogen atoms, it is "saturated." This kind of fat remains solid at room temperature. If one pair of hydrogen atoms is missing, the molecule is said to be "mono-unsaturated," one example being olive oil. If more than one pair of hydrogen atoms is missing, it is said to be "polyunsaturated." These are the thin oils that are commonly used for frying or in salad dressings.

Saturated fatty acids are found mainly in foods of animal origin, which include milk products, cheese and meats like beef, veal, lamb, pork and ham. Some vegetable products also contain saturated fats such as coconut oil. Excess saturated fats can be dangerous because the liver uses them to manufacture cholesterol and they can significantly raise the level of blood cholesterol especially the "bad cholesterol"

Polyunsaturated fatty acids are found in the greatest amounts in corn, sunflower, and soybean oils as well as some fish oils. The intake of polyunsaturated fats has been found to lower cholesterol but in excess amounts can reduce the good cholesterol and like all fats they are high in calories and should be limited in the diet. When polyunsaturated fats are altered unnaturally and hydrogenated they change to a form which is called a **trans fatty acid**. An example of this is when vegetable oils are unnaturally hardened into foods such as margarine or shortening. Studies have found that trans fatty acids can raise the "bad cholesterol" levels and in this way act similarly to saturated fats. They have also been found to be more associated with heart disease than saturated fats such as butter. Other examples of hydrogenated fats are commonly found in "junk foods" such as potato chips and cookies. They are very hard to digest and are associated with heart disease.

Mono-unsaturated fatty acids are found in nut and vegetable oils such as olive, peanut and canola oil. They appear to reduce the bad cholesterol without affecting the good so there are positive health benefits of including them in your diet but again not in excess. Fats from fish oil such as salmon and tuna are very beneficial to the body as well.

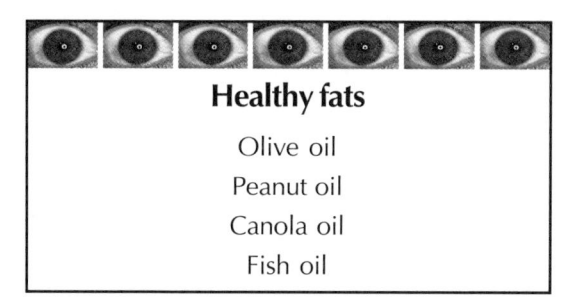

Healthy fats

Olive oil
Peanut oil
Canola oil
Fish oil

The consumption of excess fats in the diet results not only in obesity but also oxidation with the production of excess free radicals. This can subject the body to carcinogenic and degenerative effects. Excess fat has been linked to heart disease, arthritis, a variety of cancers, stroke and numerous other health problems. Excess animal fats have also been found to alter the onset of menses and menopause in women.

Remember that fats are essential in our diet but in order to lower cholesterol and stay lean and healthy, they should not be excessive in our daily intake. Polyunsaturated and mono-unsaturated are best and the intake of saturated and trans fatty acids in the diet should be reduced. If you follow the carbohydrate and protein recommendations that I have given, then fats will take care of themselves. You will not have to even think about the possibility that you will have excess fats or waste your time counting how much fat you take in with your diet.

These are the macronutrients. Since we consume them in the largest quantities they have the greatest effect on our health and well-being. Each of us has different needs for macronutrients. Later we will be able to apply this knowledge to our specific genetics. By following these important basic guidelines concerning carbohydrate, protein and fat ingestion you will be well on your way to achieving your health and weight goals.

Vitamins: Micronutrients for maintenance of growth and health

Chapter 4

Like carbohydrates, protein and fats, vitamins are essential to life. They are therefore considered essential nutrients, often referred to as micronutrients simply because they are needed in relatively small amounts compared with the three basic macronutrients.

In recent years there has been a boom in vitamin manufacturing and vitamin sales. Most vitamins can be purchased over the counter and today there are so many brands and combinations it can make your head spin when you visit your local chemist or health shop. Where do we start when we are considering what vitamins to take or should we be even taking them at all? There are no really easy answers to these questions. Every one of us is unique with different nutritional needs. That is part of the problem and controversy that surrounds vitamins. National health departments have recommended daily intakes of all the vitamins but these are usually only the bare minimums needed so that we do not get the deficiency disease. They do not take into consideration various stresses that are imposed on us that can increase our nutritional needs quite substantially. People who are active, exercise, are pregnant, those who are under great stress, or mentally or physically ill, women who take oral contraceptives, those on medication, those who are recovering from surgery and smokers and heavy consumers of alcoholic beverages all need higher than normal amounts of nutrients.

It does not matter how we look at it, vitamin supplements are processed in some way or another. The chemical forms of vitamins are not what we want and thankfully more and more manufacturers are using natural forms of vitamins now in their products. I am not against taking vitamins. I have recommended them to my patients for many years and have seen thousands of clients who have responded incredibly well to vitamin supplementation. I do believe however, that once again the public has begun to use vitamin supplementation as a crutch instead of dealing with the causes of their health problems through natural forms of diet and nutrition. Please don't get in the habit of saying to yourself, "I ate really unhealthy stuff today but these vitamin pills will compensate for it." Without eating healthy and quality foods those vitamin pills will be worth absolutely nothing. Remember they are only "supplements" which means they only supplement your diet not replace your diet. Be very careful of falling in the trap of treating vitamins like we treat drugs. Don't treat them like a get healthy quick scheme. Nothing will replace a nourishing diet complete with all the essential nutrients, vitamins and minerals in their natural purest form.

This chapter is designed to briefly give you an understanding of each of the essential vitamins and in what foods we can find a high concentration of them. Included are also the factors that increase the demand for each vitamin, some associated problems with deficiencies and toxic effects of over dosage. Toxic effects of vitamins are usually only found when taking excessive supplements not when ingesting vitamins found in natural food sources. It is always much safer to source these vitamins from the foods we eat. When taking vitamin supplements I recommend that you consult with your natural therapist or naturopathic doctor.

We will discuss the fat-soluble vitamins (Vitamins A, D, E and K) initially. The term "fat-soluble vitamins" means that they are vitamins that need fats in order to dissolve and be absorbed into our blood stream. It also means that they have a tendency to accumulate in the tissues when they are taken excessively. High levels of intake of these vitamins can have dangerous effects.

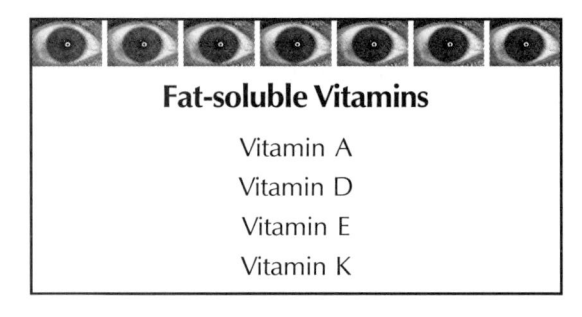

Fat-soluble Vitamins
Vitamin A
Vitamin D
Vitamin E
Vitamin K

Vitamin A, Betacarotene

Role: Vitamin A is necessary for maintenance and growth of epithelial tissues, for vision, skin, bones and reproduction.

Food sources high in Vitamin A: green leafy vegetables, liver, carrots, apricots, and fish liver oils.

Conditions that increase demand for Vitamin A: problems with fat absorption, alcohol, smog and pollution, cancer, diabetes, diarrhea, gallbladder disease, pancreatic disease, smoking, stress

Deficiency of Vitamin A may be associated with: acne, dry hair, eye inflammation, nephritis, night blindness, low immunity, slow bone growth, dry skin

Toxic effects of over dosage of Vitamin A: fatigue, headache, insomnia, bone pain, peeling skin, disturbed hair growth, anorexia, during pregnancy high intake of Vitamin A can cause birth defects

Vitamin D
Role: Vitamin D is synthesized in the skin and is required for calcium metabolism, bones and maintenance of cell membranes.

Sources of Vitamin D: sunlight, fish liver oils, egg yolk, butter and sprouts

Conditions that increase demand for Vitamin D: alcohol, Crohn's disease, intestinal disorders, kidney disorders, lactation, liver disease, pregnancy and lactation, smog, ulcerative colitis

Deficiency of Vitamin D may be associated with: Rickets, osteomalacia, cramps, diarrhea, insomnia, slow growth, softening of teeth and bones

Toxic effects of over dosage of Vitamin D: weakness, fatigue, headache, nausea, diarrhea, joint pain, kidney damage and anorexia

Vitamin E
Role: Vitamin E is a strong antioxidant that protects the cell membranes, enhances the immune system, enhances Vitamin A absorption and improves blood flow.

Food Sources high in Vitamin E: almonds, safflower, soybean and sunflower oils, nuts, egg yolk, corn, liver and green leafy vegetables

Conditions that increase demand for Vitamin E: athletes, cancer, diabetes, elderly, air pollution, excess intake of polyunsaturated oils, pregnancy and lactation, liver and gall bladder disease

Deficiency of Vitamin E may be associated with: gallbladder and liver disease, poor immunity, early aging, pancreatic disorders

Toxic effects of over dosage of Vitamin E: may affect blood clotting, may increase blood cholesterol or lipids

Vitamin K
Role: Vitamin K is required for normal blood clotting and allows clotting factors such as prothrombin to be synthesized in the liver.

Sources of Vitamin K: synthesized by bacteria in the intestines, alfalfa, cabbages, green leafy vegetables, broccoli, eggs, kelp, lettuce, soybeans, spinach, parsley and liver

Conditions that increase demand for Vitamin K: antibiotic use, intestinal diseases, Crohn's disease, liver and gall bladder disease

Deficiency of Vitamin K may be associated with: increased tendency to bleed including nosebleeds, increased clotting time

Toxic effects of over dosage of Vitamin K: vomiting, respiratory tract irritation or skin irritation

The water soluble vitamins (Vitamins B1, B2, B3, B6, Biotin, Pantothenic Acid, Folic Acid, Vitamin B12, and Vitamin C) are those that can dissolve in water which means they can be excreted through the kidneys if their levels increase in the blood. This makes these vitamins relatively safe to ingest even at higher dosages but I would still advise consulting with your natural therapist or naturopathic doctor whenever deciding to take vitamin supplements.

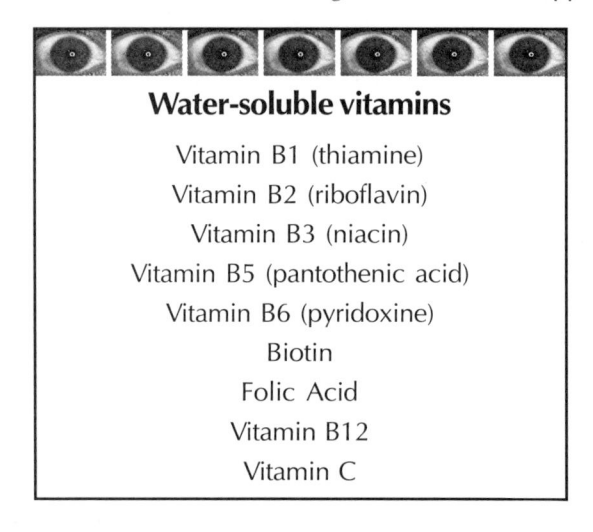

> **Water-soluble vitamins**
>
> Vitamin B1 (thiamine)
> Vitamin B2 (riboflavin)
> Vitamin B3 (niacin)
> Vitamin B5 (pantothenic acid)
> Vitamin B6 (pyridoxine)
> Biotin
> Folic Acid
> Vitamin B12
> Vitamin C

Vitamin B1 -Thiamine

Role: Vitamin B1 or Thiamine is required as a cofactor of many enzymes in metabolism, for digestion and energy production, growth and the nervous system.

Food Sources high in Vitamin B1: green leafy vegetables, legumes, liver, nuts, pork, and whole grains, yeast

Conditions that increase demand for Vitamin B1: alcoholism, athletes, coffee and tea, aging, diarrhea, pregnancy and lactation, liver disease, smoking, stress, oral contraceptive pill, high intake of sugar, fevers, infections

Deficiency of Vitamin B1 may be associated with: Beriberi, anorexia, constipation, glaucoma, low blood pressure, insomnia, memory problems, depression, muscle weakness, fatigue, tachycardia

Toxic effects of over dosage of Vitamin B1: nervousness, shortness of breath, edema, sweating

Vitamin B2 - Riboflavin

Role: Vitamin B2 or Riboflavin is essential for energy metabolism and other reactions in cellular metabolism.

Food Sources high in Vitamin B2: beans, eggs, milk products, sprouts, wholegrains, yeast, avocado, green leafy vegetables, liver

Conditions that increase demand for Vitamin B2: alcohol intake, coffee, diabetes, fevers, heart diseases, oral contraceptive pill, smoking, stress

Deficiency of Vitamin B2 may be associated with: cracking or sores on lips, dermatitis, inflammation of the tongue, blood shot eyes, cataracts, sensitivity to light

Toxic effects of over dosage of Vitamin B2: Essentially non-toxic

Vitamin B3 - Niacin

Role: Vitamin B3 or Niacin is essential for energy metabolism and other reactions in cellular metabolism

Food Sources high in Vitamin B3: Legumes, nuts, almonds, chicken, eggs, sunflower seeds, meat, peanuts, salmon, sardines, yeast

Conditions that increase demand for Vitamin B3: Alcoholism, burns, coffee, diarrhea, fever, Hartnup disease, diets based on corn, excess intake of sugar, chronic gastrointestinal disease

Deficiency of Vitamin B3 may be associated with: Pellagra, dermatitis, dementia, diarrhea, depression, headaches, schizophrenia

Toxic effects of over dosage of Vitamin B3: diarrhea, increase in pulse and respiratory rate, itching skin, flushing

Vitamin B5 – Pantothenic Acid

Role: Vitamin B5 or Pantothenic Acid is required for synthesis of acetylcholine, antibody production, cholesterol, hormone production and for most of our metabolism.

Food Sources high in Vitamin B5: organ meat, beef, fish, egg yolks, green vegetables, avocado, beans, nuts, and soybeans

Conditions that increase demand for Vitamin B5: pregnancy, stress, aging, arthritis, depression, high intake of coffee or alcohol

Deficiency of Vitamin B5 may be associated with: fatigue, headache, insomnia, nausea, vomiting, muscle cramps, depression, tingling in hands or feet, impaired coordination

Toxic effects of over dosage of Vitamin B5: Essentially non-toxic

Vitamin B6 - Pyridoxine

Role: Vitamin B6 or Pyridoxine is required for amino acid synthesis and protein metabolism

Food Sources high in Vitamin B6: yeast, chicken, egg yolk, peanuts, salmon, tuna, legumes, walnuts, soybeans, bananas and avocado

Conditions that increase demand for Vitamin B6: excess intake of protein, pregnancy and lactation, aging, diabetes, excess alcohol, liver disease, contraceptive pill, hyperthyroidism

Deficiency of Vitamin B6 may be associated with: dermatitis around eyes, mouth and nose, depression, weakness, insomnia, seizures, weight loss, poor immunity

Toxic effects of over dosage of Vitamin B6: only limited toxicity

Biotin
Role: Biotin is a member of the B group vitamins and is required for metabolism of fat, protein and carbohydrates, maintenance of hair and skin.

Sources of Biotin: some is synthesized by bacteria in the intestines, bean sprouts, liver, egg yolk, peanuts, soy beans, mushrooms, yeast

Conditions that increase demand for Biotin: excess raw egg white intake, aging, alcohol, athletes, coffee, pregnancy and lactation

Deficiency of Biotin may be associated with: dermatitis, painful tongue, muscle pain, cracked lips, anorexia, fatigue, and insomnia

Toxic effects of over dosage of Biotin: Essentially non-toxic

Folic Acid
Role: Folic Acid is a member of the B group of vitamins and is required for several metabolic reactions including amino acid metabolism and purine synthesis.

Food sources high in Folic Acid: green leafy vegetables, beans, eggs, lentils, yeast, liver, and peanuts

Conditions that increase demand for Folic Acid: pregnancy and lactation, alcoholism, aging, antibiotics, B12 deficiency, gastrointestinal disease, diarrhea, blood loss, oral contraceptives

Deficiency of Folic Acid may be associated with: anemia, anorexia, fatigue, headaches, insomnia, paranoid behavior, reproductive failures and weight loss

Toxic effects of over dosage of Folic Acid: Essentially non-toxic

Vitamin B12
Role: Vitamin B12 is required for biosynthesis of nucleic acids, protein and blood cells, metabolism of fat, protein, and carbohydrate, maintenance of growth and the nervous system.

Sources of Vitamin B12: synthesized by bacteria in the intestines, egg yolk, herring, liver, meat, milk, oysters, salmon, sardines, chicken, chlorella

Conditions that increase demand for Vitamin B12: vegetarians (vegans), aging, Crohn's disease, Coeliac disease, excess alcohol, smoking, gastrointestinal disorders, pregnancy and lactation, oral contraceptives, liver disease, antibiotics

Deficiency of Vitamin B12 may be associated with: anemia, neurological disorders, depression, fatigue, memory loss, paranoia, schizophrenia, weakness

Toxic effects of over dosage of Vitamin B12: Virtually no toxic effects

Vitamin C

Role: Vitamin C is required for collagen synthesis, synthesis of carnitine, bile acids, adrenalin, activation of folic acid, it enhances iron absorption, bone and teeth growth, blood cell formation, immunity, promotes healing and is an antioxidant.

Food sources high in Vitamin C: peppers, black currant, broccoli, citrus fruits, guava, parsley, pineapple, strawberries, rosehips, raw cabbage, brussel sprouts, and cauliflower

Conditions that increase demand for Vitamin C: smog and pollution, smoking, heart disease, high blood pressure, radiation, chemotherapy, drug toxicity, heavy metal intoxication, pregnancy, stress, surgery, arthritis, burns, allergies, high blood cholesterol, low immunity, oral contraceptive pill, infections

Deficiency of Vitamin C may be associated with: Scurvy, weakness, bleeding gums, bruising easily, depression, fatigue, susceptibility to infection, pain in joints, loosening of teeth, slow healing of wounds

Toxic effects of over dosage of Vitamin C: diarrhea, iron overload, there is some claims that possible kidney stones can occur with extremely high doses near 10 grams /day but this has not been substantiated.

Other substances that are not classified as vitamins but have vitamin-like activity are: Bioflavonoids, choline, inositol, para-aminobenzoic acid (PABA), and essential fatty acids (Linolenic Acid, and Linoleic Acid)

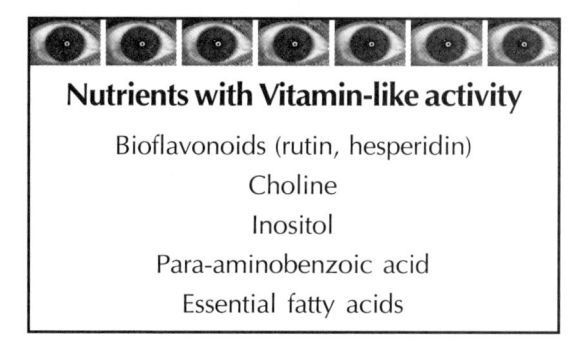

Nutrients with Vitamin-like activity

Bioflavonoids (rutin, hesperidin)

Choline

Inositol

Para-aminobenzoic acid

Essential fatty acids

Bioflavonoids (rutin, hesperidin, citrin, quercetin,)

Role: The bioflavonoids are a class of substances that are required for maintenance of capillary walls, improved blood flow and act as antioxidants along with Vitamin C

Food sources high in bioflavonoids: citrus fruits, buckwheat, berries, skins of fruits and vegetables

Conditions that increase demand for bioflavonoids: blood pressure problems, hemorrhoids, varicose veins, bruising easily, bleeding from gums, cataracts, allergies, asthma, burns

Deficiency of bioflavonoids may be associated with: bruising, poor immunity, capillary fragility, diminished vitamin C activity

Toxic effects of over dosage of bioflavonoids: No toxic effects reported

Choline

Role: Choline is needed for synthesis of lecithin; it reduces the amount of fat in the liver, plays an important role in cell membranes, and reduces blood cholesterol. It is also needed for synthesis of acetylcholine, one of the most important neurotransmitters.

Food sources high in choline: egg yolk, fish, liver, cereals, legumes, lecithin and peanuts

Conditions that increase demand for choline: high alcohol consumption, coffee, liver deficiencies, low protein diets

Deficiency of choline may be associated with: cirrhosis of the liver, fatty liver, stomach ulcers, increased blood pressure, hardening of the arteries, low, immunity, kidney and heart problems

Toxic effects of over dosage of choline: diarrhea, nausea and depression

Inositol

Role: Inositol is needed for cell membranes, fat metabolism in the liver, and in neurotransmission in the brain.

Food sources high in inositol: beans, citrus fruit, corn, nuts, seeds, vegetables, wholegrain cereals, meats

Conditions that increase demand for inositol: diabetes, high blood cholesterol, poor kidney function, lactation, stress and high blood pressure

Deficiency of inositol may be associated with: hair loss, constipation, eczema, and cataracts

Toxic effects of over dosage of inositol: diarrhea, nausea

Para-aminobenzoic acid

Role: Para-aminobenzoic acid is unclear whether it is required by humans as a nutrient but is a constituent of folic acid, facilitates intestinal bacterial activity

Sources of para-aminobenzoic acid: liver, whole grain cereals, brewer's yeast

Conditions that increase demand for para-aminobenzoic acid: excessive exposure to ozone and sun, Rickettsial bacterial diseases

Deficiency of para-aminobenzoic acid may be associated with: constipation, depression, fatigue, graying hair, headaches and irritability, digestive disorders

Toxic effects of over dosage of para-aminobenzoic acid: anorexia, fever, and skin rash

Essential fatty acids (Linolenic Acid, Linoleic Acid)
Role: coagulation of blood, growth, cell membrane and regulation of inflammatory reactions

Sources of essential fatty acids: corn oil, evening primrose oil, Omega 3 oil, tuna, salmon, seaweed, sunflower oil, tofu, wheatgerm oil

Conditions that increase demand for essential fatty acids: high alcohol ingestion, arthritis, elevated cholesterol, heart disease, obesity skin disorders, smoking, stress, diabetes, pancreatic and bile disorders

Deficiency of essential fatty acids may be associated with: skin problems including eczema, acne or psoriasis, bruising, dry or brittle hair, hormonal problems, gall stones, low immunity, impaired reproduction, inflammation, pain, poor wound healing, respiratory infections, varicose veins.

Toxic effects of over dosage of essential fatty acids: in high amounts they increase demand for Vitamin E and other antioxidants.

Chapter 5

Minerals: Micronutrients for fine-tuning and building a healthy strong body

While vitamins are organic molecules that are essential for the maintenance of our health and for growth, the minerals, micronutrients required only in small quantities, are inorganic molecules or elements found in the body. These relatively small amounts of minerals are essential to our well-being and play important roles in metabolism as well as in many aspects of function of our cells. While minerals account for only about four percent of our total human body weight, they are involved in over ninety percent of all bodily functions. Each of the major and trace minerals needed by the body are discussed below including their role, in what foods they are found in large amounts, conditions that increase their demand and associated problems linked to their deficiency. Please note again that minerals found in most foods are not dangerous but the administration of mineral supplements should be consulted with your naturopathic doctor or natural therapist as over dosages can often be toxic. I hope this chapter can give you an appreciation of what minerals are and what they do in the body. Many health problems arise due to lack of minerals in the diet. Try to familiarize yourself with each and their role in the body. Take a look at some of the foods that contain these minerals and ask yourself if you are providing your body with adequate amounts of each nutrient.

Some of the major minerals or element in our diet include calcium, phosphorus, potassium, sodium, and magnesium. These are discussed first.

Some major minerals or elements essential in the diet

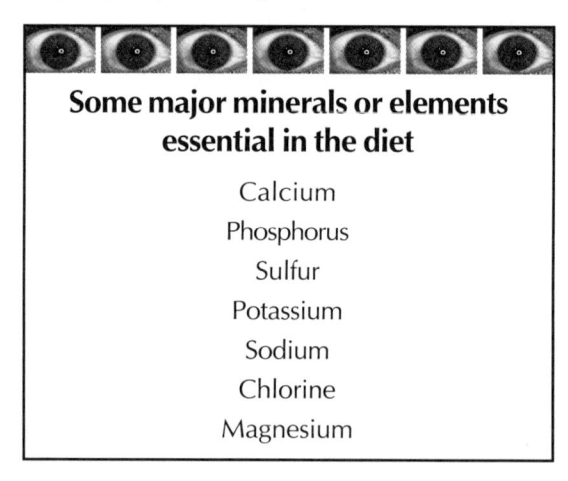

Calcium

Phosphorus

Sulfur

Potassium

Sodium

Chlorine

Magnesium

Calcium

Role: Calcium is needed for bone, teeth, muscle contraction, blood clotting, and as a cofactor of enzymes.

Food sources high in calcium: dairy products, shellfish, almonds, egg yolk, green leafy vegetables, sardines, soybeans, sesame seeds, parsley, dried figs

Conditions that increase demand for calcium: bone fractures, high caffeine, depression, high blood pressure, high intake of phosphates, high sugar or protein diets, high sodium intake, lactation, pregnancy, lack of exercise

Deficiency of calcium may be associated with: brittle fingernails, agitation, convulsions, depression, eczema, hypertension, insomnia, muscle cramps, nervousness, osteoporosis, osteomalacia, heart palpitations, tooth decay, rickets, hyperactivity

Toxic effects of over dosage of calcium: anorexia, depression, irritability, memory impairment, muscle weakness

Phosphorus

Role: Phosphorus is needed for bones, teeth, metabolism and ATP energy production

Food sources high in phosphorus: cashew nuts, almonds, chickpeas, salmon, sardines, seeds, garlic, sesame and tuna

Conditions that increase demand for phosphorus: excess calcium, lactation or pregnancy, growth, excess coffee intake

Deficiency of phosphorus may be associated with: anxiety, anorexia, fear, pain in the bones, fatigue, irritability, numbness, weakness, irregular breathing, osteomalacia, rickets

Toxic effects of over dosage of phosphorus: relatively safe, bone resorption, laxative effect

Sulfur

Role: Sulfur is needed for amino acids, for regulation of the sodium/potassium pump within the cells, for the immune system as a component of insulin and for tissue repair.

Food sources high in sulfur: brussel sprouts, horseradish, garlic, onions, radish, mustard, proteins

Conditions that increase demand for sulfur: aging, wounds, stress, arthritis, allergies, asthma, acne, low immunity

Deficiency of sulfur may be associated with: insulin deficiency, energy production, brittle hair and nails, gastrointestinal problems, poor healing or repair, poor growth and poor immunity

Toxic effects of over dosage of sulfur: None found

Potassium

Role: Potassium is the most common electrolyte in the cells, blood and tissues of the body, particularly the muscles and cartilage. Potassium is needed for normal heart beat and muscle contraction, as well as for glucose uptake, insulin secretion and nerve function.

Food sources high in potassium: all vegetables, banana, apricots, avocado, citrus fruits, dates, almonds, cashews, pecans, raisins, sardines, sunflower seeds, meat

Conditions that increase demand for potassium: stress, high level of physical activity, diabetes, diarrhea, high intake of coffee, tea, alcohol, sugar, or salt, high blood pressure, liver or kidney disease

Deficiency of potassium may be associated with: acne, constipation, depression, edema, insomnia, muscle weakness, low blood pressure, nervousness, salt retention, irregular heart beat

Toxic effects of over dosage of potassium: weakness, cardiac arrhythmia, cognitive impairment, diarrhea, mental confusion

Sodium

Role: Sodium is important in acid-base balance, maintenance of blood pressure, cell permeability and is the major electrolyte outside of the cells.

Food sources high in sodium: celery, liver, cheeses, olives, peas, salt, tuna and sardines

Conditions that increase demand for sodium: diarrhea, coffee, dehydration, excess water intake, and sweating, vomiting, lack of potassium

Deficiency of sodium may be associated with: abdominal cramps, anorexia confusion, fatigue, depression, dizziness, flatulence, headache, hallucinations, low blood pressure, muscle weakness, weight loss, seizures

Toxic effects of over dosage of sodium: diarrhea, anorexia, hypertension, edema, hyperactivity, irritability, renal failure, seizures, weight gain, tremors

Chlorine

Role: Chlorine is required for hydrochloric acid formation in the stomach and in maintaining osmotic pressure and pH in the fluid outside the cells. It also helps to keep joints, tendons and muscles healthy.

Food sources high in chlorine: asparagus, avocado, cabbage, celery, cucumber, kelp, oats, olives, pineapple, seaweed, tomatoes and turnip

Conditions that increase demand for chlorine: vomiting, excess alcohol, nicotine, cola drinks, coffee, refined foods

Deficiency of chlorine may be associated with: poor digestion, alopecia (thinning hair) baldness, cavities, edema and impaired muscle contraction

Toxic effects of over dosage of chlorine: None found for organic chlorine, inorganic chlorine toxic

Magnesium

Role: Magnesium is essential in the diet and needed as a cofactor in most metabolic reactions involving the production of energy in the cell.

Food sources high in magnesium: nuts, whole grain foods, almonds, cashews, molasses, soybeans, spinach, beets, broccoli

Conditions that increase demand for magnesium: intense physical activity, alcoholism, coffee excess, diarrhea, epilepsy, lactation, pregnancy, radiation, liver disease and high fat or sugar intake

Deficiency of magnesium may be associated with: anxiety, depression, hyperactivity, low blood pressure, insomnia, muscle pains, nervousness, seizures, rapid heart beat, cold hands and feet, muscle weakness

Toxic effects of over dosage of magnesium: nausea, nerve paralysis, respiratory distress, confusion, muscle weakness

Some of the essential trace minerals or elements, which are obtained from foods in very small amounts, are discussed below. There are many other trace elements but many of their requirements and functions in the human body are still relatively unknown.

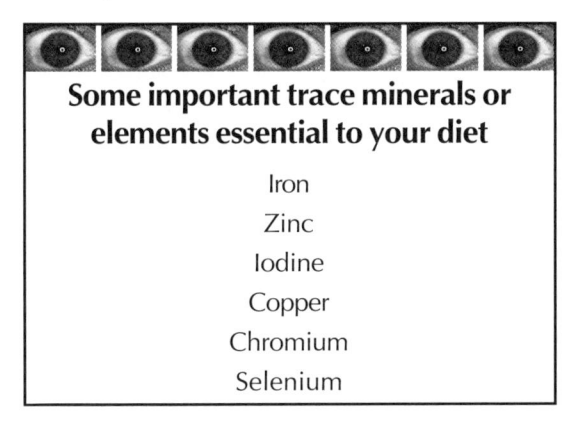

Some important trace minerals or elements essential to your diet

Iron

Zinc

Iodine

Copper

Chromium

Selenium

Iron

Role: Iron plays a vital role as part of hemoglobin, myoglobin, and as a cofactor in enzymes.

Food sources high in iron: liver, apricots, oysters, parsley, sesame seeds, soybeans, sunflower seeds and almonds

Conditions that increase demand for iron: anemia, pregnancy, copper deficiency, excess calcium intake, bleeding, ingestion of antacids, coffee and tea, vegetarian diets

Deficiency of iron may be associated with: anemia, anorexia, brittle nails, confusion, depression, constipation, digestive disturbances, fatigue, weak bones, slow growth, headaches, poor appetite, poor immunity

Toxic effects of over dosage of iron: anorexia, dizziness, fatigue, headaches, liver damage

Zinc

Role: Zinc is important, as it is required for a large number of metabolic reactions in the body as a structure of many enzymes. It is also needed for protein and nucleic acid synthesis.

Food sources high in zinc: oysters, veal, shrimp, herring, ginger, sunflower seeds, whole grains

Conditions that increase demand for zinc: burns, hypertension, pregnancy, stress, vegetarians

Deficiency of zinc may be associated with: acne, amnesia, anorexia, apathy, brittle nails, depression, eczema, fatigue, slow growth, slow wound healing, impotence, memory impairment, sterility, white spots on the nails, dermatitis, learning disorder, loss of taste and smell, changes in behavior, sleep problems

Toxic effects of over dosage of zinc: diarrhea, nausea, paralysis vomiting, anorexia, impaired immunity

Iodine

Role: Iodine is important for the synthesis of thyroid hormones.

Food sources high in iodine: iodized salt, sea fish, shellfish, mushrooms, oysters, kelp and sunflower seeds

Conditions that increase demand for iodine: diarrhea, goiter and pregnancy

Deficiency of iodine may be associated with: Cretinism, birth defects, goiter, fatigue, weight gain, heart disease, hypothyroidism, increased blood cholesterol and fats

Toxic effects of over dosage of iodine: digestive disturbances, decreased thyroid activity, diarrhea, hyperthyroidism

Copper

Role: Copper is necessary as a cofactor for enzymes, for connective tissue formation, to assist the absorption of iron, for the immune system and for brain nerve function.

Food sources high in copper: almonds, pecans, sunflower seeds, beans, mushrooms, oysters, prunes, whole grains, brown rice, eggs

Conditions that increase demand for copper: aging, excess alcohol intake, iron, sugar or zinc, pregnancy

Deficiency of copper may be associated with: alopecia, anemia, depression, diarrhea, fatigue, fragile bones, graying hair and weakness

Toxic effects of over dosage of copper: depression, irritability, joint and muscle pain, nervousness, nausea, vomiting

Chromium

Role: Chromium is a component of the glucose tolerance factor, is needed in glucose metabolism, for insulin function and for blood sugar and cholesterol regulation.

Food sources high in chromium: egg yolk, grape juice, asparagus, liver, lobster, nuts, oysters, wheat, raisins, prunes, shrimp, yeast

Conditions that increase demand for chromium: excess intake of refined carbohydrates, high cholesterol, high blood sugar, diabetes, stress, increased physical activity

Deficiency of chromium may be associated with: anxiety, glucose intolerance, growth impairment, and high blood cholesterol, fatigue, atherosclerosis, glucose in the urine, infertility and weight loss

Toxic effects of over dosage of chromium: dizziness, joint pain, nausea, vomiting, fever, tachycardia

Selenium

Role: Selenium is an anti-oxidant, and a co-factor of enzymes, which assists in detoxification of chemicals, maintenance of cell membranes as well as spares Vitamin E and inhibits lipid peroxidation.

Food sources high in selenium: alfalfa, cashews, crab, eggs, fish, liver, oysters, garlic, tuna, wholegrains

Conditions that increase demand for selenium: alcoholism, aging, cancer, heart disease, high blood pressure, liver disease, arthritis

Deficiency of selenium may be associated with: heart disease, high cholesterol, infections, liver damage, premature aging, pancreatic insufficiency and sterility in males

Toxic effects of over dosage of selenium: birth defects, dermatitis, breath odor, digestive disturbances, metallic taste, nausea

Chapter 6

Water: The fountain of youth

Mankind has searched the world for hundreds of years for miracle cures for disease and medicinal potions to prolong our lives. The human race has designed elaborate pharmaceutical preparations often with only minimal results to combat our most feared diseases like cancer, Aids or diabetes. The search for everlasting life has taken the greatest scientists and pioneers to the ends of the earth. We would all like to find a herb, a plant or a medicine that would carry with it perfect health and longevity and end our long suffering from the diseases that plague our society. I believe that we have already found it a long, long time ago. I believe that this miracle potion is found in everyone's home and accessible in some form or another to every living human being on earth. That substance is of course WATER, and one that I firmly believe is the most important nutrient of them all. I like to call it our fountain of youth.

As research unfolds the mysteries to this miraculous nutrient that most of us just take for granted, I am sure that what has been believed to be just a simple molecule will prove to be much more sophisticated than we have ever imagined. I believe that water holds many secrets to our health.

How many times have you heard that you should be drinking more water for your health? I think we have all heard someone say this to us at some point in our lives. We know we should drink more water but do we really know why? I hope this chapter will convince you that water may be the most important dietary nutrient that we can ingest in our body. I have seen miracles happen when quality drinking water is markedly increased in the diet. These miracles have resulted in substantial improvements in health including weight loss, skin improvement, relief from arthritis and back problems, reduction of blood pressure and elimination of migraine headaches.

We know that water is essential for our existence. Water really is the key to life. While we can live for a month or more without food, we cannot last more than a week without water. Our body weight is made up of about 70% water. Our brain is around 75% water, our blood is over 80% water and our lungs are 90% water. If our lungs were not moist we would not even be able to use the oxygen we inhale. The juices that are used in digestion contain a high percentage of water and many substances in our body are dissolved in water. Water is crucial in regulating our body temperature as we see by the evaporation of water from the skin or by sweating which maintains our inner body temperature. In order to eliminate wastes through the kidneys the body requires water. Remember back when we discussed the 7 essential processes of life. Water is required for each one of these processes. There are just so many important roles that water plays in the human body that makes it the miraculous substance that it is and one that we just cannot live without.

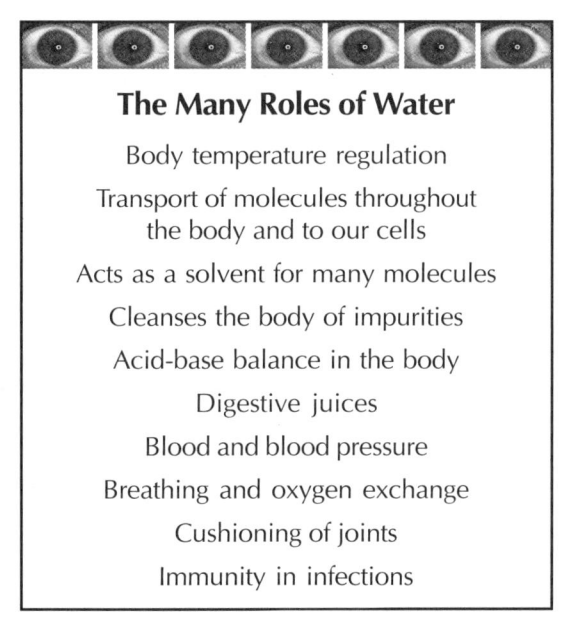

The Many Roles of Water

Body temperature regulation

Transport of molecules throughout the body and to our cells

Acts as a solvent for many molecules

Cleanses the body of impurities

Acid-base balance in the body

Digestive juices

Blood and blood pressure

Breathing and oxygen exchange

Cushioning of joints

Immunity in infections

Water is made up of two highly inflammable gases in nature, hydrogen and oxygen and if taken separately, each gas will burn. What many people do not know is that in the natural form, water has the capability to destroy many pathogenic diseases and viruses in our body. Yes, the miracle of water goes much farther than just a drink to satisfy our thirst.

Did you also know that water assists in maintaining ideal weight? It does so by cleansing the body of its impurities and toxins so that it can eliminate effectively and thus achieve healthy metabolism of proteins, fats and carbohydrates. Water must also be constantly replenished as we lose water every day. Water is lost in urine and feces, from evaporation from the skin and lungs, from saliva, tears and other secretions and well as through sweating. During normal activity levels, we generally lose about 2 to 3 cups of water a day. Under extreme conditions we can lose up to 15 liters of water in a 24-hour period due to excess sweating alone.

How we lose water

Urine

Feces

Saliva

Tears

Secretions

Sweating

Evaporation from the skin

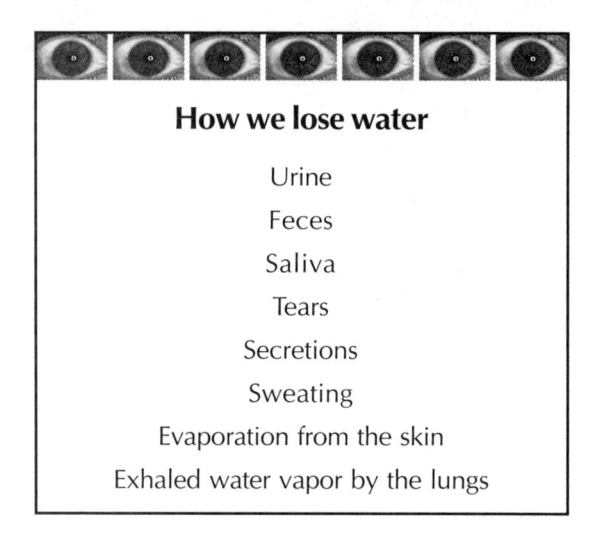

Exhaled water vapor by the lungs

Now let's take a look at some factors that can reduce the amount of water in our bodies or act as diuretics. Just take a look at the number of cups of coffee, black tea, colas or alcohol that the average individual consumes. Not only do we have the habit of drinking far less water than we require for normal health, we are guilty of substituting water with these poorly nutritious fluids. Never substitute coffee, tea, colas or alcoholic beverages for water. Both caffeine and alcohol are strong diuretics and through increased urination cause you to lose even more water. You will need to increase your water intake if you regularly drink these substances.

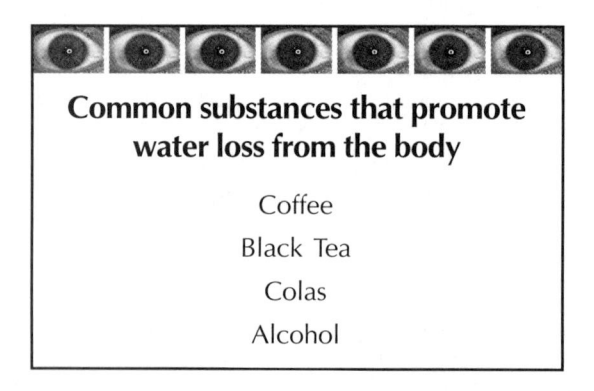

Common substances that promote water loss from the body

Coffee

Black Tea

Colas

Alcohol

What happens when the body does not receive adequate water and becomes dehydrated? A vast number of health problems can ensue if adequate water is not supplied to the body.

Probably the most common symptom I hear is fatigue. Don't be surprised if you suffer from chronic fatigue if you do not drink water. As we mentioned earlier, water allows for efficient oxygen exchange in the lungs and allows cleansing of impurities. A body full of toxic substances is a tired body. It is also not uncommon to find depression, headaches, anxiety and nervousness when water is absent. Another result of not drinking enough is the kidney stone. If water is lacking in the diet, minerals from the food that should come out through the urine stay in the body and with time harden and form stones. Drinking plenty of quality water can significantly reduce the risk of kidney stones. Inadequate water will also affect the joints with pain and stiffness occurring, particularly as we age. If you suffer from backaches or arthritis and you are not drinking enough water, it should be the first on the list when you start to implement diet or lifestyle changes. Sufficient water also can reduce blood thickness and clots and may play a factor in heart disease, arteriosclerosis, hypertension and strokes. One of the greatest causes of constipation is lack of water. So many people today suffer from obesity and spend enormous amounts on expensive diet drinks when water is a fantastic method to suppress the appetite. Drinking a large glass of water a half hour before a meal is very effective in reducing the desire to eat too much. Water is wonderful for improving your digestive, circulatory and especially detoxification processes in the entire body.

Probably one of our greatest fears is growing old. We admire those who look younger than their age. We spend thousands of dollars on cosmetic surgery to take years off our lives but you can only fool yourselves not your body. Stop wasting money on cosmetics, creams and lotions that do very little but lie on top of the skin. The fountain of youth comes in a glass not in a cream, lotion or face-lift. Most of the problems that are associated with insufficient water intake will amount to one major problem: acceleration of the aging process. Just as the leaves of a plant wither due to lack of water, so does human skin. Our skin is the largest organ in our body. Water supplies the nourishment that the skin needs to remain supple and to slow down the formation of wrinkles. Water has the remarkable ability to cleanse the body of impurities that often end up in the skin and result in eczema, acne or other disorders.

Conditions associated with low water intake

Fatigue

Stress

Depression

Nervousness

High blood pressure

Kidney stones

Backaches

Stiffness of joints

Constipation and Digestive problems

Headaches

Skin problems

Accelerated aging

Wrinkles

Slowed healing

Lowered immunity

Obesity

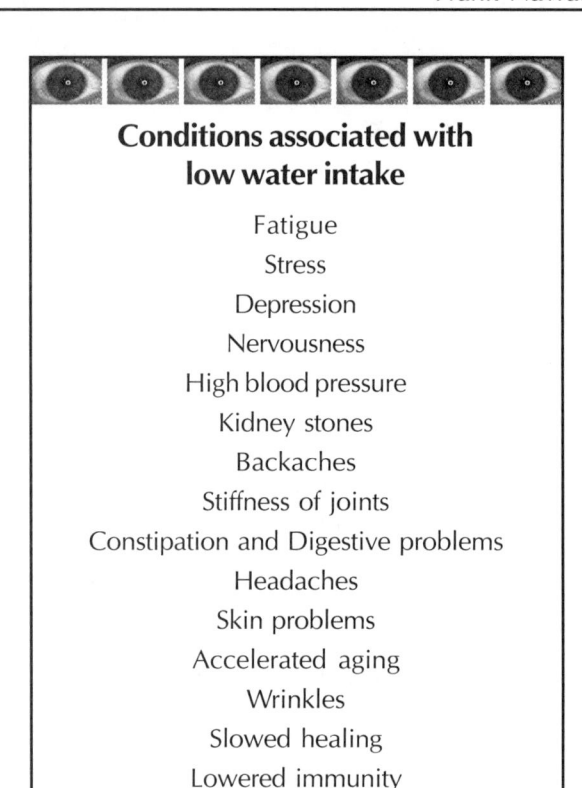

I hope by now you can at least appreciate how important water is to your health and well-being.

Now the next questions are: what kind of water should you drink, how much and when?

In order to ascertain what water to drink, we need to have an understanding of what water is made of, what chemicals it can contain and the difference between water that I call "dead" and water that is pure or "alive."

For hundreds of years we have taken water for granted. We have used water as the universal dumping ground with the belief that there is enough of it that justifies the amount of pollution that we throw into our rivers, lakes and oceans. Nature is able to regenerate our water supply but not at the rate that we are polluting it. In the end it may not be world wars that destroy our civilization but contaminated water. It is only now that we have come to the grim realization that without quality water the human race will cease to exist. Good drinking water today is becoming scarce.

Through our ignorance we have assumed that we can pull water out of its natural environment of streams, rivers and lakes, pump it along through pipes, add chemicals to disinfect it to reach our households without any effect on its quality to our health. Water is not a simple substance. Research is revealing that water may hold many mysteries. First of all, water is a fragile substance and not all water is the same. Most of the water we drink from taps or bottles is what I call energetically "dead."

It is no wonder that we have the chronic health problems that we do. To understand what "dead" water is we need to know what pure water or water that is "alive" means.

If we search back to nature, which I believe is always the greatest school for learning about health, we find that water circulates in rivers, lakes and streams. Nature's purification system of water consists of evaporation from the ground, condensation and falling back to earth as rain. During that process it is exposed to the purifying ability of the radiation of the Sun. Yes even though water has no calories it does possess energetic qualities that the body requires and that the cells can utilize. Nature has also provided us with waves, waterfalls and winding obstacles in creeks and rivers that allow water to naturally tumble, breathe, become oxygenated, mix and reform its crystalline structure. Nature's water comes with minerals. Water from melted snow is one of the most purest forms of water as freezing is another method that Mother Nature uses to regenerate the properties of water. The longevity and rare incidence of disease of the people of Nepal has often been attributed to pure water from the melted snow from the Himalayas. We have also seen that water from its sources in some of the famous spas and natural occurring springs around the world has therapeutic effects, including alleviating digestive disorders, kidney stones, arthritis and many other ailments. Water from nature's environment is water that is "alive" and bioenergetically available for utilization by the cells.

Mankind's purification system of water is entirely different from what nature intended. First of all, molecules of water are fragile and very sensitive to mechanical abuse. Most transport of water from a river, well or lake is achieved using a centrifugal pump, which experiments have found deplete the natural energy of water. It is typically then transported to water treatment areas where particles are removed by adding chemicals such as aluminum sulfate or ferric chloride, then filtered and finally disinfected using ozone, UV or chlorine. Fluoride may then be added and often the pH is adjusted by adding acid or alkaline chemicals. It should be interesting to note that aluminum and iron have been associated with heart disease and other chronic problems. While chlorinated water is effective in killing organisms that cause cholera, typhoid or dysentery, it has also been associated with thousands of cases of bladder and rectal cancer. Studies have also shown that it may be linked with arteriosclerosis and the reduction of HDL, the good cholesterol. Fluoride, once a popular addition to our water supply as it was believed that it builds strong bones and teeth is finding less and less support in most countries as it has been correlated with birth defects, allergic reactions, mottled teeth, diarrhea, headaches, osteoporosis and cancer.

Do we really want these added chemicals in our drinking water? Is this the way nature intended our water to be? The pipes that transport the water to our homes also contain contaminants and some older homes or areas may have lead plumbing, which adds lead to the drinking water. Lead is a highly toxic metal that can affect the brain, kidneys, as well as behavior. If that isn't bad enough once we have the water in our homes we subject it to microwave radiation when we heat it, which studies have found destroy the subtle properties of water. This is what I call "dead" water with very poor bioavailability to the cells.

What about bottled water?

Bottled water has the benefit that you can avoid contamination but energetically it is no better than tap water that has been filtered. The fact that it is bottled means that it loses its ability to breathe. All bottled water whether it comes from the most famous world's spas loses its energetic properties after a day or so after packaging. Moreover, if it is stored in a plastic container, water is able to dissolve it so it is much better to store water in glass bottles to preserve its natural properties. Stay clear of carbonated water or other carbonated beverages as they contain phosphates that leech calcium from the bones and have been associated with osteoporosis.

Where does that leave us? It seems that in order to find pure water that is energetically alive we need to get it direct from nature or live by a natural occurring spring or spa. Unfortunately, pollution and contamination of our water supply places us with too great a risk of contracting disease from most urban water sources. What can we do to get the best possible "live" water? I would suggest if you want to use tap water to get a quality carbon filter, which will at least remove chlorine and heavy metals like lead. I do not recommend distilled water as it may be dangerous over long-term use and may leach minerals from the body. If you drink bottled water try to find glass bottles not plastic. As I mentioned earlier, freezing water is one of nature's methods to regenerate the properties of water. You can apply this method that nature uses to activate water at home. Heavy water freezes at a higher temperature than pure water, so the isotopes of water will first migrate to the surface and form a skin while freezing. This frozen skin can be removed. Let the rest of the water freeze. You can then remove it, let it melt and then drink it.

How much water should we drink and when?

The final question about how much water we should drink and when we should drink depends on several factors. Remember the ways we lose water. If we are in a hot environment, or we are exercising we will lose more water so our intake needs to be higher. A general rule that I like to promote is to aim for one eight-ounce glass of water per day for every 20 pounds or every 9 kilograms of body weight. For example an average 150 pound / 70 kg man should drink a minimum of 7.5 glasses of water a day. In extreme hot climates or during high activity, water intake will need to be much higher. The same applies if we consume alcohol, coffee or black tea. Water should be minimized with a meal or for approximately 30 minutes after eating as liquids with food may interfere with the digestive process. If you are not used to drinking that much water, you may feel initially bloated in the first several weeks. This water retention will usually release after this time and should not be a problem once adequate water is being replenished on a regular basis.

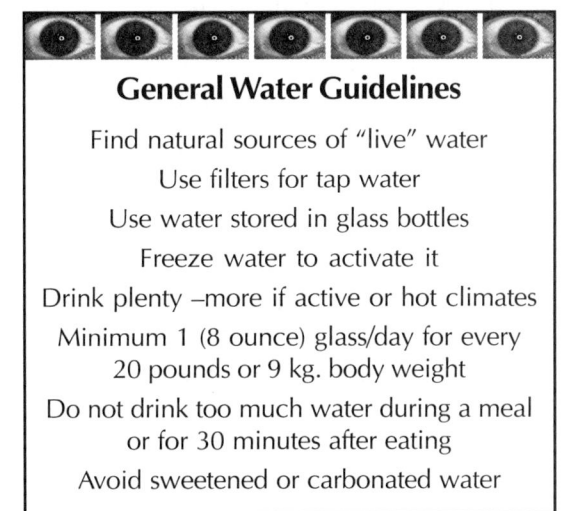

General Water Guidelines

Find natural sources of "live" water

Use filters for tap water

Use water stored in glass bottles

Freeze water to activate it

Drink plenty –more if active or hot climates

Minimum 1 (8 ounce) glass/day for every 20 pounds or 9 kg. body weight

Do not drink too much water during a meal or for 30 minutes after eating

Avoid sweetened or carbonated water

Once upon a time the water on our planet was clean, activated by nature and alive. That time is almost gone and through our industrialization we are rapidly destroying our most valuable resource. I hope that you learn to respect that water is one of our most hidden treasures and we need to find ways to keep it activated and clean through the laws governed by nature. Always remember that it should never be taken for granted or referred to as just "plain water." Water is anything but plain and may just be that miraculous "fountain of youth" that will cure the chronic health problem that you have been suffering from for years.

Chapter 7

Fiber: The essential garbage-disposal nutrient

It is interesting to find that when I was working in Eastern Africa and conducting a survey on health status I found that typical Western conditions like obesity, constipation, appendicitis, colitis, diverticulosis or cancer of the colon simply just did not exist or only very rarely. Also very interesting was that consumption of processed foods, white sugar, white flour and refined carbohydrates were almost absent in the diet. Their diet was very high in unrefined cereal grains, fresh vegetables and fruit. These foods contain what is commonly referred to as dietary fiber. I call fiber the essential garbage-disposal nutrient because it acts so well to cleanse the digestive system.

What is fiber and what does it do in the body?

Although most fiber is not digested, and not actually considered by common standards an essential nutrient, several important health benefits have been associated with its increase in the diet. Fiber has been referred to as plant cell wall material that contains substances like cellulose or pectin that the body cannot digest. Sources of fiber in foods include bran, dates, prunes, whole meal foods and bananas. Fats, oils, sugars and cakes on the other hand contain no fiber or extremely little fiber.

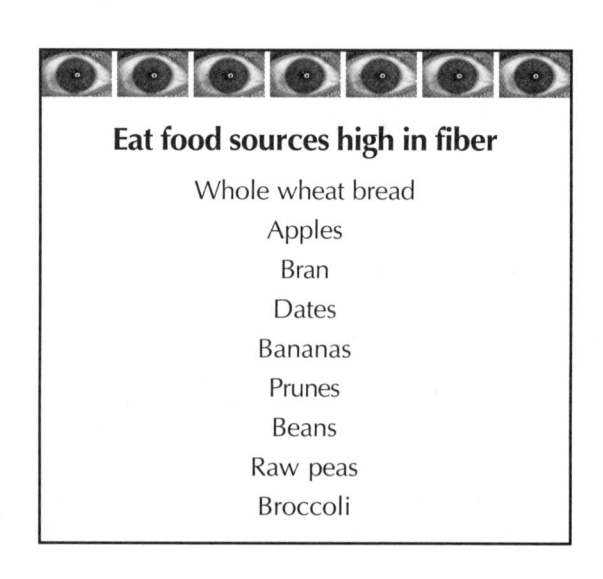

Eat food sources high in fiber

Whole wheat bread
Apples
Bran
Dates
Bananas
Prunes
Beans
Raw peas
Broccoli

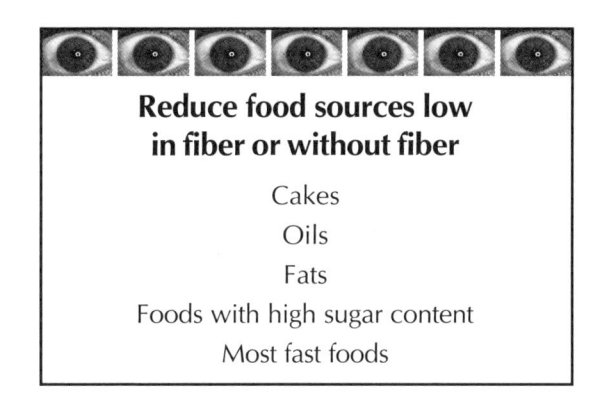

> **Reduce food sources low in fiber or without fiber**
>
> Cakes
>
> Oils
>
> Fats
>
> Foods with high sugar content
>
> Most fast foods

I believe fiber is crucial for our digestive system and I really consider it like an essential nutrient because it has a number of beneficial effects on digestion and absorption of food. First of all, fiber increases the bulk of the food contents in the digestive system. We feel fuller and this action has the ability to reduce our appetite. Increasing the fiber in our diet is an excellent way to maintain weight throughout our lives and to avoid obesity. Also by increasing the bulk of the food contents, the rate that food passes through the digestive system is increased. This allows food to keep moving along and speeds up transit and elimination time. This has the advantage of reducing gas formation and putrefaction. Food contents that stay in the digestive tract too long may become toxic to the body. A high-fiber diet also reduces the risk of colon cancer, perhaps by speeding the rate at which stool passes through the intestine and by keeping the digestive tract clean.

Secondly, fiber retains water that results in softer and bulkier stools which assists in their elimination. Populations that lack fiber in their diet often suffer from straining when going to the toilet and this has been associated with conditions such as constipation, hemorrhoids, hiatus hernias, diverticular disease and varicose veins.

Fiber also has the remarkable ability to bind to some molecules and assists in the removal of cholesterol and fats from the body. This effect has been associated with a lowered risk of atherosclerosis, heart disease, high blood cholesterol and gall stone formation.

Another beneficial role that fiber has for the digestive system is bacteria that normally reside in the lower parts of the gastrointestinal tract can ferment it. This results in a well-nourished bacterial population that can synthesize some important vitamins and maintain normal function of the intestinal tract.

The final role of fiber is its ability to slow down the absorption of sugars, which reduces the requirement for insulin following their ingestion. This is particularly significant for diabetics because if they increase their fiber intake, their need for insulin is often reduced. The incidence of diabetes may also be reduced by a high fiber diet.

Be careful of too much bran in the diet as some studies have shown that vitamins and minerals like calcium, zinc and iron may become deficient in the body with extremely high intakes of fiber in the diet.

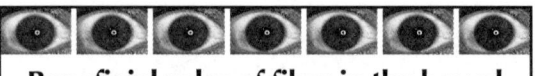

Beneficial roles of fiber in the bowel

Increases the bulk of the food contents
Increases bowel transit time
Retains water to produce softer bulkier stools
Removes cholesterol and fats from the body
Allows fermentation for beneficial bacteria in the bowel
Slows down the absorption of sugars

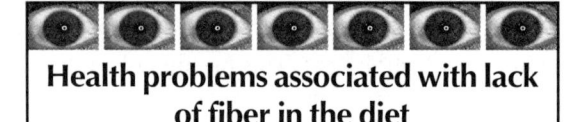

Health problems associated with lack of fiber in the diet

Cancer of the colon
High blood cholesterol
Atherosclerosis
Constipation
Gallstones
Diverticular disease
Hemorrhoids
Hiatus hernia
Varicose veins
Carbohydrate intolerance or diabetes
Decreased synthesis of some vitamins

The average Western diet is generally low in fiber as seen in the predominance of refined carbohydrates and proteins that contain little or no fiber at all. As you can see so many of our health problems can be associated to some extent with the lack of fiber in our diet. As these conditions are seldom encountered in some cultures in Africa, it is obvious that diet and fiber have a strong protective influence on our health. Whether you are trying to lose or maintain weight or whether you are suffering from cancer or diabetes, an adequate amount of fiber in the diet has many positive effects and should hold a firm place in your overall health goals.

Chapter 8

Food Group Choices: Is the traditional food pyramid valid?

From early childhood we have been led to believe that we must follow the nutritional food pyramid and select food items from each of the recommended food groups. While balance in nutrition is very important we have to be careful from what food groups we select that make up a balanced and nutritious diet. Again the various food producers and food associations supply most of the nutritional information that is given to the public and to children in schools. Remember they are concerned about selling their products not about the long-term health of the individual. This was listed as one of the many illusions that we tend to have in relation to health and nutrition.

Most of the dietary nutritional information that is available lists six or seven commonly recognized food groups with recommended daily servings. It is interesting to see the nutritional board's insistence on including a substantial amount of milk products even though many are responsible for a variety of health problems not to mention that a large proportion of the population of the world cannot even digest milk protein. We can thank the wonderful worldwide advertising campaign that effectively convinced us all of the benefits of milk and I find that even most doctors recommend it. Milk and milk products will be discussed in greater detail in a later chapter. Another interesting note is that butter and margarine really do not provide the body with anything more than just fat and calories and in the case of margarine, harmful trans fatty acids. Why do we need to include them in our diet? We don't. Further, the bread and cereals group does not differentiate between refined white flour products and unrefined wholegrain products. Refined white bread, pasta and rice are consumed in far too high quantities and lack several vital nutrients. Take a look at what many health departments recommend for food choices in the table below. Despite current research, many health departments still recommend the food choices in the table below.

Common Food Groups and Typical Government Recommendations

Bread and cereals group – bread, pasta, rice, grains	**6 to 11 servings a day**
Meat and meat alternatives group – beef, chicken, pork, fish lamb, turkey, eggs, peas, beans, lentils, nuts	**2 to 3 servings a day**
Milk and milk products group – milk, cheese, cream, yogurt, cottage cheese	**2 to 3 servings a day**
Fruit group – citrus fruits, berry fruits	**2 to 4 servings a day**
Vegetables group – vegetables	**3 to 5 servings a day**
Butter, oils, margarine group	**Only sparingly**
Sweets group – soft drinks, candy	**Only sparingly**

A good balanced diet certainly needs to include variety. We need to provide all the essential nutrients in the appropriate amounts. These include protein, carbohydrates, fat, vitamins, minerals, water and fiber. The problem with these food group pyramids is that we are all different and our requirements for food differ from each other. In that case although all of us can benefit from a base of the same healthy foods most of us have individual requirements in addition to these basic standards in order to maintain health or prevent disease. That is where genetic eye constitutions can really assist us in understanding those extra requirements that our body requires due to genetic factors. Remember we are all born with different bodies. It is logical that each one of us needs a special nutritional program above and beyond what is generally recommended. In Section 3 we will become familiarized with genetic constitutional types and their nutritional deficits and requirements. We will soon be able to use this information to add to our food group pyramid. Through my years in nutritional counseling, I have designed what I believe a much more sounder approach to achieving individualized nutritional health. I call it the "Eye for an Eye Diet" Food Pyramid. Try to implement it in your daily nutritional program.

Our genetic heritage is the base of who we are. It is therefore appropriately indicated at the base of the "Eye for an Eye Diet" food pyramid and we will learn more about it in the next section of this book. You will see that foods at the bottom of the pyramid should be consumed in greater amounts while those at the top of the pyramid should be used only sparingly.

Frank Navratil BSc. N.D.

ACHIEVE
INDIVIDUALIZED NUTRITIONAL HEALTH

- **SWEETS, WHITE FLOUR PRODUCTS, POTATOES** (Sparingly)
- **RED MEAT, CHEESE, ALCOHOL, BUTTER** (Sparingly)
- **YOGURT OR SOUR MILK** (1 serving a day)
- **HEALTHY OILS** (use in salads)
- **NUTS AND LEGUMES** (1 to 2 servings a day)
- **FISH, POULTRY, EGGS** (1 to 2 servings a day)
- **WHOLEGRAIN, UNREFINED BREAD AND CEREALS** (2 to 3 servings a day)
- **LOCAL FRESH FRUITS AND BERRIES** (2 to 3 raw servings a day)
- **VEGETABLES** (Min. 5 servings a day of which 2 are of the dark green variety) At least 60 percent in raw form
- **WATER** (Minimum 1 (8 ounce) glass/day for every 20 pounds or 9kg body weight)
- **INDIVIDUAL NUTRITIONAL SUPPORT BASED ON GENETIC EYE CONSTITUTION**

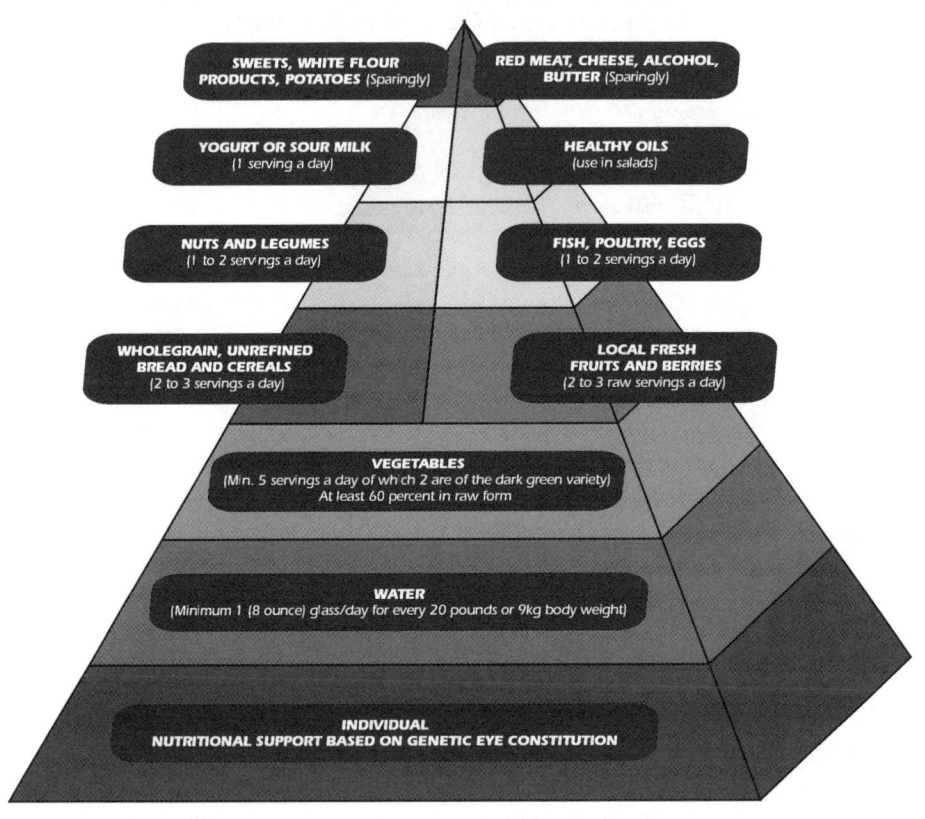

The "Eye for an Eye Diet" Food Pyramid

I believe that generally we consume far too much milk products, cheese, bread and starch including potatoes and refined pasta. We need to increase our intake primarily in the vegetables group including more of the dark green variety and start to use wholegrain cereals and wholegrain pastas. We need to draw from our local sources for freshly ripened fruits and berries. At least 60 percent of our fruits and vegetables should be eaten in the raw form. Red meat is high in cholesterol and saturated fat. We can replace it with alternatives such as nuts, beans, lean poultry, tofu or fish. The foods that we should use cautiously and sparingly include sweets, white flour products, potatoes, red meat, butter, margarine, and alcohol. We will learn why their excessive consumption can be detrimental to our health in later chapters. While oils do contain a fair amount of calories we should not be aiming for a zero percent fat intake. Our body needs fat. Our body needs fats and cholesterol to build cell membranes, to make bile acids for digestion and to form essential hormones such as testosterone and estrogen. Don't get on the bandwagon of a zero percent fat diet. I often see consequences of this with my female patients who suffer then from hormonal problems. Remember the food manufacturers were quick to pick up on this and now offer anything fat-free that we could possibly desire. Be smart. Remember nature's laws.

Below are some foods that are recommended from the various food groups of the "Eye for an Eye Diet Food Pyramid." Definitions of serving sizes are included as well.

Sound Healthy Food Choices from the "Eye for the Eye Diet" Food Pyramid

1. **Water group** — 1 glass/day for every 20 pounds or 9 kg. body weight

2. **Vegetables group** — Serving size = 1/2 cup vegetables or 1 cup leafy vegetables or 1 cup vegetable juice
   – vegetables including broccoli, green beans, parsley, sprouts (potatoes only sparingly)

3. **Wholegrain Bread/Cereals group** — Serving size = 1 slice of bread or 1/2 cup pasta, rice
   – wholegrain breads only, unprocessed grains and natural rice, wholegrain pastas (no refined white flour products)

4. **Local Fresh Fruit and Berries group** — Serving size = 1/2 cup berries or 1 piece of fruit
   – fruits, berry fruits (use preferably those that are grown locally)

5. **Fish, poultry and eggs group** — Serving size = 2-3 ounces fish, poultry or 1 egg
   – fish, chicken, turkey, tuna, salmon, eggs (red meat only sparingly)

6. **Nuts and legumes group** — Serving size = 1/2 cup nuts, beans, lentils
   – peas, beans, lentils, nuts

7. **Natural Yogurt or Sour Milk group** — Serving size = 1/2 cup yogurt or soured milk
   – only natural yogurt, soured milk, raw goats milk (hard cheeses or goats cheese sparingly only)

8. **Oils group** **Use unheated on salads or in fish oil supplements**

– olive oil, canola oil, sunflower or other vegetable oils, fish oil (butter sparingly and no margarine)

9. **Sweets, white flour, potatoes group** **Use sparingly only**

–(use sparingly soft drinks, candy, cakes, chocolate, potatoes)

10. **Red Meat, Cheese, Alcohol, Butter** **Use sparingly only**

– (use sparingly, alcohol maximum 1 drink daily)

Nutritional benefits of Primary Food Groups

Water group- essential for every metabolic process

Vegetables group- source of fiber, vitamins A, C and folate, and iron and magnesium

Wholegrain bread/Cereals group- source of complex carbohydrates, fiber, vitamins, minerals

Fresh Fruit/Berries group- source of vitamins C, bioflavonoids and fiber

Fish, Poultry, Eggs group- source of high quality protein and Omega 3 fatty acids

Nuts and Legumes group- source of protein and beneficial fats

Natural Yogurt/Soured milk group- source of calcium and beneficial bacteria

Oils group- source of healthy monounsaturated and polyunsaturated fats

I do not believe in counting calories. Life is too short to be referring to calorie tables every time we consume a food. When we eat meals we also need to be relaxed and not feeling stress that we may be eating more calories than we should. This is not an intelligent approach to a diet. It is a desperate approach. If we need to be counting calories this means that we do not have the discipline to follow sound nutritional guidelines. It also means unfortunately that we will often include combinations of foods that may be low in calories but not necessarily good for our health. In the past there have been various recommendations that have been made on how many calories we need daily for categories of women who are sedentary, for active women, children, teenage girls, active men and women and teenage boys. We are all different and each one of us has different needs according to our genetics, our activity levels, our inner metabolism and the stresses that we place on our bodies every day. If we are eating the right foods, obtaining the right nutrients, eating at regular times during the day and exercising, we will not become obese. There is therefore no need to count calories. The danger of counting calories and crash dieting is that we try to starve ourselves and don't listen to our bodies. This kind of dieting does not work. We will just gain the weight back again. Your lifestyle needs to change and you have to adopt a new way of eating. The body will respond and your detoxification channels will be efficient if and only if you feed your body the right foods. Stop wasting time counting calories and start making intelligent choices.

Chapter 9
Factors that affect the nutritional value of foods

The road that leads to the end consumer of food is often a long one and most often the item of food that ends up on your plate is usually not the same as it was in its original natural state. We need to understand this concept because even if we eat what we believe are the right kinds of foods, there is no guarantee that we will be satisfying the nutritional needs of the body one hundred percent. In today's society finding fresh unaltered nutritious food is becoming more and more difficult. Many of us do not have the luxurious option of growing our own fruits and vegetables and getting them fresh in our meals. I don't want to sound negative but I believe it is next to impossible to maintain and prevent disease if we do not have a constant supply of fresh, natural foods in our diet. For every problem however there is always some kind of solution. The good news is that some factors that affect the nutritional value of foods are within our control. Our goal should be to retain as much of the natural qualities of food so that when it ends up on our plate it contains a large quantity of the nutrients that we require. Let's take a look at the many factors that affect the nutritional quality of our foods.

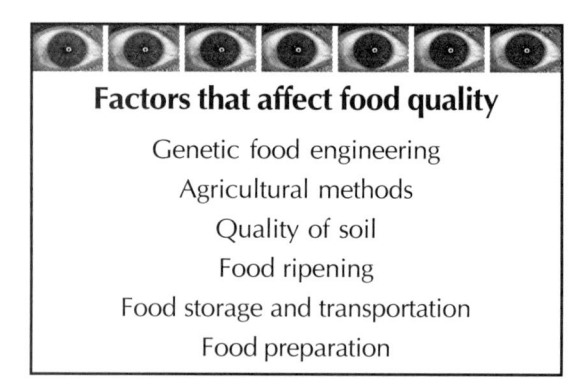

> **Factors that affect food quality**
>
> Genetic food engineering
> Agricultural methods
> Quality of soil
> Food ripening
> Food storage and transportation
> Food preparation

Genetically engineered foods
We can start with that word that we are hearing more and more often, genetically engineered foods.
Once again the scientists claim that they have a hand over God and much due to our insistent demand for beautiful large and perfect fruits, grains and vegetables they are experimenting with food that may not follow the rules

of nature. Why don't we learn? Mankind has produced chemically altered fats that we call margarines that only now after years of use are revealing negative health effects on the heart when they were supposed to produce the exact opposite. We have played with synthetic low calorie sugars that often result in migraines. We have produced chemical vitamins that were supposed to be exactly the same as natural vitamins but research is showing the exact opposite as well as numerous other attempts to so call improve our food supply. When we play God and start to alter DNA and the natural properties of food, we inevitably suffer the consequences. It may take years to scientifically correlate the negative health effects of genetically engineered foods or synthetic products. By then mankind will have a whole new set of diseases and we will not be any further ahead in our attempts to improve our health. Take my word for it, there is just so much money involved in this worldwide food business that I would not be surprised that we will soon hear all about the positive health benefits of various genetically engineered foods. I hope that you are intelligent enough not to fall into this trap of media advertising. Sources estimate that already up to 60 or 70 percent of the foods on shelves in some countries contains genetically engineered components and is often not even labeled. These foods contain substances and combinations of genes that have never been a part of the human food supply. Genetic engineering is the largest food experiment in the history of the world and we are the guinea pigs. Remember if it is at all possible, go natural and you cannot go wrong.

Agricultural methods and the quality of the soil

We have already discussed in an earlier chapter about the quality of our soil and its effects primarily on the minerals and nutrients in plants. This is a factor that is difficult for us to control but if we have a choice then organically grown produce is recommended. The use of various fertilizers will influence the nutritional value of the food grown as well. If you grow your own fruits or vegetables, use earthworms, nature's aerator and purifier of the soil. Understanding what minerals may be deficient in the soil in your area where produce is grown can assist in indicating where deficiencies can be in your diet.

Foods and the ripening process

You may have wondered whether the not quite ripened fruits or vegetables that come into the supermarket or to your home are really that healthy for you. Fruits and vegetables contain their highest level of nutrients when they are harvested at full ripeness and eaten soon thereafter. The most nutritious produce consists of homegrown fruits and vegetables picked at full maturity. This means avoiding picking them prematurely and allowing them to then ripen. To retain the most nutrients they should also be eaten immediately. Unfortunately many fruits are often picked as early as six weeks before their maturity date, which provides advantage for storage and transportation but little advantage to you. Fruits that are commonly picked early include oranges, grapefruit, tomatoes, peaches, avocado, apples, pears, bananas, apricots and others. Citrus fruits especially are not that healthy to consume in large quantities when they have been picked too early because they then tend to add more acidity to body tissues. Every food grown has a natural cycle and nutrients such as beta-carotene and vitamin C may be deficient if the cycle is broken. Many nutritionists promote only eating fruits and vegetables that are grown in your local area. I tend to agree even though I believe that all natural fruits and vegetables from around the world are beneficial to us. The fact remains thought that the only real way to get it fresh is to pick it straight off the vine or tree when it is ripe and growing in your backyard.

Nutrient losses in food due to storage and preservation

Not only does picking produce before it is ripe affect the nutritional quality of food but there are also significant losses during storage and transportation. The factors that are usually responsible for these nutrient losses include effects of air, light, moisture and heat. Most vitamins lose their stability under these conditions. Vitamin C and E is particularly sensitive to all these factors. For this reason it is never advisable to purchase fruits from outdoor stands that are exposed to heat and sunlight because often their Vitamin C content is far less than fruit that is stored in cooler conditions. Vegetables and fruits stored in the refrigerator as compared to room temperature lose fewer nutrients. In room temperature over a period of 48 hours, some vegetables and fruits can lose over half their vitamin C alone. This fact indicates that since most fruits and vegetables are stored at least two days before they reach our hands, a considerable loss of nutrients has already occurred even before we make the purchase. Foods such as green leafy vegetables quickly deteriorate after only a short period of time while under refrigeration potatoes have a very slow uptake of oxygen and can retain most of their nutrients for a month or more. It is inevitable that some nutrients will always be lost with time and are accelerated under heat, light, air and moisture conditions.

Another method of storage of food is freezing. Frozen foods are a fairly good choice for produce because they are generally picked at their peak, quickly processed, and stored at nutrient preserving cold temperatures. Although freezing is effective for storing foods for long periods of time with relatively small nutrient losses, often Vitamin C, B and beta carotene levels are quite significantly reduced. These just happen to be antioxidants that our body desperately needs. The rate of loss of nutrients while freezing varies from product to product and not only vitamins can be affected but also the levels of carbohydrate, fat, and protein can be altered in some frozen foods. I am not trying to say that freezing is entirely bad as it is one of the better methods of storage, but expect that it will result in foods that have some degree of nutrient loss from their original, natural state.

Canning food is another popular storage technique. Usually canning eliminates the problems of air, light and growth of microorganisms in foods but at the expense of adding usually large amounts of sugar, salt, and preservatives as well as heating the foods to sterilize them. Most of the canned foods incur losses of vitamins. Again at the top of the list of vitamin losses are vitamins C, B and beta-carotene.

The final few methods include freeze-drying, sun drying, salting and smoking foods. Freeze-drying is a very expensive method that relies on the process of removing all the water from food so that microorganisms cannot operate. It is usually done at very low temperatures, allowing for maximum retention of nutrients for very long periods of time. Sun drying or salting can also preserve foods but there are still nutrients that are lost and in the case of salting, large amounts of salt are added to the diet. Smoking foods is a method of preservation that creates a layer of soot on the outside layer of the food that acts as an agent against microorganisms and an antioxidant that prevents oxidation of the food. I do not recommend smoked foods of any kind as they have been found to contain carcinogens as well as nutrient losses.

Be aware of the nutrient losses in foods due to storage and preservation techniques and understand that there is always a compromise to make when using these foods in the diet. Every storage technique results in some losses of nutrients and these foods will contain a less than optimum nutrient content. Store foods properly to prevent significant nutritional losses. A cool, dark place is generally best since degradation of vitamins accelerates at higher temperatures and several of the water soluble vitamins such as vitamin C and the B vitamins in particular, are very light sensitive.

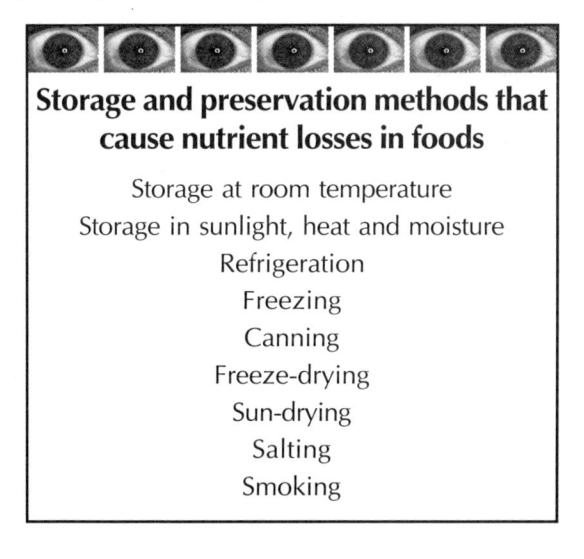

Storage and preservation methods that cause nutrient losses in foods

Storage at room temperature
Storage in sunlight, heat and moisture
Refrigeration
Freezing
Canning
Freeze-drying
Sun-drying
Salting
Smoking

Nutritional losses due to food preparation
So now that we have finally purchased the food product we wish to consume after it has undergone some sort of storage and preservation, we are faced with a variety of options on how to prepare it. We know that we most likely already, unless we have picked it from the garden, have a food product that contains less than the optimum amount of nutrients before we even start to do anything with it. Preparation of food generally in most cases, involves heating the product. Any method of preparation of food that involves heat will significantly affect those vitamins that are heat-sensitive. Let's discuss some of the ways that our society cooks and prepares food.

Most commonly when we prepare a food we **boil it, fry it, steam it, pressure cook it, bake it, broil it, grill it, microwave it or toast it.** The extent of mineral and vitamin losses during cooking methods depends on the type of food, the length of cooking time and the amount of water used. The type of cookware used plays a role as well. Stainless steel cookware seems to be the best. Do not use teflon or aluminum pots and utensils. Aluminum can react with food, especially acid foods, and elemental aluminum can react with digestive enzymes to deactivate them. Alzheimers disease and other degenerative CNS diseases have also been associated with chronic aluminum poisoning while Teflon is susceptible to release of fluorinated hydrocarbons, especially if it is overheated or damaged. Remember high temperatures damage food so those methods such as **deep-frying, broiling or grilling** can result in substantial nutrient losses as well as in the case of grilling and broiling the generation of carcinogens. **Frying** a food in fats or baking in fats can drastically add unnecessary calories as well as heating the food to very high levels where many nutrients are destroyed. The most sensitive vitamins to heat are the B vitamins, ascorbate (Vitamin C) and the beta-carotenes. When we **boil** vegetables in water, vitamins and minerals are leached into the water and usually thrown out with the water. There can be losses of vitamin C of up to half the original amount. While minerals are generally not destroyed by heat, they can dissolve in water and be lost from the food when boiling. **Steaming** is a much smarter cooking choice because the less water that surrounds the food item, the less mineral loss. However, we still cannot escape the fact that the food is heated and this will always result in some degree of vitamin loss. When we use a pressure cooker, the cooking temperature is increased but the cooking time is reduced. This has some degree of advantage in that less nutrients are lost due to shorter cooking time. I would strongly recommend not using microwave ovens. The chemical structure of the food is altered much more than in conventional cooking and microwave heating has been shown to change cis-fatty acids to trans-fatty acids which are toxic, like those found in margarine. Each year more and more research is revealing health hazards in association with **microwave cooking** due to radiation exposure and changes in the food structure. As almost every restaurant and household uses microwaves, it may be something to seriously consider as these foods may lack nutrients and may be transformed into forms that the body cannot digest and assimilate as effectively. Finally **toasting** of bread results in losses of the B vitamin, thiamine.

Nutrients in food are retained the best when cooking times are reduced to the minimum, when cooking temperature is reduced and when we use minimal water or oils in our cooking methods.

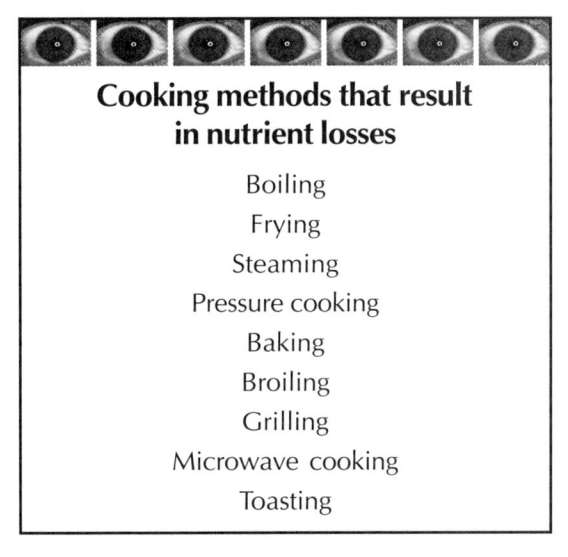

> **Cooking methods that result in nutrient losses**
>
> Boiling
> Frying
> Steaming
> Pressure cooking
> Baking
> Broiling
> Grilling
> Microwave cooking
> Toasting

We should have an understanding of each of these factors that affect our food quality so that we can make intelligent food choices. Remember the goal is to get our food from sources that are as close to the way that nature intended. If you really follow this advice you will minimize the amount of processed or altered food in your diet and prepare food by reducing cooking time and temperature so that it contains the most in nutritional value when it ends up on your plate. Remember it is always wise to eat at least 60 percent of your dietary fruits and vegetables in the raw form.

Chapter 10

Food Contaminants

As early as the year 1910, only about ten percent of the food eaten was processed. Today this figure has grown to well over eighty percent. Every year we dump billions of tons of toxic waste into dumpsites that inevitably have an effect on our soil, the air, the water and food supply. Billions of pounds of pesticides are sprayed on fresh fruit and vegetables every year and hormones and antibiotics are used in the diets of cows, chickens and pigs so that they can fatten and be suitable for sale. An intelligent study of food and nutrition therefore would not be complete without a thorough understanding of what the contaminants are that may be ingested along with the foods we eat.

Contaminants are different than food additives, which are the topic of the next chapter. While additives are included in foods intentionally, contaminants are considered accidental or non-intentional additions to our foods. In most cases contaminants carry with them chemicals that impose additional burdens on our body's detoxification system and are responsible for many ill health effects. Although it is impossible to ensure that there are no contaminants in foods, most governments have set up maximum levels of dangerous chemicals that are permitted in food items. For us, the consumer, contaminants pose several difficulties because they are not advertised on the food items we buy and they are often beyond the control of the food manufacturers themselves. As mankind develops even more new chemicals, their long-term effects with interactions with our food supply may only be evident after a few generations. One thing is for certain though; they do have some negative effects on our state of health.

One of the greatest sources of contaminants in our food supply are fertilizers used to grow our produce as well as pesticides, herbicides and fungicides used to spray our foods. There are a great amount of pesticides and herbicides used today and in the past. Some of those that have been banned include the chlorinated hydrocarbons like DDT, which find their way into the food chain and can accumulate in our fatty tissues. They have been associated with cancer and genetic damage. Many pesticides are organophosphates that block acetylcholine in our nervous system and have been known to cause nausea, headaches, diarrhea, numbness and visual disturbances. Dioxins, such as PCB's (polychlorinated biphenyls) originated in agricultural and industrial chemicals and persist in the environment for many years. This chemical has found its way into animals, plants, fish and fresh water supplies and is stored in the fatty tissue of our body once it is ingested. Overexposure can result in liver damage, damage to the digestive system, skin problems, as well as other systems in the body. Dioxins have been found in milk and fruit juice paper cartons and in breast milk. What are the effects then on newborn babies? Pesticide contamination of fresh fruits is often incredibly high.

Another source of contaminants are metals such as lead, mercury and tin. Lead is finding its way into our food supply in increasing amounts. Leaded fuels contribute to lead pollution in the air which then gets into plants and soil. Animals grazing on plants contaminated with lead concentrate the heavy metal in their bones. Lead may appear in soups made with boiled animal bones or in plants. It also appears in water supplies. It is interesting to note that the decline of the Roman Empire has also been associated with lead poisoning from the lead plumbing and dishware containing lead that they used to use. Mercury is another metal whose toxicity has been associated with health problems such as damage to the nervous system, blindness, paralysis and mental retardation in children. Much of the mercury contamination has been due to factories that have released wastes into the streams or the ocean affecting fish and seafood. Dental amalgam also provides a constant source of mercury in our bodies as it slowly vaporizes from fillings and combines with chemicals in the mouth. Amalgam has been associated with a long list of medical problems from headaches to leukemia. Another contaminant is tin, commonly used in canned foods and in tin foil.

The Chernobyl incident demonstrated quite clearly how radioactive isotopes can enter the food chain. Increased levels of radiation were found almost immediately in leafy green vegetables grown in contaminated soil. Soils contaminated by this radioactive fallout produce food crops with increased radioactivity for many years to come.

We should not forget that a hidden source of food contamination is often from some packages that our foods come in. Traces of chemicals from plastic containers have been found in margarine and other food products as well as in plastic food wraps used extensively in microwave cooking. Bottled water also can dissolve some chemical substances in the plastic bottles in which they are contained. Another source is ink from food labels that leaches into our food.

Antibiotics and hormones that are fed to animals also contaminate our food supply. These substances have been found in meats, chicken and eggs as well as milk products. The effects on our health I believe have been seriously underestimated.

The final groups of food contaminants are microorganisms. These include the harmful bacteria Salmonella, Staphylococcus, and E. coli and moulds such as mycotoxins and aflatoxins. These microorganisms lead to spoilage of foods or the release of toxins into the food itself. Salmonella a is very common form of food poisoning and symptoms which usually appear 8 to 48 hours after the meal, can include vomiting, headache, diarrhea and intense cramping. Staphylococcus bacteria produce toxins that are released into the food itself with similar symptoms. Botulism is another bacterial food poisoning that multiplies in under-processed foods such as in sausages, canned or preserved foods. It can cause death from respiratory failure 3 to 6 days after the infected meal. E. Coli is usually associated with poor hygienic conditions or poor sewage conditions where the food is grown. Ways to control bacteria is improving food handling and storage including refrigeration as bacterial growth is slowed under these conditions. Freezing will not kill bacteria only stop further growth, but boiling will kill it. Mycotoxins are toxins produced by some moulds that enter the food. One toxin called aflatoxin has been found to be a carcinogen in animals and potentially for humans as well and has been found in nuts such as peanuts or in peanut butter.

Sources of Food Contaminants

Fertilizers

Pesticides

Herbicides

Lead, mercury and tin

Radioactive isotopes

Plastic food containers

Ink from food labels

Antibiotics and hormones fed to animals

Microorganisms

So now that we have learned about what nasty substances have contaminated our food supply, what can we do about it? Again, as I mentioned, it is nearly impossible to completely avoid some sort of food contaminants in our diet. What we can do however is make intelligent food choices. Organic produce is one way that we can reduce the ingestion of many contaminants that come from fertilizers and insecticides. Generally strict guidelines are set down to control levels of these substances in the soil that the food is grown. We can also make sure to adequately wash our fruits and vegetables. Use warm water and there are a number of natural organic food washes that are available as well. Purchase eggs and poultry from free-range farms where they are not trapped in small cages and where they are only fed natural feeds.

Often these caged chickens are deficient in minerals as are their eggs because they are not in their natural environment. Be careful of milk products as they often contain hormones and other contaminants. Be careful of lead or mercury poisoning. Avoid using too much canned foods and opt for more fresh produce. Stay clear of too many processed foods and drink water from clean sources and glass bottles. Refrigerate foods to avoid spoilage and buy from only clean hygienic sources where you know that the food product will be fresh.

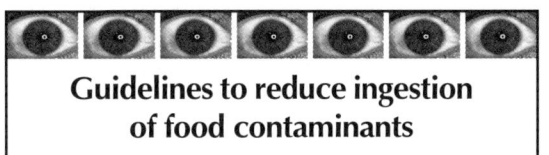

Guidelines to reduce ingestion of food contaminants

Purchase organic produce
Adequately wash fruits and vegetables
Purchase free-range eggs and poultry
Limit canned and processed foods
Source clean drinking water
Avoid spoilage of foods
Purchase foods that are from hygienic sources

Our body has enough work to do cleaning up waste products from daily normal metabolism. Our detoxification organs are the digestive organs, liver, kidneys, skin, lungs and lymphatic system and if they are already weakened they may not be able to keep up with the additional burden of contaminants that mankind has introduced into our food supply. This will increase the toxicity of our body tissues and lead to a variety of health problems. Be aware that those of us with a strong genetic make-up and lucky enough to be born with strong detoxification organs are few so that sooner or later most of us suffer health problems. If we understand how to minimize the ingestion of toxic substances while strengthening our genetic weaknesses as well, we may be able to prevent or cure our diseases and minimize the dangerous effects of food contaminants.

Chapter 11

What has been added to your food lately?

Mother Nature, when she invented food, probably never foresaw where modern technology would eventually take and abuse that food which at one time held most of the natural answers to our current health problems. Originally, when Mother Earth was unpolluted and her oceans, lakes and rivers were clean, foods were able to be grown in mineral rich soil, fish were able to be caught from unpolluted waters and there was no need for the thousands of chemical substances that we add to our food today. As the human population grew, expanded and traveled, techniques for food preparation and preservation such as salting, pickling and smoking were developed to deal with newly introduced problems of food storage and food-borne illnesses. With advanced technology, the food industry was able to add substances intentionally to foods that would improve its shelf life, flavor, nutritional value, convenience and appearance. For decades now the food industry has found new methods to transform our foods and to artificially color and alter our foods to make them more convenient so they look fresher for longer periods of time. Every food has a cycle, it grows, it ripens or ages, it reaches a peak in nutritional value and then it rots or decays and returns back to Mother Earth to be recycled again. Modern technology seems to think that it can manipulate this natural sequence of events with the use of chemicals that can now extend shelf life and alter color to mask its natural appearance. Are we really moving forward or have we just taken another giant step backward. As I have mentioned several times, you cannot abuse Mother Nature's laws. Eventually we will pay the price or perhaps we are already, we just don't know it yet.

As one of the goals of this book is to learn how to make intelligent food choices we need to know what food additives are safe and what food additives can endanger our health. Our body has enough work to do cleaning itself up of toxins and waste products produced through our own metabolic processes. It was never intended to handle all those extra unnatural substances we take in with the foods we eat. Some of us who have strong genetic constitutions will be able to get through this onslaught of chemical warfare. Those of us who do not, which are the great majority, will perish and succumb to some sort of disease. Is it really a surprise why cancer is on the rise, why there is a greater incidence of allergies in children and why every other person suffers from migraines? Think about it. Don't wait until the health authorities find out that a chemical substance in food is linked to cancer because that can take years or even decades. Many chemicals that were used in foods that are now banned had been on the shelves for years. Don't wait until the food manufacturer decides to stop selling their dangerous foods with added chemicals because that won't happen because they won't risk losing profit but they will go ahead and risk your life with no problem. Don't fall into the illusion that there is someone out there that will protect you from the risk you take by eating these chemically altered foods. Artificial substances in my belief will never take the place of natural food. We cannot fool Mother Nature we can only fool ourselves. The sad thing is that the average person is so misguided by the food companies, so influenced by mass advertising and so naive in believing that a product could not be sold in stores if it were not completely safe.

Avoiding or reducing this chemical onslaught on our bodies is an extremely important step towards lowering your risk of disease and enhancing your health. Immediate effects from chemical additives in foods can range from headaches, asthma attacks and stomach upsets to psychological reactions and hyperactivity in children. Long-term effects can increase your risk of many degenerative conditions such as heart disease, cancer and diabetes. Although there are just so many chemicals added to our foods today, there are some that should be avoided or at lease not consumed on a regular basis. This chapter will take a look at the various classifications of substances that are added to our foods today as well as their effects on our health.

Food Additives

Colors
Preservatives
Flavors
Sweeteners
Modifying agents
Bleaching agents
Vitamins and minerals
Other agents

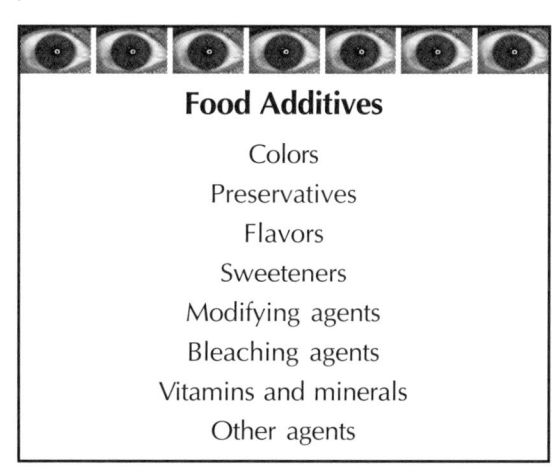

The list of the most frequently added substances to our foods today includes colors which are used to increase the attractiveness of foods, preservatives that prolong shelf life, flavors which make the food more palatable or desirable, sweeteners that are generally used to reduce the caloric content of the food, modifying agents that are used as emulsifiers or thickening agents, bleaching agents used often in bread-making, vitamins and minerals used to replace those that have been lost in processing as well as many others.

Colors

Colors added to our foods are probably the most controversial additives in human nutrition as their role is almost exclusively cosmetic and do not have any function other than making the food more attractive. Many colors are added to commercial drinks, ice creams, cookies, cakes, potato chips, soups, desserts, sauces and jams. Their intake is especially high for children as colors are very attractive to them. What is particularly dangerous with colors is that they often disguise the quality or freshness of the food. While nature has its own methods of revealing when the food item is no longer fit for consumption, color additives can make even stale foods appear fresh. It is unknown what the effects of enormous quantities of ingested colors that we ingest with foods have on our health but they have been associated so many times with allergic reactions, hyperactivity in children, asthma and some cancers. While natural food coloring agents such as chlorophyll and carotenes are also used in foods, it is especially important to stay clear of those foods that contain artificial colors.

Preservatives

Preservatives are of two kinds, the **antioxidants** or those that prevent unwanted oxidation reactions in foods such as in protecting fats from going rancid and **antimicrobial** agents which are used to prevent growth of bacteria, fungi and moulds in foods. Common antioxidants used in foods include lecithin, the tocopherols (Vitamin E) and ascorbic acid (Vitamin C), which are used in preserving fruits and vegetables and in pickled and salted meat. Antioxidant additives that have been suspect of being carcinogens are butylated hydroxyanisole (BHA) and butylated hydroxytoluene (BHT), which are used to prevent spoilage in foods with oil or shortening and to preserve many dried soups and breakfast cereals. They have been associated with accumulation in body tissues, liver enlargement, allergic reactions, hyperactivity and cancer.

The antimicrobial preservative agents include additives to foods that have been used for centuries and include salt, alcohol, sugar and vinegar. In preserving and enhancing the flavor of cured meats such as luncheon meats, ham, bacon, sausages and hot dogs, nitrites and nitrates are used extensively. Sodium nitrate is commonly used in the preservation of these meats to prevent botulism and to keep them looking red when normally they would decompose to an unappealing gray. The blue shimmer on the surface of luncheon meat is the result of sodium nitrate. Nitrites and nitrates have been associated with cancer in laboratory animals as they can develop into nitrosamines in the body, which are known to be carcinogenic. As botulism is one of the most deadly of all toxins, one has to weigh the risks. I would recommend to stay away from all luncheon meat and other cured meats. Another group of microbial agents used are the sulfites. They are synthetically produced to reduce discoloration in such foods as dried fruit, dehydrated soup mixes, processed seafood and syrups. Their ingestion has been associated with worsening asthma, allergic reactions and other health problems.

Flavors

Flavors include one of the largest number of food additives available and they can be either natural or synthetic. Food flavorings include those substances that enhance a flavor that is already present in a food and substances that offer a brand new flavor. Substances that are used to enhance flavor include salt and monosodium glutamate. Excessive salt has commonly been associated with fluid retention and high blood pressure. New flavors can be added to tasteless foods, as today it is possible to simulate the flavor of almost any fruit and vegetable by creating synthetic flavorings.

Probably one of the most well-known and controversial flavorings is monosodium glutamate, commonly associated with Chinese take-out food but added to many foods to enhance flavor including frozen foods and instant soups. Studies have associated the ingestion of this substance with over-stimulation and death of neurons in the brain, headaches, dizziness, burning sensations, tingling, allergic reactions, chest pains, depression and mood changes.

Sweeteners

Two types of sweeteners also exist that are commonly added to our foods. The first set of sweeteners are those that provide energy and include sugars such as sucrose, glucose, fructose, lactose, maltose and sorbitol. Health problems that have been associated with high intakes of these sugars are obesity, diabetes, hypoglycemia, dental cavities, increased triglycerides and candida infections. The other group are those that provide very little energy and are used primarily for diet foods and drinks. They include substances such as saccharin, cyclamate and aspartame. They are used commonly in diet soft drinks, chewing gum, puddings and desserts. These artificial sweeteners have been banned in some countries and their use has been associated with a variety of health conditions. These include headaches, migraines, tinnitus (ringing in the ears) dizziness, hyperactivity and nausea. Aspartame is definitely unsafe for those with phenylketonuria, which is a congenital condition that affects a small percentage of the population.

These artificial sweeteners have also posed dangers for pregnant mothers, infants and small children. My recommendation: If they are unsafe for pregnant mothers and infants they are unsafe for you adults as well. Using diet products with artificial sweeteners to lose weight is a desperate way to achieve your health goals. We need to understand how additives such as artificial sweeteners are not beneficial and are just part of that crash diet scheme that I hope by now you have abandoned and replaced with the much more intelligent approach that we are trying to learn here in this book.

Modifying agents

Most of the modifying agents are naturally occurring and do not pose health problems when introduced into foods. They are commonly used to alter the physical characteristics of foods usually by thickening the substance. They include vegetable gums such as pectin, emulsifiers such as lecithin and thickeners such as gelatin and starches.

Bleaching agents

These additives are primarily used in bread making to quicken the process so that the yellow color of the wheat flour that is freshly milled and made into dough bleaches out faster than when the dough is matured by standing. Processed bread is subject to a fair amount of chemistry and chemical agents such as those that slow down the staling process, soften the crust and lengthen the shelf life are commonly used. Try to find freshly baked whole grain bread that is not subject to chemical processing. The ingestion of refined white flour, which has very little nutritional value is associated with constipation, carbohydrate imbalances, altered insulin production and alteration of micro flora in the intestines.

Vitamin and minerals

Vitamins added to foods are also considered additives. Many are added to replace those lost during processing. Examples include adding vitamins to bread to account for losses in processing and the addition of Vitamin C to many fruit drinks. In some cases vitamins are added to prevent deficiencies in society such as Vitamin A and D to margarine so that they have the equivalent of butter and iodine to salt to prevent goiter in communities where soil may be deficient in this mineral. As we have seen earlier, Vitamin E and the tocopherols are used as antioxidants in high fat and oily foods and Vitamin C is also used as an antioxidant. It seems ironic that we must add vitamins to our processed foods. This demonstrates the importance of including in our diet as much natural unprocessed foods that contain natural vitamin sources that we can.

Other agents

Although we have covered the great majority of food additives there are many others. Additives are added to powdered foods such as salt and powdered milk to prevent them from clumping together and maintaining their flow properties. There are **lubricating agents** added to chocolates and toffees to prevent them from sticking to our teeth or to paper. There are **food waxes** that are used as a protective and cosmetic coating for cucumbers, pepper and especially apples. These waxes have been associated with allergies and can contain pesticides and fungicide sprays. **Aluminum compounds** are common leavening agents in baked goods and aluminum has been associated with Alzheimer's disease. **Phosphorus compounds** make soft drinks bubbly and keep canned vegetables firm and their excess use can disturb the body's ability to absorb calcium, increasing the danger of osteoporosis. Ice cream producers use propylene glycol, the same substance in antifreeze and paint remover. Carboxymethylcellulose is a stabilizer used also in ice cream, salad dressings, cheese spreads and chocolate milk and is a suspected carcinogen. **Brominated oils** have for many decades been added to bottled fruit juice to maintain the look of freshness even after several months of storage. They have been associated with side effects such as enlargement of the thyroid and kidney or liver damage.

It should be kept in mind that most of these additives that I have mentioned have been associated with some degree of danger to our health yet despite this they are still found in increasing amounts on our store shelves. When you take the fact that there are now thousands of chemical substances that we regularly ingest into our bodies, no expert can predict their cumulative long-term effects. There are also obvious dangers to the fetus of the pregnant mother who ingests these toxic substances. These toxic additives disrupt the natural chemistry in the cells of the body and increase the workload of your detoxification organs. Eventually they cannot keep up and diseases may begin to take over the body such as cancer, diabetes, heart disease, kidney and liver disease, allergies and premature ageing. Our bodies have amazing capabilities of self-regeneration and as we have learned our old cells are constantly being replaced with new ones. The raw materials for this regeneration process come from the blood stream that transports nutrients. When the blood stream contains toxic additives, the process of regeneration slows down and resistance to disease diminishes. If you have genetic weaknesses in organs in your body like most of us have, the cumulative effect of toxins will increase your chance of being a host to disease or suffer premature death. Try if at all possible to avoid as many foods that are processed and that contain harmful synthetic additives. You will not only add years to your life but you will also allow your body the best chance to work at optimum capacity for the best of health.

Chapter 12

Foods that Steal

This chapter and the following one discuss some of the negative effects of the food items that we commonly eat. I usually try not to advocate one particular food over another, as I believe that food in its natural form the way nature intended is food that is positive for the human body. There have been just so many claims that one food causes cancer or another causes arthritis or yet another increases the risk of osteoporosis. I believe that it is generally not the food but the additives and the processing that goes into it that are generally responsible. It is the preserving techniques, the cooking methods, and the host of factors that we have become familiar with in the last several chapters. I believe that no one should be allergic to natural foods that are meant for human consumption, but we should and we are allergic to the chemical substances that are found in our food sources as well as the host of synthetic drugs we take for our many ailments.

Foods that steal are unnatural foods. Foods that steal are those that take more nutrition away than they give to the body. They are what I call "dead" foods. If the proportion of dead foods that we ingest is greater than our body's need for foods that are rich in nutritional value or "alive" then we will succumb to disease and ill health. It is that simple. The fact is, that some of us need more nutrients than others and some of us need specific nutrients in far greater amounts due to our genetics and the stresses that we place on ourselves. If we have a weak genetic constitution, we will need higher amounts of foods that are "alive." If we have a strong genetic constitution we may get away with less.

Although this list is not in any way meant to be all inclusive of foods that steal, they are some of the most important foods that I would recommend to minimize in your diet.

Milk and milk products

Milk products would probably not be as bad if they were produced fresh from healthy cows but that option rarely exists today. The fact is that milk and milk products cause more stealing than giving to our health and that is why it has made my list of foods that steal. The media and dairy producers have performed a great job of promoting the benefits of milk and the result is that they has produced a host of misinformation that has convinced the majority of the world that they cannot live without milk. The truth is unfortunately the exact opposite. We have always heard that milk builds strong bones. This is what we have always believed so we made sure to give it to our children as often as they could fill their glasses. The truth is that milk and dairy products have been found to weaken bones and speed up osteoporosis and calcium loss. Remember how it is important to learn from other cultures and not from the mass media machine. Cultures that drink less or no milk have the lowest rates of osteoporosis. The affluent nations have the highest incidence and also the highest milk and milk product consumption rates. Milk allergies are very common in children and can cause sinus problems, chronic ear infections, asthma, diarrhea, constipation and fatigue. The high content of fat in milk, cheese, ice cream and other dairy products is also a growing concern and can add to our problems of heart disease. I have seen in many cases that asthma attacks completely cleared up after milk and milk products were stopped. A large percentage of the population cannot even digest milk, are what is called lactose intolerant because they just don't have the enzymes to digest lactose. The controversial bovine growth hormone, which is being administered to cows to dramatically increase milk production, has been associated with breast cancer in women and prostate cancer in men. Because the cows are now producing milk far faster than nature had intended due to this hormone, the incidence of infections of the cow's udders has dramatically increased. This shows up as blood and pus in the milk. It also leads to treatment with antibiotics, which as you probably have guessed, also show up in our milk and milk products. The processing of milk involves heating and pasteurization, which destroy much of the goodness we find in natural milk. Nature intended milk for baby cows just like nature intended breast milk for our newborn children. The popular practice of formula feeding of babies in the past is now returning back to more women breast-feeding as research has discovered once again that nature produces the best start for the immune system and for disease prevention in the growing child. I believe that soured milk or natural yogurt has a place in our diet but only in minimum quantities. The beneficial bacteria contained in it have been found to have positive effects on our digestive system.

Much more healthier alternatives to milk are soymilk, rice milk or raw goat's cheese or milk. If you stick to that one half cup of milk product daily and have an abundant source of dark green vegetables, avocado, alfalfa and nuts like almonds and sesame seeds, you will supply the body with its daily calcium needs.

Refined white flour, white sugar and white rice

We eat far too much refined carbohydrates in the form of white flour, white sugar and white rice. Refined foods are stripped of their nutritious outer layers which contain powerful phytochemicals and antioxidants that may be, in part, responsible for the reduced risk of cancer and coronary heart disease associated with a high-fiber diet. Often the bran and germ is removed which is an incredible source of minerals and vitamins such as the B vitamins and chromium.

The refined carbohydrates as they are often called are the basic components of most refined or processed foods. They are produced in mass quantities and contain additives and preservatives that extend shelf life. They offer very little in terms of human nutrition and include any products made with white refined flour such as white bread, pastries, breakfast cereals, most pasta, products made with white sugar and finally white rice.

Devoid of nutrients and containing chemicals our bodies are not genetically equipped to handle, these foods have dramatic negative effects on our health and well-being. A trend to a decline in health is often seen when using these products in excess, which most people do. Associated health problems with refined carbohydrates include diabetes, cardiovascular disease, constipation, diarrhea and cancer and tooth decay. Refined carbohydrates are also rapidly absorbed, characterized by a high glycemic load and can aggravate glucose intolerance and cholesterol levels. They feed the non-beneficial bacteria that live in our intestines and disturb the micro floral environment. Individuals who are obese and insulin resistant are even more prone to the effects of a high dietary glycemic load. Substituting whole grain for refined grain products has been associated with a lower incidence of diabetes. Refined grains were also found to increase the risk of cancer of the pharynx, esophagus, larynx, stomach and colon.

Some of the worst dead foods come in the form of refined carbohydrates that desperately lack the vital nutrients that we need. Think about it when you reach for that next slice of white bread. I recommend that you exchange these poorly nutritious foods for their whole food alternatives such as products made only with wholegrain flour, raw sugar, rice syrup or honey and natural rice.

Artificial sweeteners

As we learned in the last chapter, artificial sweeteners are chemical additives that are found in diet foods, soft drinks, chewing gum and other desserts. I would recommend staying clear of them. Their use has been controversial and many of these products such as aspartame and saccharin have been banned in several countries. They do not offer anything of nutritional value and their sole purpose is to sweeten foods without adding calories. Many people have reported headaches, migraines, ringing in the ears and other conditions when they use artificial sweeteners.

Soft drinks

Soft drinks have made their way into most households and especially into the diets of our children and teenagers. They have absolutely no nutritional value but have plenty of white sugar or artificial sweeteners, phosphates and in the case of colas, caffeine. Every carbonated soft drink or water has elevated amounts of phosphates and as we have learned they leach vital minerals like calcium from the body. The high level of sugar in these popular drinks causes the pancreas to produce an abundance of insulin, which can cause fluctuations in blood sugar and other sugar metabolism problems like diabetes, not to mention hyperactivity in young children. Soft drinks do not substitute the body's need for water and can create a dehydrated state in the body. The caffeine and high amount of sugar has drastic effects on the digestive system and can block the absorption of vital nutrients. The diet soft drinks contain artificial sweeteners, which as we have learned have been associated with a variety of negative health effects. Soft drinks are extremely acidic and this is the last thing we need to ingest into our bodies.

Smoked, salted, pickled or grilled foods

Smoked, pickled and salted foods often contain nitrosamines produced from nitrates and nitrites. These have been found to be potential carcinogens and linked with stomach and esophageal cancer. Foods such as pickled vegetables, salted fish and smoked meats, sausages and cheeses are particularly associated with these health problems. Many experts suggest limiting consumption of charcoaled and grilled foods because they may contain hazardous compounds formed when fats and proteins come into contact with high heat.

Fast foods

Fast foods are a phenomenon of western countries. They include meals like hamburgers, French fries, pizzas or fried chicken and are generally relatively cheap and very convenient to purchase. The problem is that they are most often loaded with saturated fat, trans fatty acids, salt and excess calories, not to mention being very low in fiber and nutrients like calcium, vitamin A, E, C and folate. Due to high temperature cooking and frying methods many nutrients in these foods are lost. They are "dead foods" that give us a feeling of satisfaction due to high caloric content but very little in nutritional value. Countries that have adopted fast foods from western cultures soon begin to suffer similar health consequences. These include obesity, heart disease, high blood cholesterol, diabetes, constipation, high blood pressure, cancer and others. Is it no wonder that over half the American population is overweight? Our stressful and hectic lifestyles do not make it easy to ignore the growing convenience of fast food outlets. Remember, if you concentrate on eating regular meals and taking something with you that is more nutritious, you will be less tempted to reach for the quickest food available when those hunger pangs begin. Stay away from fast food outlets. Don't use the excuse that you just don't have time because when you do have that "heart attack" or "cancer" you will have all the time in the world, but then it is usually too late.

Instant foods

We are often presented with a wide variety of instant food preparations on our store shelves and due to our relentless search for high convenience foods, we often make the wrong food choices. Instant foods or foods to which you just add water or milk include instant powdered soups, instant puddings, instant noodles and instant mashed potatoes among many others. Is this food that is alive? Just barely. Most of these products contain chemical preservatives, loads of salt and sugar and possess very low nutritional value yet they are appearing in enormous amounts and people are more often opting for convenience rather than nutrition. The food companies love to manufacture these products and I am sure more and more will appear on our store shelves because guess what, they have incredibly long shelf lives. Don't fall into the instant food trap. Don't sacrifice nutritional value for mere convenience. You are not doing your body any good.

Margarine

Due to the public's demand for low cholesterol foods, margarines were created to simulate natural butter. They were hailed as being responsible for reducing heart disease and high blood cholesterol but they forgot one thing. You can't fool Mother Nature. Since vegetable oil is naturally liquid at room temperature it needs to be made more solid so hydrogen is added to it transforming it into a hydrogenated oil or margarine. Hydrogenated oils also extend the shelf life of margarines. Now research is showing that in the body the hydrogenated fats become trans fatty acids and may increase the bad cholesterol (LDL) and decrease the good cholesterol (HDL). So we are back to square one again. As I have mentioned many times in this book if you go natural you cannot go wrong. As much as we try to simulate real foods, nature always has a way of getting us back.

Potatoes

The reason I include potatoes in my list of foods that steal is that we generally eat too many of them in the form of French fries, baked potatoes, potato chips or mashed potatoes. While potatoes do contain substantial vitamin C, potassium, and other nutrients and are low in fat, high temperature cooking methods generally add fat and destroy nutrients so that we are left with a poorly nutritious food. Most often, people eat potatoes covered with high-fat sour cream, butter or gravy or as deep-fried French fries. These foods unfortunately are not good nourishment for the heart or the arteries by anyone's standards. The typical western meal is a large piece of meat with potatoes and possibly a garnish of salad. What potatoes do is fill us up and "steal" room for the quantity of vegetables that we need. Potatoes have also been known to spike blood sugar in similar ways that white sugar and white bread do and they are known to have a high glycemic index. This means that if you are a diabetic or one that is on the borderline it makes sense to restrict the intake of potatoes. Because of our extremely high intake of potatoes, I would recommend that you use them sparingly in the diet. Unlike the other vegetables that are high in the carotenes they do not seem to protect that much against cancer.

Condiments

Often a hidden source of foods that steal are from our assortment of various condiments such as sauces like mustard, ketchup, steak sauce, soy sauce, mayonnaise, salad dressings, horseradish and many others.

These foods are very acid forming and mucus forming in the body. Many contain excess salt, sugar, artificial flavors and preservatives. Take a look in your fridge and on your shelves and you will be surprised just how many condiments you have. Make sure you take a close look at what ingredients they have or what chemicals have been added to them.

Excess meat and animal protein

The average western diet has just too much meat and protein. This creates excess acidity in the body and puts a strain on the digestive system as well as the kidneys. High meat consumption has been associated with colon cancer, constipation, high blood cholesterol, high blood pressure and heart and kidney disease. Many of these health problems do not even exist in some cultures such as in Africa where meat consumption is very low. The meat that we consume often includes red meat and poultry, which contains many chemical substances, saturated fats and hormones that in excess can cause significant health problems. I am not saying that you should eliminate meat altogether unless you are a vegetarian, but try to limit intake and enjoy a variety of alternatives such as fish, nuts and legumes and soy products. Refer back to the "Eye for an Eye Diet" Food Pyramid in Chapter 8 to make sure that you have a balanced nutritious diet.

Other foods that steal

I have purposely not included several foods and drinks that we regularly consume on a regular basis as they form the group of food items that I call "food addictions." They also steal or take more than they give in terms of nutritional value and affect our health in negative ways. These addictive foods are the subject of the next chapter.

Chapter 13

Food Addictions

When we think of addictions we usually associate them with chemical drugs, and what goes on in some dingy dark alleys in the bad part of town. Most of us do not associate them with foods or drinks that we consume on a regular basis in our clean, well-lit suburban kitchens. What I call a food addiction is when you crave a food item and when it causes withdrawal symptoms when you are without it. This in my opinion is not a good sign of health and indicates that the addictive property in the food item begins to take control rather than the other way around.

Natural foods do not cause cravings. You never feel guilty about eating too much fruit. You never hear little voices in the back of your head or a devil on your shoulder saying *eat, eat, apples*. No, because natural foods balance the body and physical cravings are caused by biochemical imbalance. Alcohol, caffeine, salt, saturated fat, refined starch and refined sugars cause cravings because they imbalance the body's chemistry.

In our society there are several acceptable food and drink items that I call food addictions. What they have in common is that they can cause health problems when in excess and some come with withdrawal symptoms after terminating their consumption. The list includes items like coffee, black tea, alcohol, white sugar, salt, saturated fat and chocolate.

In moderation, these items have their place at the top of the food pyramid, which means they should be used only very sparingly. One should not completely wipe them off our diet list as some studies have even shown that they contribute some benefits to our physical as well as psychological health if used in moderation. Now, this term moderation will vary from individual to individual. If you are born with weak liver function then even one drink of alcohol a day may affect your liver and your health in a negative way. If you are born with a weak pancreas then a bar of chocolate a day may contribute to blood sugar fluctuations and your pancreas may just not be able to handle this glucose load after time. If you are born with weak kidneys for example then ingestion of salty food on a regular basis may be just what is causing your high blood pressure. Do you see what I am getting at? We learned in Part 1 that each one of us is different. It is very difficult to ascertain how these addictive foods will affect your health but my advice is to keep them at a minimum, just as they appear on the top of our food pyramid. If you are one of the lucky few who have all their organs in perfect shape you may be able to get away with it but those who don't may just be subjecting themselves to health conditions anywhere from heart palpitations and insomnia, to diabetes, cirrhosis or hypertension.

Food Addictions

Coffee and tea
Alcohol
White sugar
Salt
Saturated fat
Chocolate

Let's take a look at each of these food addictions one at a time.

Coffee and tea

Probably the most commonly used drugs in the whole world are the group of stimulants known as the methylxanthines. Included in this group are caffeine, theophylline and theobromine which are easily absorbed across the walls of the gastrointestinal tract and which can readily cross the placenta into the fetus or be ingested by an infant through breast milk. These substances are found in coffee, tea, chocolate, cocoa, guarana and cola drinks and are undoubtedly the most abused substances to ever find such an acceptable place amongst the children and adults in our society. I am not saying that in moderation they pose any harm but generally we consume too much on average and this comes with a price to pay.

While coffee is often consumed to stay awake and alert, the caffeine it contains is mildly addictive. If you're like many people and you don't get your daily fix of coffee, your body can go into withdrawal. Signs of withdrawal include sleepiness, fatigue and headaches in both adults and children. This withdrawal headache, well known among coffee drinkers, usually lasts anywhere from one to a few days, and is commonly alleviated with analgesics such as aspirin or with just another dose of caffeine.

Caffeine is a stimulant, which may cause nervousness, irritability, anxiety, insomnia and disturbance of heart rate and rhythm and breathing. It is also a diuretic, which increases urination, meaning that both children and adults need to increase water intake if they regularly consume caffeine in their coffees or colas. Since caffeine is a diuretic, it can also increase calcium loss in the urine, which may contribute to the possibility of osteoporosis later in life.

The average cup of coffee contains around 100 mg of caffeine, the average tea around 50mg and the average cola around 40mg. Don't forget that cocoa and chocolate also contain significant amounts of caffeine. My patients often report effects of excess caffeine ingestion because they begin to feel anxious, excitable, restless or irritable. Often as a result of too much coffee they suffer from gastrointestinal upsets, headaches or migraines, arrhythmia, insomnia, tremors or dizziness. The blood vessels are also affected by coffee and tea as they can cause a decrease in the diameter of blood vessels in the brain, reducing cerebrovascular blood flow. Ingestion of caffeine has been associated with refluxing where acid contents of the stomach back up and irritate portions of the respiratory tract. It also raises the blood pressure and may affect the incidence of heart disease. Coffee can also stimulate the stomach to produce more hydrochloric acid and pepsin, which has been associated with the development of peptic ulcers.

There have been plenty of studies about caffeine and pregnancy, and it is generally considered best to eliminate it altogether or decrease the amount of caffeine you consume when you're pregnant. Evidence suggests an increased risk for difficult conception, miscarriage, and delivery of low birth weight babies with certain amounts of caffeine intake. If it is risky for newborns you can bet it is not that good for you as an adult.

Theophylline is found in tea and can also increase the heart rate or cause arrhythmias in some individuals. It has a stronger effect on the heart and breathing than caffeine and for this reason it is often used in home remedies for treating asthma, bronchitis and emphysema because it is a potent bronchial dilator. It does however have undesirable effects on the brain and nervous system similar to caffeine. Theobromine is found in cocoa products and tea and is also a cardiac stimulant as well as a diuretic.

Associated adverse health effects with excess coffee and tea

Nervousness
Irritability
Headaches or migraines
Decreased blood flow to the brain
Insomnia
Arrhythmia
Anxiety
Loss of water by increased urination
Loss of minerals and calcium
Tremors
Dizziness
Hyperactivity
Restlessness
Increased acidity in the stomach
Heartburn and reflux
Increase in blood pressure
Problems with pregnancy

Alcohol

The drinking of alcohol goes back probably to the early history of mankind and today is considered normal human practice as almost all societies consume some form of alcohol. Again for those who do not have specific health problems drinking alcohol in moderation can be tolerated and perhaps even offers some physical and psychological health benefits. Its abuse however is responsible for the majority of automobile deaths, for marriage breakups, for considerable violence and crime, not to mention a host of associated health problems.

As alcohol can be metabolized to generate energy I classify it as a food. The problem is that this food is a very high energy-providing nutrient that in excess can make us obese. The other problem is that it offers very little in terms of nutrition and takes away or steals even much more than we may realize.

Alcohol is absorbed almost totally and passes readily across the walls of the gastrointestinal tract primarily in the small intestine but also in the stomach and colon. The liver metabolizes most of the alcohol ingested into the body. Most of us know that this organ is the one most affected. As the liver is responsible for an incredible amount of processes and reactions in our body, serious health problems can occur if there is too much ingested alcohol. Fatty liver leading to the condition called cirrhosis is one of the most common liver problems found in heavy drinkers. For some as little as a drink a day can affect their liver in a negative way.

The other organ affected by excess alcohol is the stomach, which has been associated with damage of the stomach lining, peptic ulcer formation and interference with digestion. The small intestine suffers as well, as excess alcohol impairs the mucosal lining and the absorption process. People who drink too much alcohol will have impaired ability to absorb vitamins such as B1, B2, B12, vitamin C and folate. Most alcoholics have deficiencies in these vitamins. Look back at the chapter on Vitamins to see what effects this can have on your health. The pancreas also becomes damaged with excess alcohol leading to deficiency in secretion of digestive enzymes, which will impede the absorption of fats and protein. This is not a good thing as these are all essential nutrients the body needs to heal and to maintain health. The heart is another organ affected. Excess alcohol depresses the activity of cardiac muscle and the associated thiamine deficiency can damage the heart muscle. Finally we cannot forget the effects of alcohol on the brain. Memory deficits, poor judgment, loss of coordination and disturbed behavior are all drastic effects that alcohol has on the brain. Just as termination of excess coffee drinking causes withdrawal symptoms so does alcohol withdrawal. This is particularly noted in alcoholics as they often experience a set of symptoms called delirium tremens, which includes tremors, hallucinations and delusions after they stop drinking.

Alcohol excess has been associated with a greater risk of cancer and pregnant mothers should definitely avoid it, as there is a much greater chance of congenital deformations and growth retardation for the newborn infant.

What is more important to realize is that not only is alcoholism on the rise but that group of borderline alcoholics that abuse alcohol is in far greater number. If your social drinking habits amount to more than 1 or 2 drinks a day you are in this category and are subjecting yourself to a greater incidence of disease.

White sugar

We have already discussed white sugar to some extent in the last chapter. It is mentioned here because it is what I call a food addiction for many people. It really is an empty food source in the same way that alcohol is because it contributes calories to the diet but nothing much else.

White sugar is just an unnatural substance produced by industrial processes (mostly from sugar cane or sugar beets) by refining it down to pure sucrose, after stripping away all the vitamins, minerals, proteins, enzymes and other beneficial nutrients. What is left is a concentrated unnatural substance which the human body is not able to handle, at least not in anywhere near the quantities that is now ingested in today's modern lifestyle. In my opinion, sugar probably does the greatest amount of damage to our health than all the other food addictions out there. We develop a craving for sugar from early life and many of the products that we purchase contain what has often been referred to as "white death." Its effects are slow and insidious and it can take years before sugar ruins your pancreas and adrenal glands or throws your whole endocrine system out of balance. I often hear from my patients that they do not add extra sugar to their meals but when I enquire further I find that they regularly use products that contain high amounts. This is what I call the hidden sugar sources as sugar is often found in soft drinks, chocolate, sauces, ketchup, breakfast cereals and soups as well as in most processed food items available on our store shelves. What does sugar really do in the body that is damaging?

First of all, sugar is pure carbohydrate and a very high source of energy in the form of calories. Excess sugar is stored in two ways in the body, in the liver and muscle where it is stored in the form of glycogen or in adipose tissue as triglyceride or fat. This means that excess intakes of sugar can lead to obesity. Further, another dietary mistake we often make is that after we fill up on excess sugar in foods such as candy and cakes, we do not feel hungry and this results in displacement of nutritious foods that we should be eating. Most people with a high intake of white sugar do not get the necessary nutrients in the form of vitamins, minerals and dietary fiber. Sugar is by far the leading cause of dental health problems resulting in cavities, bleeding gums and loss of teeth. Within minutes of ingestion of sugar in the mouth, glucose is metabolized by the bacteria on the surface of your teeth to produce lactic acid, which eats into the tooth enamel to cause a cavity. It is therefore important to immediately brush your teeth after ingestion of a sugary meal.

Because white sugar is so quickly and readily digested and absorbed into the blood, it causes a rapid rise in blood glucose, which is detected immediately by the pancreas. The pancreas then secretes insulin that brings the level of glucose in the blood down to normal stable levels. This is a normal part of the automatic regulation of glucose in the blood. The problem arises when we eat a lot of sugar throughout the day because this will in turn demand a constant secretion of insulin from the pancreas. It soon becomes depleted and exhausted and the ability to regulate blood glucose levels through insulin secretion is impaired. This can result in insulin resistance and the conditions known as diabetes, hyperglycemia or hypoglycemia. Those who consume a lot of sugar often have a deficient intake of fiber and chromium. Fiber is especially necessary for those with high intakes of white sugar because it has the ability to slow down the uptake of glucose from the digestive tract. In this way it can prevent exhaustion of the pancreas. For this reason I would recommend if you do consume sugar, have some high fiber foods along with it such as fruit, vegetables or whole grains.

A high intake of sugar has also been linked with an increased risk of heart disease. As sugar consumption can raise triglyceride levels as well as circulating levels of cholesterol in the blood, this can contribute to coronary heart disease.

The effect of excess sugar on the blood sugar levels can also result in a variety of mood changes, which include depression as well as hyperactivity, which is quite often found in many young children.

Finally white sugar is what feeds the non-beneficial bacteria in the gut such as Candida albicans, which can lead to low immunity to varieties of yeast infections. As the micro floral environment in our digestive system is crucial to our health, I would highly recommend limiting your intake of white sugar.

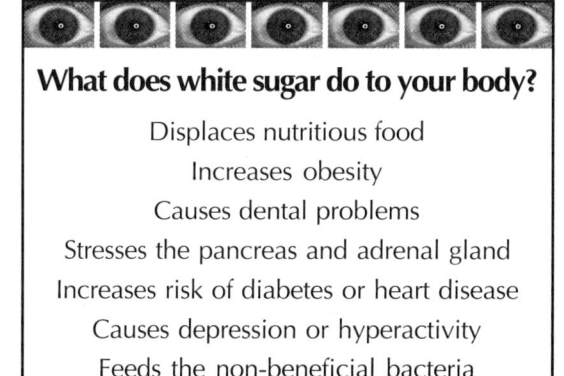

What does white sugar do to your body?

Displaces nutritious food

Increases obesity

Causes dental problems

Stresses the pancreas and adrenal gland

Increases risk of diabetes or heart disease

Causes depression or hyperactivity

Feeds the non-beneficial bacteria

Disrupts the hormonal system

Salt

Salt is another one of those food addictions that plague our modern society. While some salt is necessary for our body functions, the amount that is normally consumed is far greater than our requirements. Do we really need all that salt? Our general daily need is the equivalent of the salt in one piece of bread. Salt is an acquired taste and often quite addictive as usually those who use a lot of salt say that their foods would be tasteless without it. This is really not true. Try this experiment. Reduce your salt intake dramatically for 6 weeks or so and you will find that the foods will regain their taste. Your tongue just takes a while to get used to the change. Also remember that even if you do not use a saltshaker on the table or add salt while cooking there are an incredible amount of hidden sources in the foods that we eat. Considerable amounts of salt are found in most canned foods, sandwich meats, butter and margarine, packet soups, bread, cheese, ice cream, salad dressing and salted nuts.

Probably one of the most well known reasons for reducing salt intake is high blood pressure or hypertension. Excess salt in the diet is associated with a higher risk of hypertension. I have witnessed falls in blood pressure when salt was reduced in the diets of many of my hypertensive patients. Salt affects the water balance in the body and the function of the kidneys. Kidney stones have also been associated with possible excess salt consumption. When large amounts of sodium are excreted with excess salt intake, this involves some loss of calcium in the urine. For this reason a high salt diet can also contribute to osteoporosis in some individuals due to loss of calcium from the bones.

In most western societies, inadequate salt intake is not a problem, rather the opposite. Surely if you are active or engage in extreme physical activity you will need more salt then the average individual. Most of us however will better our health if we cut out unnecessary salt in our diet.

Saturated fat

The craving for something greasy or fatty is a common food addiction. The problem is that saturated fats found in many fried or fast foods are associated with a greater risk of heart disease. Saturated fats are usually from animal origin and found in meats, oils and milk products. One of the most significant adverse health effects from eating excess saturated fats is obesity. Obesity is associated with a number of health problems such as diabetes, gallstone formation, heart disease and high blood pressure. Remember a body that is in proper chemical balance will be resistant to these cravings for foods such as saturated fats. Avoid stress, fast food outlets, eating on the run, not eating regularly and you will find that you will be less inclined to opt for the unhealthy alternative when you make your food choices.

Chocolate

A list of food addictions would not be complete without including one of mankind's all time food cravings, chocolate. You are probably just waiting for me to tell you the bad news about chocolate but although there have been several associated adverse health effects of its consumption including links to migraines or acne, many recent studies have also found some positive benefits as well. Chocolate is usually high in sugar and contains a considerable amount of caffeine, which as we noted earlier has negative implications. Processed or commercial chocolate especially milk chocolate contains a fair amount of saturated fat as well. Chocolate also contains theobromine which is a compound similar to caffeine and that is poisonous to dogs.

The good news though is that cocoa butter which is a prime ingredient of chocolate contains monosaturated fatty acids, which may have some beneficial effects on the heart. Further some studies have shown that chocolate contains an antioxidant that may have protective properties for the heart as well. Dark chocolate seems to have more health benefits than milk chocolate.

Other studies have revealed evidence that chocolate can increase the level of the neurotransmitter, serotonin. Serotonin levels are often decreased in people with depression or in those experiencing symptoms of pre-menstrual syndrome. The ingestion of chocolate may increase their level of serotonin production in the brain along with their reported feelings of well-being. As these studies are not conclusive, it is important to use chocolate in moderation. Its place remains at the top of the Food pyramid along with any sweets and this means it should still be used sparingly.

Chapter 14

Foods that Heal

In the past few chapters we have focused on the damaging effects of some foods and the toxic substances that we find in many of our food items. This information has been presented so that you can make intelligent food choices and to provide a solid nutritional background for you to apply the Eye for an Eye Diet. It is time now to move in a new direction and to take a look at some of the foods that have remarkable healing qualities. As I believe that 90 percent of all disease can be prevented if quality nutrition is restored to the body, this chapter is particularly important in our quest to find the answers to our growing health problems.

Although I believe that most foods in their natural unprocessed form have the ability to heal, I have selected those groups of foods that I feel are some of the most important in a superior quality nutritional diet.

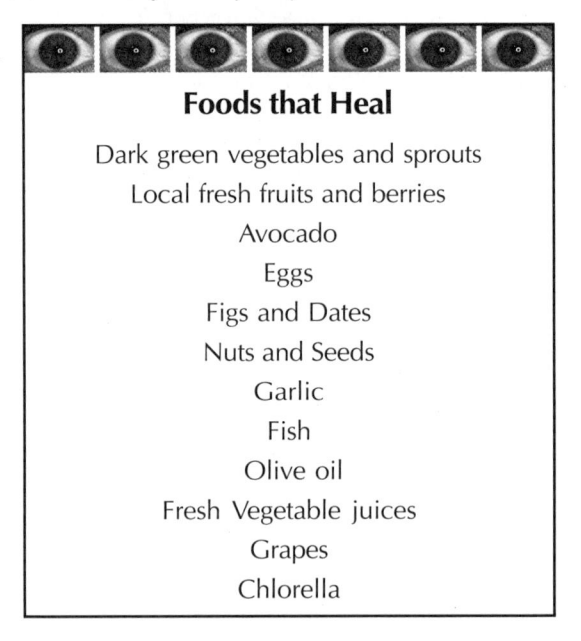

Foods that Heal

Dark green vegetables and sprouts
Local fresh fruits and berries
Avocado
Eggs
Figs and Dates
Nuts and Seeds
Garlic
Fish
Olive oil
Fresh Vegetable juices
Grapes
Chlorella

Dark green vegetables and sprouts

Dark green vegetables such as broccoli, green beans, brussel sprouts, spinach and peas are a rich source of beta-carotene, fiber and other vitamins and are linked to reduced risks of breast, colon and stomach cancers. Broccoli is particularly important as it also contains a large amount of Vitamin C and many minerals. Vegetables should always be only lightly cooked or better eaten raw to preserve their nutrients. Spinach is loaded with iron and folate. Sprouts are a superb source of nutrients that should always be added to your salad. These include varieties like alfalfa, radish, mung bean and soybean and they all have curative abilities to protect against disease. Sprouts such as alfalfa also contain an abundance of plant estrogens that are particularly helpful in preventing osteoporosis and female disorders like pre-menstrual syndrome, fibrocystic breast tumors, hot flashes and menopausal symptoms. Alfalfa sprouts are one of our finest food sources of another compound, saponins. Saponins lower the bad cholesterol and fat but not the good HDL fats. Sprouts are also beneficial for improving the immune system and contain an abundance of highly active antioxidants that prevent DNA destruction and protect us from the ongoing effects of aging.

Include five servings of vegetables a day with at least two being of the dark green variety, eat sixty percent in their raw form and always add a handful of sprouts to your salad.

Local fresh fruits and berries

The benefits of eating fresh local fruits in season are many. As we have learned valuable nutrients are lost in the transport and storage of fruit. By the time that tropical piece of fruit arrives in your food store significant amounts have been lost. Further, with regards to many of these fruits, they are usually picked much too early and long before they are fully ripe so you are not getting what nature has really intended. Eating the whole fruit as opposed to just fruit juices has further benefits because we are getting other nutrients like bioflavonoids and valuable fiber that allows a steady slow uptake of fruit sugars into the bloodstream. Lemons are excellent cleansing fruits and lemon juice can be added to drinking water to assist the toxic elimination from the body. Apples are high in pectin, which has the ability to take up water in the intestines and make a soft bulk. This serves as a fantastic digestive aid to improve the movement of food or peristalsis through the digestive tract.

Berries are another source of valuable nutrients and many have been used for their curative properties as well. They have the most fiber of any fruits and are valuable sources of calcium, iron, potassium and folic acid. Strawberries are very high in Vitamin C and bioflavonoids. Blueberries are high in pectin, which lowers cholesterols levels and they may contain more antioxidants than any other fruit or vegetable. They seem to have anti-aging benefits and some experiments have shown improvements with short-term memory. Another benefit of blueberries is that like cranberries, they seem to fight off urinary-tract infections by preventing E. coli bacteria from adhering to the bladder wall. Cranberries have long been used as a folk remedy for bladder and kidney infections and recently their medicinal properties have been supported by scientific research. Other quality sources of berries include blackberries and raspberries. Remember the majority of us eat berries in the form of cooked jams or jellies that contain large amounts of sugar with significant losses of nutrients.

Try to include at least two to three raw servings of fruit or berries daily.

Avocado

The avocado is a fruit that is full of nutrients and fiber. It is also a rich source of monounsaturated fat, the good kind of fat that actually lowers cholesterol levels. Known for their vitamin E, the avocado may provide protection against heart disease. Avocado consumption also has been found to help the body combat other major diseases including diabetes, cancerous tumors and osteoarthritis. Some research studies have found that by eating avocado, the risk of heart disease in diabetics is lessened, especially those with insulin resistance or type two diabetes. The reason is because they guard against after-eating increases in blood sugar. Consuming avocado has been shown to give knees and hips afflicted with osteoarthritis extra lubrication. As a result, sufferers gain better joint mobility and endure less physical pain. Researchers in Japan have discovered that they also contain potent chemicals that may also reduce liver damage. In addition to benefiting the liver, these green-skinned fruits are rich in vitamins E and C, high in potassium and fiber and contain large amounts of folate, a vitamin that helps reduce birth defects in pregnant women.

An alternative to spreading butter or mayonnaise on bread is to try mashed avocado instead. This will reduce your intake of saturated fat and increase the amount of monounsaturated fat as well. Consuming avocado provides a great variety to a low-fat, well balanced diet but you should eat them in moderation if you are trying to lose weight, as they are high in calories.

Eggs

I have always considered eggs one of the most perfect protein foods available and have recommended them to my patients for years. They allow slow rises in blood sugar and are relatively easy to digest. Despite having a reputation of being high in cholesterol, recent research has shown that they are not as bad as we used to think because they also contain lecithin, the element that breaks down cholesterol so it can be properly metabolized. Eating one boiled or poached egg a day has been shown to have no significant affect on cholesterol levels or heart disease. If eggs are cooked with the yolk exposed to air as in frying, their cholesterol is oxidized and becomes worse for the body because it can be deposited in the inner lining of arteries. Make sure that the eggs you eat are from uncaged chickens that have been ideally fed vegetarian organic feed. Caged chickens have been found to be mineral deficient as well as their eggs. Vegetarians who are not vegans can also use the positive protein benefits of eggs to balance the nutrients in their diets.

Figs and Dates

The fig has been around since ancient civilization and contains a high amount of calcium. Figs are also laxative due to the pectin they contain. They are high in carbohydrates and produce energy very quickly. Dates have also been cultivated since ancient times and are a high source of energy and calcium as well. Some research has found that they may be even able to reverse the progression of some cancers.

The main reason I included figs and dates in my list of foods that heal is because they are excellent sweet alternatives to white sugar products like candy, cookies and cakes. They are best eaten fresh but do provide a good source of nutrients when they are dried. They also reduce the chance of constipation, which is a huge health problem in modern society and provide a high source of calcium that is necessary to maintain strong bones and prevent osteoporosis.

Nuts and Seeds

Nuts are very high in natural oils and there are many nutritious nuts but I have to give credit to the almond as being one of the most important to include in your diet. Almonds are very high in protein and contain no bad cholesterol. They have significant amounts of Vitamin E, which is a potent antioxidant with anti-cancer properties and most of the fat in almonds is monounsaturated or the "good" fat. The almond is also packed with minerals like phosphorus, zinc, magnesium and folic acid, as well as plenty of healthy fiber. They are also excellent sources of calcium to maintain strong healthy bones. In addition, almonds have been known to improve the health and shine of the hair.

Seeds are also a valuable source of nutrients and have long been considered a health food with the power to slow down aging and prevent various diseases like high blood pressure and heart disease. Sesame seeds are one of the most superior forms as they have natural antioxidant properties that can prevent oxidative damage in the body, a contributor to increased cancer risk. They are also a rich source of thiamin. Other nutritious seeds include sunflower seeds and pumpkin seeds.

Try to include a daily serving of nuts and seeds especially almonds and sesame seeds.

Garlic

The health qualities of garlic have been celebrated since ancient times. This wonderful odorous substance has been used for an endless list of ailments over the times. The odor factors are sulfur-based compounds known as allyl sulfides and many scientists agree that allyl sulfides and the other phytochemicals present in garlic may actually help protect the heart. Garlic claims on health include abilities to reverse high blood cholesterol and triglycerides, lower high blood pressure, detoxify the body of toxic metals like lead, cadmium and mercury and boost the immune system. It has been used in the treatment of goiter due to its high iodine content and scientists are fairly confident that garlic also has antibacterial and antifungal powers. To release garlic's potent compounds, you need to mash or mince it. Be careful of cooking it for a long time or at a high heat as it may destroy its beneficial substances. For some people, especially those with existing digestive problems, garlic can irritate the lining of sensitive stomachs. Be careful of excess raw garlic as it can cause stomach problems and heartburn. If you use raw garlic, limit it to no more than two cloves, as excess has been known to cause anemia over long-term use. You do not have to worry about cooked garlic.

I would recommend you consume one clove of garlic a day preferably in the raw form or next best to take some garlic supplements if you are concerned about odor.

Fish

If you are not a vegetarian, I believe that eating certain fish has the ability to offer amazing health benefits as well as offer superior nutritive value. Remember way back how we discovered that it is important to learn from other cultures. We learned about the Greenland Eskimo whose traditional diet is high in fat and protein and low in fruit, fiber and leafy green vegetables, yet they experienced little evidence of heart disease. Researchers concluded that the key to the Eskimos' good health was due to the highly unsaturated omega-3 oil found in the fish and other marine animals these people ate. Omega-3 are long-chain polyunsaturated fatty acids found in fish and other seafood; mainly the fattier species of fish, such as salmon, tuna, sardines, mackerel and herring. A growing body of scientific opinion suggests that omega-3 fatty acids provide significant health benefits. They seem to prevent platelets in the blood from clumping together and sticking to arterial walls in the form of plaque. They also decrease triglycerides and bad cholesterol. Researchers suspect that omega-3 fatty acids may block the production of inflammatory substances linked to autoimmune diseases like rheumatoid arthritis and lupus. In my practice I have used Omega-3 fatty acids for eczema and skin problems, for high cholesterol and high blood pressure as well as for migraines with great success.

I would highly recommend that you consume a serving of fish, primarily salmon or tuna at least 3 times a week.

Olive oil

Olive oil has often been described as the "miracle of the Mediterranean." This impressive title is based on the finding of numerous research studies that have confirmed that a diet containing olive oil offers many health benefits. The best way to learn is from different cultures. People who live around the Mediterranean Sea, where olive oil is a major component of their daily diet, have much lower death rates from heart disease and certain cancers. Olive oil is very high in the antioxidants vitamin A and E, which neutralize cancer-causing free radicals in our bodies. It is also monounsaturated and lowers the "bad" LDL cholesterol without reducing the "good" HDL cholesterol. This results in improved circulation, reduced cholesterol, lower blood pressure and less risk for heart disease. Recent research also indicates that olive oil may be especially effective in preventing both breast cancer and osteoporosis and assists in regulating the body's blood sugar levels which can be helpful for diabetics.

Olive oil is suitable for all types of cooking except frying. It is excellent to use on salads and as a substitute for animal fats such as butter and lard. Make sure you choose "extra virgin" olive oil in a dark bottle as it means the oil is from the first pressing, uses top grade olives with low acidity and has the highest nutritional value and taste.

Fresh vegetable juices

What I mean by fresh vegetable juice is not the commercially prepared variety that is often so processed that the nutritional content is largely lost and the healthy enzymes are killed by heat sterilization. Due to this you will often find that vitamins have been added to the juices to replace what has been lost not to mention a lot of added sugar and salt. Commercial juices do not have the same health benefits as freshly squeezed juices made from a juice extractor and consumed immediately. Freshly squeezed vegetable juices contain naturally occurring vitamins, minerals and enzymes that are easily absorbed into the bloodstream and reach your cells much faster. They do however lack the fiber of the whole vegetable but they offer a much more concentrated quantity of the other beneficial nutrients found in vegetables. Their therapeutic uses have offered benefits for cancer and terminally ill patients, they are valuable in relief of high blood pressure, heart and kidney disease as well as obesity. I have seen dramatic results with the treatment of chronic diarrhea, colitis and general toxicity of the digestive system. Their high buffering capacities offer valuable treatment for excessive hydrochloric acid in the stomach or any over-acidity of the tissues and body fluids.

It is important to use a quality juice extractor that does not destroy the valuable enzymes that the juices contain. Some excellent healing juices can be made with spinach, parsley, celery, cabbage, tomatoes, alfalfa, cucumbers, carrots or beets. Avoid too much carrot juice as it contains a fair amount of sugar. Remember to drink immediately after juicing to avoid unnecessary loss of nutrients. I do not recommended too much fruit juice as it can often be quite acidic and contains concentrated fructose concentrations that can raise blood sugar levels quite quickly. Try to eat fruits as much as you can in the whole form. If you do juice them, make sure that they are diluted fifty percent with water.

Grapes

Grapes are one of the oldest fruits in our history. They have also been used for curative purposes throughout the world. They are high in magnesium and iron and are excellent for cleansing the bowel and liver and for assisting kidney and bladder function. Grapes have a lot of water content and contain grape sugar that gives quick energy. They are very high in antioxidants and the flavonoids, especially in the red grapes, have led to some research on potential health benefits of red grapes and red wine. A potent anticancer agent called quercitin is found in red grapes. They also seem to protect arteries as the grape skins contain resveratrol, which has shown to inhibit blood-platelet clumping or blood clot formation. Grapes are ideal as cleansing food and have been used during fasts for treatment of cancers and other chronic diseases. I would recommend that you include grapes in your diet especially the red grape varieties but make sure that they are properly washed as they often contain many chemicals.

Chlorella

I have used chlorella for many years in my naturopathic practice and because it has proved to provide so many health benefits for my patients, I have included it here in my list of foods that heal. Chlorella is a single-celled freshwater algae and nutritionally it is considered almost a perfect food. Chlorella contains more than twenty vitamins and minerals including B complex, beta-carotene, vitamins C and E, iron, iodine and calcium. It also contains B12, which is good news for vegans. It has an extremely high percentage of protein (almost 60 percent) that is very easily digestible. Chlorella has the highest percentage of chlorophyll of any known plant source and probably for this reason it has been the subject of intense study especially by the Japanese who regularly consume this food. Chlorophyll is well known as a liver detoxifier and a bowel cleanser. Research has shown that Chlorella is a very high source of the nucleic acids DNA and RNA and these factors are known to stimulate tissue repair, speed up healing and slow down the aging process. The unusual cell wall of this algae binds with heavy metals such as cadmium, lead and mercury as well as pesticides and carries theses toxic substances safely out of the body. Chlorella also contains a substance called Chlorella Growth Factor, which has been found to strengthen immunity by improving the activity of T and B-cells and macrophages (components of our immune system) and some studies have found that it can inhibit some tumors. I have especially used Chlorella for a variety of digestive disorders including colitis, Crohn's disease, inflammatory bowel syndrome, diarrhea and constipation with very effective results.

Due to the fact that the food we eat contains many chemicals and preservatives and because Chlorella has many positive health effects as a liver and bowel cleanser, I would definitely recommend using Chlorella regularly in the diet. It can usually be purchased as a food supplement from your health store.

Chapter 15

Contemporary Issues in Human Nutrition

One of the most difficult realizations that one has to come to terms with when we deal with nutrition is that there is just so much nutritional information out there. We have nutritional advice coming to us from all angles, including our doctors, the radio, TV, health magazines, books and countless other forms. Just a brief surf on the internet and you can find nutritional advice on every topic imaginable, which can leave the average person quite overwhelmed, confused and undoubtedly intoxicated from information overload. There are just so many companies flaunting their supplements and nutritional programs and products that it is quite easy to not know which way to turn. Nutritional advice and scientific expertise also varies quite considerably.

Who can you believe or trust? The answer is, only yourself. You are the master of your own destiny as well as your own health and I hope that you are intelligent enough to put all this nutritional advice into proper perspective. As I have mentioned before, one of our greatest illusions is that we believe that food companies out there are concerned about our health. In this day and age, we have to learn to rise above the hype and glamour of media advertising and start thinking for ourselves. When the media started us thinking and panicking about cholesterol, we allowed the food companies to produce products like margarine without cholesterol. Now the bitter truth is coming back at us. It turns out that margarine is not as healthy as we had believed for years. The reason: because this is not how nature intended it. When we allowed the processed milk producers to convince us that their milk is good for our bones, we made them rich but as a result many of us suffered more from allergies to asthma or osteoporosis. When we wanted to lose weight, the food companies created low calorie artificial sweeteners so that we could have our cake and eat it too. However nature fought back with greater revenge with incidence of other serious health problems. As consumer demand for bigger, better and more beautiful food produce is increasing it is no wonder that companies are gathering their scientists together to genetically engineer our wishes and desires. Who knows what nature's reaction will be but you can be assured that it won't be pretty and you will probably have to wait at least ten years before any long-term effects are brought to public attention. Just think of how many years baby food companies have been selling and convincing us the benefits of formula over breastfeeding and only now are mothers beginning to realize the drastic effects on the immune system.

Frank Navratil BSc. N.D.

Nature is the only force that we really can and should believe in. When I examine research papers on nutrition or food products, it doesn't matter if the scientist has won a Nobel prize, if the food does not conform to Nature's laws, I cannot be convinced otherwise. Remember there is just so much money behind some of these research endeavors and so many are funded by the food manufacturers themselves.

I want to bring up a few contemporary health topics that surround nutrition, which in my opinion and experience are worthy to examine. As a fair amount of controversy surrounds these issues, I hope they will clear up some possible misinformation that you have been subject to in the past and offer some new insights into means of preventing and dealing with disease using natural methods.

Breast-feeding versus Formula feeding

Unfortunately, there is just no money to be made in marketing breast-feeding but there is plenty to be made by advertising formula feeding for infants. Hence another common misconception is that baby formula can be substituted for mother's milk. What many of you may not realize is that bottle-fed babies are more likely to contract a variety of illnesses, including ear infections, diarrhea, pneumonia and Sudden Infant Death syndrome. Nature has always intended that newborn infants be fed mother's milk that contains nutrients and antibodies that the child requires for the rest of its life. We cannot simulate such a formula no matter how smart we think we are. One of the most critical and responsible decisions a mother can make is to breast feed her child in the first stages of life. The other responsible decision is to make sure that what she eats or drinks is nutritious for her as well as for her baby.

Many research studies have shown that infants who were formula fed often had lower mental and cognitive development, a higher incidence of allergy and respiratory problems, greater gastro-intestinal illness and incidence of diarrhea. They also were found to be at greater risk of developing diabetes, childhood lymphomas or succumbing to cot death or SIDS.

Give your child the best possible start he or she can possibly have. Achieving optimum health in this day and age is difficult enough without going through life already weakened by the effects of formula feeding during infancy.

Skipping meals does not help you to lose weight

Skipping meals is something that many of us believe will cause us to lose weight. However, this common practice sets the body up for a fall in the effectiveness of the metabolic system. Each time you skip a meal, the body goes into a state of shock or crisis. It begins to wonder where its next meal is going to come from so it begins to slightly conserve energy. If one meal is missed per day and this continues every day, your body's metabolic rate will slow down. Soon the body begins to burn fewer calories at rest than it did prior. For a few days, the body will lose weight mostly in the form of water but will then begin to hold on to stored calories. When food intake is resumed, the body may hoard however many calories it takes in and can store them as fat. This method of cyclic dieting sets the person up for a roller-coaster ride of constant weight gain and loss. Don't deny the body of nutrients just because you want to lose weight. It will backfire on you. Your body is an intelligent and sophisticated instrument and for every action on it there will be a reaction. Shocking the body and depriving it of adequate nutrition is not the way to go. Stick to our intelligent program, exercise and you will not need to count calories. The ultimate goal of your nutritional program should always be to focus on quality eating and lifestyle habits, not habitually counting calories and skipping meals.

Enzymes are the difference between raw and cooked foods

I believe that so many chronic degenerative diseases are caused or aggravated by digestive problems. I also believe that the average diet is responsible for the development of chronic degenerative diseases such as heart disease, atherosclerosis, cancer, diabetes, stroke and others. It is no mystery that many of the most common health complaints revolve around that mucus-lined tube we call our digestive tract, which directly interacts with our outside environment. Digestion is one of our essential life processes and its job is to transform the food we eat into a useable form that our body can absorb. In order to perform its job effectively, enzymes are required. Enzymes are powerful biochemical catalysts, which speed up burning or building reactions in the body according to need. They are made from specialized proteins and often have names that end in "ase" such as protease, lipase and amylase which assist the digestion of protein, fats and carbohydrates respectively. They come from our salivary glands, in the form of amylase that starts the digestion of carbohydrates right in our mouth. Our liver and pancreas also supply enzymes that are secreted into the small intestine and assist with protein and fat digestion, while the lining of our stomachs and digestive tract has its own enzymes that further the process.

Enzymes are also found in raw foods. They are destroyed in cooked foods.

Now, you may be asking why do we need enzymes in raw foods when we already have such an elaborate system of enzyme production in our body? The answer is that although the enzyme-producing organs continue to function over the entire course of a healthy life, they eventually wear down, especially with our standard diet which includes regular cooked or canned foods. What's more is that we are not starting our lives with perfect livers, pancreas organs or digestive systems. With cooked foods our pancreas is forced to work harder as well as our other digestive organs and the more they are used, the faster they wear out. This extra activity can be detrimental to our health because it continually taxes the reserve energy of our organs. Furthermore, cooked food passes through the digestive tract more slowly than raw food, it tends to ferment, and may cause toxins to be thrown back into the body. Colon cancer is one of the greatest killers in our society and it is surely related to our dietary habits as well as poor supply of enzymes. A toxic intestinal system may manifest itself by symptoms of bloating, fatigue, gastro-intestinal discomfort, recurrent infections, headaches, arthritis, skin eruptions, hormonal disturbances, allergies or asthma. I have witnessed all of these conditions showing positive response to therapy directed to correcting bowel toxicity and digestion. It is important to have fiber in the diet as we have mentioned in an earlier chapter to scrub the colon walls clean but in order to allow proper digestion and assimilation of vital nutrients we need adequate enzymes. Cooked food is often not digested adequately enough and molecules of this food can pass into the bloodstream and cause several health problems as well as compromise the immune system that responds unnecessarily to the influx of foreign food particles.

Raw foods have special properties that assist the body's natural enzyme processes. Ideal sources of enzymes are sprouts and other fruits and vegetables that are uncooked. You can think of raw food as "live food" that relieves the stress imposed on the liver, pancreas, stomach and intestines by a predominantly cooked food diet. I would recommend that 60 percent of your fruits and vegetables that you consume be in the raw form.

Overeating Sugar is worse than overeating fat

Many food products are being manufactured today with reduced fat or zero percent fat. Our compulsion with reducing our fat intake when we are dieting is leading to the habit of replacing fat by an overindulgence of sugar consumption. Overeating sugar is actually worse than overeating fat because it can cause blood sugar imbalances, and has been associated if abused enough, with adult onset diabetes, digestive problems and hormonal imbalances. Saturated fats may be correlated with heart disease over time, but remember, that's only part of the story. Monounsaturated fats are necessary and healthy for bodily functions. Eating fat from sources such as flax seed oil, walnuts, olive oil, almonds or avocado is good for the body. We need fat to survive and remain healthy. We don't need table sugar for any reason. It is not an essential nutrient. Keep in mind that the body turns all carbohydrates into glucose (sugar) in order to digest it and feed the body. Sucrose or table sugar, on the other hand, or high fructose corn syrup are never necessary for the body and only end up raising blood sugar levels and wreaking havoc on the pancreas. Choose fat, the healthy kind over sugar when you are making a food choice.

Vitamins alone do not replace quality food

The next chapter deals more closely with vitamin supplements but one key issue in nutrition that must be understood is that vitamins are not meal replacements. They are as their name implies, "supplements" to the diet. There are usually no calories in vitamins. Calories are found in proteins, carbohydrates and fat and they come from our meals. Vitamins are essential nutrients needed by the body in relatively small amounts depending on the need of the individual. They assist in driving cell processes and help other nutrients to be absorbed, digested and metabolized but they will not replace a quality meal. Don't get in the habit of thinking that if you throw a few vitamins into yourself you don't need to eat anything of any value.

Eggs and cholesterol

For years we have been led to believe that we should use eggs sparingly because they contain high levels of cholesterol. In recent times, studies have shown that although it is true that eggs contain high amounts, the absorption of cholesterol is reduced by another compound found in eggs, lecithin. The lecithin or phosphatidylcholine in eggs was found to decrease the lymphatic absorption of cholesterol.

This means that much of the cholesterol that is eaten with eggs becomes unavailable for absorption in the body in the presence of lecithin. If you have normal cholesterol levels and no family history of cardiovascular disease, eating one to two eggs a day should pose no problem, as long as they are not fried or the yolk is not exposed to air. This means that boiling or poaching are the only acceptable cooking methods. As eggs are what I consider a healing food that is extremely nutrient rich and contains superior quality protein, there are more overall nutritional benefits to gain from eating them than there are risks. Eggs are also a significant source of vitamins A and E as well as the B vitamins and folate. As I have mentioned before, try to source your eggs from free-range hens that are fed only natural vegetarian feed.

Meat eating versus vegetarianism

I believe that the decision to be a vegetarian or a meat eater is entirely up to you. I myself was a vegetarian several years ago for a good period of time and I have worked with hundreds of vegetarian patients but for health reasons I see no dramatic health benefits one way over the other. I certainly respect anyone who wishes to be a vegetarian due to beliefs in animal rights or religious practices and the fact remains that a large percentage of the population in the world lives without any eat meat at all. When strictly talking about health though, in my experience it is not the fact that meat causes health problems but the high quantity of meat that the average person consumes along with the low intake of vegetables that is the culprit. I see many vegetarian patients who eat no meat but gorge themselves with sweets and have associated health problems. I also see many patients who eat some meat or fish as well as lots of vegetables and stay healthy. The opposite occurs as well.

Of course eating meat does come with its own specific set of problems. With the increased incidence of contamination, Mad Cow's disease and other risks of food poisoning or additives in meat, a vegetarian diet may offer a safer alternative. However, vegetables are often subject to pesticide spraying and genetic alteration, so their ingestion also poses other forms of health risk. The advantage of eating vegetables is that it usually comes with an increased intake of fiber and other essential nutrients, which have been associated with a reduced risk from cancers, heart disease and digestive disorders. Vegetarians however need to watch that their protein intake is sufficient as some protein from vegetables may be more difficult to absorb or be assimilated in the body.

The other environmental factor is the effect of livestock farming on the earth's resources. It has been said that it takes about ten kilograms of vegetable protein to produce one kilogram of meat, which means that this is very wasteful and not a very efficient means of producing food. Other environmental reasons for becoming a vegetarian are that millions of hectares of rain forests are destroyed yearly to make grazing pasture for livestock not to mention that the earth's oceans have been over fished. Animals are also subject to horrendous living conditions, caged in confined spaces and often fed an unnatural diet laced with antibiotics and chemicals.

Although each side of the vegetarian versus meat-eating story comes with its own set of problems as well as benefits, I strongly recommend that if you are not a vegetarian, make sure that the majority of your food comes from plant sources.

Cholesterol and heart disease

One of the most misleading issues in human nutrition is cholesterol and its association with heart disease. While there are many studies showing that people who suffer from heart disease often have high blood cholesterol, no one as yet has ever been able to prove that high blood cholesterol causes heart disease. The Greenland Eskimos who had a diet that was extremely high in fat and cholesterol rarely had any heart disease or heart problems. The Masai people in Kenya drink half a gallon of milk from the African Zebu cattle (which is much fatter than cow's milk) each day and eat mainly meat and very little vegetables. In spite of this the cholesterol of the Masai tribesmen is among the lowest ever measured in the world. Furthermore we have to ask ourselves what causes an atherosclerotic plaque to form in an artery. Some scientists believe that cholesterol just cannot stick to the walls of an artery for no reason. In order for these plaques to begin to form or stick there must be some form of injury or assault to the walls of the arteries. What causes weakness or stress in the blood vessel walls? One possible reason is high blood pressure, which has been implicated in causing stress or damage to the arteries and may possibly encourage plague formation. Another theory is that the lack of Vitamin C, which produces collagen, may cause stress fractures in the vessel walls and promote the binding of cholesterol. If this is the case, then how did the Eskimos obtain their source of Vitamin C if they ate only fish and seafood? The answer to this mystery is that their vitamin C was obtained from raw narwhal and beluga whale skin, which contains as much as oranges and raw seal liver provided their vitamins A and D.

Maybe we should look at atherosclerosis as not a disease but a healing process. Remember for every action on the body there is an intelligent reaction. The body does not form a clot or plaque just for the sake of it. Just like a scab forms when we have an injury, plaques form after a lesion or injury is imposed to the walls of the blood vessel. Advocates of vitamin C therapy have proposed that many people today are chronically deficient in vitamin C and if they restore their vitamin C levels then the arteries will heal and plaque formation along with heart disease can be prevented.

According to conventional wisdom it is smarter to lower your cholesterol if it is too high. The main reason for this advice is due to the observation that people with high blood cholesterol more often get heart attacks than people with normal or low blood cholesterol. Although this observation is correct, it still does not mean that the high cholesterol is the cause of the heart attack. It may possibly be due to lack of vitamin C or some other factor that we still don't know about.

Chapter 16

Nutritional Supplements

I have always been a strong believer that diet and lifestyle changes are the only way to achieve optimum and lasting health and to cure the body of disease. Ideally, one should achieve the nutrients the body requires through food, sunlight and the air we breathe. The modern reality is however, that our food supply is low in quality and as we have discovered is often contaminated with chemical fertilizers, additives and preservatives while smog and pollutants often deplete the oxygen in the air we breathe.

How can one stay healthy in such an environment?

It is becoming increasingly difficult to maintain health as we can see in rising rates of cancer incidence and chronic diseases like diabetes, allergies and asthma. As each one of us has different genetic requirements for nutrients, often for many the nutrients from processed foods are not enough to prevent disease. Very few of us can say that we eat quality nutritious foods each and every day.

The stresses that we incur in our modern lives are taxing our body's ability to fight disease. Often many nutrients are lost through the processes of freezing, packaging and canning foods. Many fruits that are transported from other countries are picked before they are ripe and stored for long periods of time and the final consumer often gets a low quality, vitamin poor product. We have learned that we consume thousands of different chemical additives to foods in the form of colors and preservatives that our livers and cleansing organs must detoxify. The variety of drugs we take for symptoms of constipation, headaches, high blood pressure, colds and flu are also reducing our body's ability to absorb and utilize nutrients. The exposure to damaging radiation from the power lines around us to mobile phones is an additional drain on our nutrients. Add this to the stresses of life in modern society and it is not surprising that it is a rare individual today that can really say that he or she is truly healthy.

A new branch of natural medicine has recently gained more and more acceptance by doctors and naturopaths around the world called the field of nutritional therapy. Nutritional therapy is a method that combines diet, vitamins, minerals and concentrated nutritional supplements to cure or prevent disease. Often these vitamins and supplements are used in much higher dosages than standard recommended daily dosages set by government health departments. It is therefore recommended that if you are endeavoring to undergo nutritional therapy or take nutritional supplements to first consult your naturopath or doctor who specializes in this therapy and who can advise you on safe dosages.

I have used nutritional therapy for many years for a variety of health conditions with enormous success. While I admit that concentrated nutrients in the form of vitamins and other supplements are not the way that nature intended, in our modern society we have very little alternatives. If the quality of our food supply is decreasing, we will not fulfill the nutrient demands of our bodies and the grim reality is that we will eventually succumb to disease. We need to combat this problem by not only working on ensuring that we have the best quality food that we can obtain and in the right amounts but also supplying our body with extra essential nutrients that may be lacking. Often these nutrients are used in specific combinations for treatment and prevention of a variety of health problems and for general maintenance of health.

Vitamin and supplement therapy should never replace a good quality diet of fresh food and vegetables, it should as the name implies, only supplement a diet that may often be low in nutritive value.

It is also very important that the supplements are in the most natural form possible. Many years ago it was commonly believed that synthetic vitamins, as they were identical in chemical structure to natural vitamins, would have the exact same effect on the body. Today we are learning otherwise. Again, we cannot fool Mother Nature. I would always recommend first and foremost getting the most vitamins, minerals, proteins, carbohydrates and fats from natural whole foods. Then secondly, find the most natural supplements that you can find that will supply the body with nutrients that are as close to the way nature has intended because they will have the greatest effect on the body.

Most people are familiar with the use of vitamins or supplements in some sort of way, but most are unaware of which supplements they may need and in what quantities. In Part 3 of this book you will learn more about your genetic nutritional needs and this will provide you with the background information on what your body is most probably lacking.

Frank Navratil BSc. N.D.

What are some nutritional or herbal supplements that are used today in the field of nutritional therapy? Here are just a few of the hundreds that are commonly available today.

Vitamin C	Zinc	Betaine hydrochloride
Vitamin E	Lactobacillus acidophilus	Glutamine
Vitamin B-complex	Digestive enzymes	Chlorella
Beta carotene	Chromium piccolinate	Spirulina
Multivitamins	Bioflavonoids	Kelp
Calcium	Omega 3 fatty acids	Coenzyme Q-10
Magnesium	Potassium	Garlic
Iron	Selenium	Ginseng
Folic Acid	Lecithin	Propolis
Cranberries	Gingko biloba	Shiitake mushrooms
Echinacea	Shark cartilage	Valerian
Alfalfa	Amino acids	Evening Primrose oil
Methionine	Glucosamine sulfate	Carnitine
Lysine	Royal Jelly	Antioxidants
Rutin	Hesperidin	Licorice
Inositol	Pectin	Acerola

I would like to describe a few nutritional supplements that I believe deserve special attention.

Lactobacillus acidophilus

There are many types of bacteria that reside in our intestinal tract, some of which are beneficial and others that are non-beneficial and if not kept in check can cause significant health problems. These bacteria populations are kept in balance in order to maintain pH in the digestive tract so that enzymes and reactions work at their most optimum rate. This is what we call our intestinal flora and it ensures that we properly digest our food as well as being responsible for producing some vitamins and an environment that is favorable for efficient absorption of nutrients into our bloodstream. This delicate balance can be easily disrupted. It is very common to see digestive problems in our society and it is no wonder as the assault of various drugs we take including antibiotics plus chemical additives in our foods, destroy that delicate balance, reducing the amount of favorable bacteria. Unfavorable bacteria such as Candida albicans or Escherichia coli then have a breeding ground to proliferate. The increased acid environment then causes damage to the intestinal mucosa or the inner lining of the digestive tract and toxins and larger food particles are then able to get into our bloodstream. This causes havoc for our immune system, creates allergies and a free radical cascade that may cause anything from arthritis to hormonal disorders. Digestion is the foundation of our health. If it is not is order then our cells will not receive the nutrients they require and they will die and we will succumb to disease. Only in recent times it has been discovered that once the micro floral environment is disrupted it is very difficult for the body to return it back to normal. Lactobacillus acidophilus bacteria are friendly or favorable bacteria that are normally present in our digestive tract. They are the same bacteria that are found in soured milk or naturally made yogurt. Keep in mind that most commercially made yogurts contain very little beneficial bacteria despite their claims. It is also very difficult for the beneficial bacteria in these products to survive through the acidic environment of the stomach in order to reach the duodenum. Some bacteria will survive but it may be inadequate to treat digestive disorders. If you have undergone treatment with antibiotics or other drugs or if you just want to prevent disease and ensure that your flora are kept in check, I would recommend taking lactobacillus acidophilus supplements. They are usually specially coated or protected to last in their journey through the stomach so they can reach their destination and begin to re-colonize the area. They displace the Candida albicans and reduce the numbers of unfavorable bacteria such as Escherichia coli to manageable proportions, allowing favorable flora to then proliferate. Lactobacillus acidophilus supplements can be extremely beneficial for treatment of candidiasis, hyperchlorhydria, hypochorhydria, duodenal ulcers, irritable bowel syndrome and colitis.

Enzymes

Another common modern problem is insufficient enzyme production in the body. As we discussed in the last chapter, our excessive ingestion of cooked or canned foods leads to more stress on our body to supply enzymes for digestion. I also see much more incidence of insufficient liver or pancreatic function these days so again it is not surprising that our bodies just cannot digest our food as well as we would like. Common health problems associated with lack of enzymes can be bloating after meals, excessive gas production, constipation, diabetes or diarrhea. Enzyme supplements may relieve this stress on some of our organs that produce enzymes so that they can once again regenerate.

Chlorella

Chlorella is a fresh-water alga that contains an incredibly high amount of chlorophyll as well as nucleic acids and many vitamins and minerals. We have come across Chlorella before as I have listed it in the chapter, Foods that

Heal, due to its remarkable abilities to cleanse the bowel and liver. It usually comes as a supplement and I would strongly recommend it as part of a detoxification program for the body.

Lecithin

Lecithin is a phospholipid, a fatty food substance, which serves as a structural material for every cell in the body. It is an essential constituent of our brain and nervous system and is also an important component of the endocrine glands and the muscles of the heart and kidneys. Lecithin is a rich source of choline, which the body requires to make acetylcholine, a neurotransmitter, which is essential for normal nerve function. Nervous, mental or glandular over-activity can consume lecithin faster than its replacement and this may cause irritability and exhaustion. It is therefore, of utmost importance to add lecithin to the diet, if the body's own supply decreases as in old age or when the body is under stress.

Rich sources of lecithin include egg yolk, vegetable oils, whole grain cereals, soybeans and liver. The cells of the body are also capable of synthesizing it as needed, if several of the B vitamins are present. Since these B vitamins are generally removed when grains are refined, people who eat exclusively white flour products or refined carbohydrates are often lacking them and require lecithin in greater amounts.

Studies have demonstrated that lecithin has positive effects on controlling blood cholesterol, aiding in the digestion and transportation of fats. It has also been suggested that lecithin intake can assist organs and cells that need it, notably the kidneys, heart muscle and endocrine glands. For the older generation, lecithin intake has been associated with improvements in memory, alertness, blood pressure, nervous exhaustion, senility, Alzheimer's disease and elimination of yellow or yellow-brown plaques on the skin or around the eyes caused by fatty deposits. It has also proved valuable in the treatment of certain skin ailments, including acne, eczema and psoriasis. Since lecithin has the ability to make cholesterol more soluble it can also reduce the risk of gall stone formation. Lecithin is a natural product and comes in supplement capsules or in granular form.

Omega 3 fatty acids

Omega 3 fatty acid supplements are generally made from fish oils such as salmon oil. One of the prime reasons for producing them has been for the health benefits that these oils have primarily on the heart and circulatory system as seen by studies of the Greenland Eskimos, who despite a diet high in fats, suffered only rarely from heart disease. Their regular use has been associated with a decrease in heart disease, blood triglycerides and high blood pressure as well as improvements in kidney disorders, depression and skin diseases like eczema. For those who do not regularly eat salmon, tuna, sardines or mackerel, I would recommend Omega 3 fatty acid supplements.

Echinacea

Echinacea is a very popular herb and it is used throughout the world. Echinacea was first used in the United States by Native Americans who used the herb to heal wounds including snakebites. The root of the plant was used to treat toothaches, sore throats and other irritations in the mouth. The herb was later introduced in Europe. All parts of the Echinacea plant are used, including the leaves, roots and purple flowers. Echinacea has been well researched and many studies have been conducted to test its curative properties. Today, Echinacea is widely used and its healing and infection-fighting properties are well known. Scientists and the medical community have proved many of the herb's benefits.

Numerous studies have shown Echinacea to be effective in strengthening the body's immune system. Echinacea seems to stimulate the immune system and promotes T-cell activation and assists white blood cells to attack germs.

Another way Echinacea seems to help the body to fight infection is through the stimulation of the liver, lymph glands and mucous membranes. The major use of Echinacea is to treat colds and flu. It is also used for urinary tract infections, skin wounds that aren't healing well, and skin conditions such as psoriasis and eczema. It has been well documented that Echinacea is valuable in boosting the immune system of cancer patients, especially after chemotherapy treatment.

Gingko biloba

In the last few decades numerous studies have given clinical evidence that ginkgo biloba has positive effects on the entire body. This herb is gaining recognition as a brain tonic that enhances memory because of its positive effects on the vascular system, especially in the cerebellum. I have used it in treatment for tinnitus (ringing in the ears) and a variety of neurological disorders and circulation problems, including varicose veins and hemorrhoids. Ginkgo biloba may help to counteract the effects of aging, as it seems to show improvements for mental fatigue and lack of energy.

This herb seems to have a remarkable ability to increase blood flow to the brain and throughout the body's network of blood vessels that supply blood and oxygen to the organ systems. Benefits of enhanced circulation in the brain include improvements in short and long-term memory, mental clarity and reaction time. Ginkgo is often used to assist elderly persons with Alzheimer's disease, poor memory, absentmindedness, confusion, depression, dizziness, tinnitus and headache. It acts as a powerful antioxidant and contributes to the oxidation of free radicals, which are believed to contribute to premature aging and dementia. The herb has also shown to have positive effects on other circulation-related disorders such as diabetic peripheral vascular disease, Raynaud's syndrome, hemorrhoids, varicose veins, eye and ear disorders. It can also aid in the treatment of insufficient circulation and complications from stroke and skull injuries.

Studies have confirmed that ginkgo biloba increases blood flow to the retina, and can slow retinal deterioration resulting in an increase of visual acuity. In clinical tests ginkgo has improved hearing loss in the elderly. It also improves circulation in the extremities relieving cold hands and feet or swelling in the limbs.

Propolis

Propolis is a brownish resinous material collected by the bees from the buds of various plants and trees and used by them to fill cracks in their hives and as a cleanser for cells before placing honey or pollen in them. Before the queen lays her eggs in a cell, the bees clean it out and line it with this microscopic coating of propolis. It is only then that the queen will lay her eggs in what has become a sterile environment. Bee propolis, which has been used since ancient Egyptian and Roman times is considered a very effective all-natural antibiotic and antibacterial/antifungal agent that has shown to provide benefits in the treatment of many health conditions, including sore throats and infections, sinus and bronchial ailments, allergies and asthma. It is readily available as a supplement in most health food stores.

Ginseng

Ginseng is probably the most famous Chinese herb and the most widely recognized plant used in traditional medicine. Various forms of ginseng have been used in medicine for more than 7000 years. Several species grow around the world, and though some are preferred for specific benefits, all are considered to have similar properties as an effective general rejuvenator and an agent that balances the body functions. Ginseng is native to China, Russia, North Korea, Japan, and some areas of North America.

Reported health benefits of ginseng include resistance to stress, improvements in circulation and mental functioning, reduction of risk of cancer and improved control of blood sugar levels. It has been known to normalize blood pressure, increase blood circulation and aid in the prevention of heart disease. The main active ingredients of ginseng enable it to balance and counter the effects of stress by acting on the adrenal glands, helping to prevent adrenal hypertrophy and excess corticosteroid production in response to stress. Ginseng is used to restore memory, and enhance concentration and cognitive abilities, which may be impaired by improper blood supply to the brain. It has been shown to increase energy, stamina, and help the body resist viral infections and environmental toxins.

Ginseng is also used to improve performance, boost energy levels, enhance memory, and stimulate the immune system. Oriental medicine considers ginseng a necessary element in the prevention and cure of disease. Men have often used this herb to improve sexual function and impotence and women have even found improvement with menopausal symptoms and hormonal disorders.

Acerola

Malpighia glabra is a small tree or shrub that grows up to 5 meters in height and can be found growing throughout Northeast Brazil, the West Indies as well as South America, Central America and Jamaica. Acerola is the fruit of the tree. It is bright red and 1 to 2 cm in diameter with several small seeds and has an appearance similar to the European cherry. The acerola tropical cherry contains about eighty percent juice and is one of the richest known natural sources of Vitamin C. It can often provide over 4 percent Vitamin C compared to 0.05 percent in an orange. For this reason it is often used in Vitamin C supplements.

Bioflavonoids

Bioflavonoids are a group of naturally occurring plant compounds, which act primarily as plant pigments and antioxidants. Some of the best known include rutin, hesperidin, citrin, and quercetin. Food sources high in bioflavonoids include citrus fruits, skins of fruits and vegetables, and buckwheat. They are most noted for their powerful antioxidant properties. Bioflavonoids work with other antioxidants to offer a system of protecting vitamin C from oxidation in the body, which allows the body to reap more benefit from vitamin C.

Besides their important antioxidant effects, bioflavonoids help the body maintain health and function in many ways. They have been shown to be anti-carcinogenic, anti-aging, and provide assistance to the structure and function in the circulatory system. Their health-promoting effects include better eyesight, improved cardiovascular health, improvement for varicose veins and hemorrhoids, increased capillary strength, improved structure of connective tissues and appearance of skin and a stronger immune system.

Vitamin E

In recent years, many researchers have reported that vitamin E, packed in shiny amber capsules can protect the heart and blood vessels, help prevent cancer, boost the immune system and slow the progression of Alzheimer's disease. Vitamin E has also been known to help in the aid of wound healing and slow down the effects of aging due to its strong antioxidant properties. I have used vitamin E supplementation in the treatment of cardiac arrhythmias, heart and circulation problems and clot formation. Taking vitamin E can significantly lower your risk of heart disease and enhance the functioning of your immune system. Natural sources of vitamin E include vegetable oils, such as soybean and sesame seed oil, most nuts and in lesser amounts, wheat germ and most vegetables. As a supplement the best form of vitamin E to take is its natural form, which is labeled d-alpha tocopherol. The synthetic form of vitamin E is labeled dl-alpha tocopherol.

Some health problems that have been benefited by nutritional therapy are:

Diabetes	Allergies	Heart problems
Cancer	Osteoporosis	Circulation problems
Constipation	Thyroid	Nervous system
Digestive problems	Migraines	Diarrhea
Liver disease	Infertility	Eczema
Kidney disease	Skin problems	Hair loss
Difficulty in sleeping	Bladder infection	Low immunity
Chronic Fatigue Syndrome	Sexual problems	Varicose veins
Arthritis	Hemorrhoids	Vision problems
Asthma	Psychological	Menstrual problems
Prostrate problems	Candidiasis	Cataracts
High cholesterol	High blood pressure	Colitis
Crohn's disease	Depression	Gallstones
Obesity	Schizophrenia	Stress

Over the last several years I have recommended making lifestyle and diet changes based on genetic eye constitution supplemented with combinations of many of the above supplements with great success for the numerous health problems that plague our modern society. For most health problems that exist there are natural ways to deal with them through this fascinating growing field of nutritional therapy.

Chapter 17

Restricted Diets

I chose this chapter to write about the various types of diets that exist in our society. When we hear the word "diet" we generally associate it with giving up something that we like and that means we feel we will have to suffer a bit when making any kind of change in our eating plan. Most crash diets involve counting calories and as I mentioned before I am much against any kind of short-term program. A change in our diet does not necessarily mean we have to suffer. We have to be willing to change our habits somewhat but like anything else it takes some time to adjust to a new way of living. Health fads come and go and there are many diets that have endured and have been used in a variety of ways to conquer some of our health problems. I believe that ninety percent of our diseases are due to improper food and lifestyle decisions. This means that it is crucial that we adopt a diet that will suit us and from which we can gain the required nourishment for all our daily activities. No matter what type of diet we choose, the same guidelines that we have discussed in this book up to now always apply.

Eating a wide variety of different foods, including some from each of the major food groups of the pyramid that we have constructed, is an important step towards achieving a healthy and nutritionally balanced diet. There are some people however who choose to omit certain foods or food groups from their diet due to religious, ethical, health or moral grounds and others who may be forced to exclude certain foods because of a medical condition. In most cases, it is still possible to ensure that the diet contains all the essential nutrients for good health. The important thing to remember however is to be aware of the potential nutritional deficiencies which may arise and to develop a strategy to avoid these pitfalls. In order to make responsible food choices we should be familiar with some of the types of diets that many people in society adopt along with their advantages and disadvantages, health benefits and health risks.

Vegetarian diets

Probably the most popular type of diet is the vegetarian type. Being vegetarian means to avoid eating meat or animal products in the diet. There are however many types of vegetarian diets. **Vegans** are strict vegetarians who eat absolutely no foods from animal sources. This includes no meat, poultry, fish, dairy products or eggs. There are **ovo-lacto-vegetarians** that eat both dairy products and eggs but no meat or fish. These are the most common vegetarians. **Lacto-vegetarians** on the other hand eat dairy products but no eggs. **Fruitarians** are similar to vegans but they avoid processed or cooked foods and their diet consists of mainly raw fruit, grains and nuts. Still others who class themselves as semi-vegetarians avoid red meat and poultry but eat fish.

The vegetarian diet is often criticized for two main reasons. First, there is a higher risk of not obtaining enough quality protein, because the vegetable proteins are generally incomplete and lack one or more of the essential amino acids. There are exceptions as is in the case of soybeans, which are a very good source of complete protein. Some sulfur-containing amino acids like methionine are lacking in foods like black beans and lentils and legumes. Grains often lack lysine and lentils are often deficient in the amino acid tryptophan. In order to compensate for these deficiencies, vegetarians must combine two vegetable types so that the complete set of essential amino acids is obtained in the diet. Examples of complementary protein pairs of vegetable foods include legumes with cereals, lentils with wheat or rice, peas and wheat, leafy vegetables with seeds or beans and corn. Ovo-lacto-vegetarians can combine eggs or dairy products with some deficient vegetable protein and create complete protein in their diet but vegans must be much more careful.

The other reason why the vegetarian diet is criticized is because of a greater risk of inadequate vitamins and minerals that are normally found in food from animal sources. Vitamins and minerals that may be in short supply include vitamin B12, calcium, iron, zinc and vitamin D. Vitamin B12 deficiency is usually not a problem for vegetarians other than the vegan who may need to take some supplements or ingest certain types of seaweed including Chlorella that contain some source of this vitamin. Vitamin D as it is usually adequately synthesized in the skin by the action of sunlight, is usually not a problem unless the vegetarian has very limited exposure to the sun. Excellent calcium sources for vegetarians are almonds, sesame seeds, leafy vegetables, legumes and fortified soymilk. Iron deficiencies have also been reported in vegetarians. Iron is abundant in vegetable sources but may be more difficult to be absorbed in the digestive system as most of the iron remains bound to the food fiber which is excreted from the body. However, iron absorption from vegetables can be greatly assisted with vitamin C and fruits eaten at the same meal. Zinc deficiencies can also arise in vegetarians as the metal also binds to some fibers, so an adequate intake of whole grains is important in the diet. Pregnant or lactating women and growing children are often those at greatest risk from nutrient deficiencies in a vegetarian diet, especially a vegan diet.

Although there are some guidelines that must be followed in order to avoid nutritional deficiencies in a vegetarian diet, in general, vegetarians enjoy many beneficial effects on health. Since they have a much lower intake of fats, especially saturated animal fats, they often report lower blood cholesterol levels along with a lower incidence of coronary heart disease. Since they have a very high intake of fiber, it absorbs fat, cholesterol and bile salts in the digestive tract and reduces uptake into the bloodstream. A lower incidence of cancers has also been reported in vegetarians especially cancers of the bowel, breast, pancreas, ovary and prostate.

I don't think that it is necessary to be completely vegetarian to enjoy some of the health benefits. If you follow the "Eye for an Eye Diet" Food Pyramid, you will be getting a large proportion of your food from vegetable sources and at the same time you will be supplying your body with complete protein, fiber, vitamins and minerals.

High Protein Diets

There is a common misconception that high protein intake will help build more muscle mass and promote one to lose weight. Protein is required for muscle growth but unless you are an athlete or engage in high physical activity, excess protein intake above your basic needs will never add more muscle. High protein intake can actually be very dangerous. It will overwork your liver in order to turn it into uric acid resulting in the kidney working overtime to excrete the surplus uric acid in your blood stream. A consistently high uric acid level in your blood will make you more prone to kidney stones and other kidney diseases. High-protein diets can interfere with mineral absorption such as calcium, placing you at an increased risk of osteoporosis. Gouty arthritis is another disease related to high uric acid in blood. When uric acid level is too high in the blood stream, uric acid crystals start to form in kidneys and joints.

The popularity of the high-protein diet is beginning to fade as people discover the dangers involved. Another effect can be a strong body odor as well as the smell of ammonia of your breath. Many high protein foods such as meat and dairy products are likely to be loaded with saturated fat, and a diet high in this kind of fat increases your chances of developing heart disease. Limiting complex carbohydrates will also mean your diet is lacking in fiber, leading to constipation and other health problems. Remember, if you follow the guidelines in this book, you will keep the right kind of quality protein levels adequate while at the same time achieving a supply of complex carbohydrates in your diet that will provide enough fiber and other nutrients important to your health.

No - Fat Diets

In recent times the increased rate of obesity in western cultures has led to extreme obsessive dieting programs, which often include methods to reduce as much fat from the diet as possible. Many zero-percent fat products are on the market including yogurts and other items. Although it is desirable to reduce saturated and trans fatty acids, it can be detrimental to health to reduce all fats. As we mentioned before, our body needs fats, especially the healthy types from vegetable sources such as the polyunsaturated and mono-unsaturated variety. Extremely low fat diets can cause hormonal and metabolic problems and contrary to popular belief, substituting fat with calories from carbohydrates does not always lead to weight loss. Furthermore, the fat-soluble vitamins require fat for their absorption in the body. If you eat no fat, the carotenes, those found in vegetables and those that are vital to our health pass through our system and literally go to waste. Cholesterol is a fatty substance that is made mostly by the liver and we all need some cholesterol, as it is required to build cells and make vital hormones. There's no need to follow a fat free diet, just cutting down on saturated fats and ingesting unsaturated fats, found in food items like olive oil and avocado will help you achieve your goals.

Fasting Diets

Fasting goes back to Biblical times as a way to purify the body and the mind and has been used as part of spiritual exercise that dates back to cultures including the Greeks. It is the voluntary abstinence from eating for an extended period of time. Fasting is believed by many to be a way of giving the digestive system a rest to allow the body to rid itself of toxins and wastes. It is also thought to stimulate metabolism and promote healing by strengthening the immune system. The main argument offered by those who advocate fasting is that it is a means of detoxifying the body, or getting rid of natural waste and environmental chemicals that build up in our bodies. The principle is based on the fact that an incredible amount of energy is required to break down the food we eat, energy, which can be better spent healing our bodies.

There are many types of fasting, the most popular is probably the juice fast where only fresh fruit and vegetable juice or herbal teas and vegetable broth are consumed. Since all of these liquids are high in nutrients, it is more of a restricted diet instead of a real fast. Fasting is often a controversial procedure about which opinion is seriously divided. What I consider acceptable is no more than a one-day fast that is supplemented with plenty of water. The body contains its own detoxification system and if all the organs are functioning well it should be able to cleanse itself of unwanted toxins. The problem arises when these organs are not functioning well. In my opinion, the body must be ready to perform its detoxification tasks and the only way to do this is to strengthen weak detoxification organs. If toxins are released in the body and the liver, kidneys and other detoxification organs are not prepared to handle this release it can cause an overload that the body will not be able to handle. Dangers of fasting can include symptoms of lightheadedness, dizziness or headaches. Longer fasts can lead to sodium and potassium depletion. Yes, fasting has been used to cure cancer and other terminal illnesses but I really believe that depriving the body of nutrition that it needs to survive and perform its detoxification tasks is not the sole answer for long term health.

Low calorie diets

At any given time, millions of people are dieting in the world. Most people view the diet as a temporary means of losing weight quickly and then they just return back to their old ways of eating. This as I have mentioned before just does not work. Companies continuously advertise fast weight loss, liquid diets and crash diet programs targeted to those who want a "quick fix" for their weight problems. Weight can be quickly lost but is gained right back, because people return to their old eating habits. Despite the fact that millions of dollars are spent each year on these programs, they do not work. I would recommend you stay away from any low calorie type of diets. Stop counting calories and start an intelligent approach to your health. After spending a few weeks on a low calorie diet, your basal metabolic rate, which is the rate at which the body burns up calories, drops. At this time, the body also begins to use muscle as its energy resource. The body thinks that it is starving, so its natural reaction is to save energy. Muscle is consequently lost and fewer calories are burned. The weight lost from the low calorie diets comes from water and muscle tissue along with the fat. When you return to normal eating habits, the water and fat are regained. However the muscle tissue is not regained unless exercise is used to promote its development.

You must realize that very low calorie diets will cause your body to become less efficient at burning fat. In the long run this causes more fat to be gained. This dieting results in what is popularly called the Yo-yo effect and over time, when weight is constantly lost and regained you will become fatter instead of leaner. You can achieve much healthier and more permanent fat loss results by following the guidelines in this book which include eating a nutritious well balanced diet, enjoying regular exercise and strengthening your genetic weaknesses which we will learn more about in the next section.

Specific diets for medical reasons

Under certain medical conditions particular foods must be excluded from the diet. For example, patients with celiac disease must avoid gluten, found mostly in wheat, which can lead to nutritional deficiencies. Others suffer from lactose intolerance and must not ingest dairy products that contain lactose otherwise they get severe diarrhea or abdominal cramps. There are a variety of allergies to foods that exist for some people and in those cases they need to be avoided.

Chapter 18

Exercise: The essential nutrient your body cannot live without

I like to think of exercise as a nutrient because it really is something that the body takes in and uses and which remarkably improves its function. It also improves the ability to ingest another nutrient, oxygen that is essential for our cells. If you begin to view exercise as an essential nutrient and develop an understanding and respect for what it can achieve for your health, you will soon dismiss the idea that it is only for sports-minded people but actually something that every body needs and cannot live without.

You have come this far with me and I hope that I have shown you that nutrition is not a fad or a crash diet but a change in lifestyle habits. There will never be a fast way to lose weight or regain your health overnight. The natural processes in your body cannot be rushed. What you need to learn is more about how your body works as each of you are individuals with your own set of individual physical and emotional characteristics. The more we learn about ourselves the more we uncover the secrets to our own health. We can then be able to assist our bodies so that they work at their optimum rate. Exercise works hand in hand with nutrition. Like nutrition it is something that we need to ingest regularly whether we are eight or eighty.

It always helps to be informed about a topic, as it will motivate us further to achieve our goals. Let's take a look at what exercise can offer in relation to our health and well-being. Remember that exercise assists all of the seven essential processes of life.

I would always suggest finding a type of exercise that you can do at least 3 or 4 times a week and that you enjoy because the chances are very high that you will quit after the first few weeks if you are anything like the average person. Take a look at the list below and ensure that you adhere to each of the conditions.

1. Find an exercise activity that you enjoy and that you will not get easily bored with.
2. Find an exercise activity that provides aerobic training as well as strength and flexibility training.
3. Find a partner who will motivate you in times of weakness.
4. Make sure that the location of where you exercise is easily accessible as there will be times when it may be too much of a bother if the exercise facility is too far to get to.
5. Provide time in your weekly schedule for exercise just as you do for meals.

6. Put together a list of alternative activities should your first choice fail for some reason.
7. Be strict and discipline yourself - the first 6 weeks are the toughest.
8. Accept the fact that you may be more tired the first six weeks of your program than you were before and keep in mind that the body is adjusting to new changes.
9. Remind yourself that you will always feel better after the exercise session even if you have no motivation to exercise right now. With experience you will come to appreciate this fact.
10. Don't use sad excuses.

What can we expect from a sound exercise program? Here are 50 reasons why you cannot afford to not exercise.

Benefits of exercise
1. Improves heart and lung function
2. Relieves stress and improves ability to handle stress
3. Controls weight
4. Increases physical and muscular strength
5. Improve endurance
6. Increases lean muscle mass and decreases body fat
7. Increases energy levels
8. Improves resistance to disease
9. Increases flexibility and the range of motion
10. Protects the body and back from potential injuries
11. Improves stamina and endurance
12. Improves muscle tone
13. Assists in better sleeping
14. Reduces depression, anxiety and psychological problems
15. Increases confidence and self-esteem
16. Improves sexual function, vigor and vitality
17. Improves peristalsis and digestive function
18. Prevents constipation
19. Improves lymphatic flow
20. Increases the resistance of the immune system
21. Reduces blood cholesterol
22. Strengthens the heart and entire circulatory system
23. Improves balance and posture
24. Improves muscle and nerve interaction
25. Prevents calcium loss from bones and osteoporosis
26. Increases the metabolic rate and burns calories
27. Increases blood flow and oxygenation

28. Improves skin function
29. Improves physical appearance
30. Protects against heart disease and stroke
31. Reduces the risk of developing high blood pressure
32. Helps reduce blood pressure in people who have high blood pressure
33. Protects against noninsulin-dependent diabetes
34. Reduces the chance of obesity
35. Protects against back pain
36. Improves strength of tendons and ligaments
37. Reduces the risk of developing colon cancer
38. Reduces the incidence of hip fractures
39. Improves the quality of life
40. Increases maximum oxygen consumption
41. Increases the cardiac output
42. Increases the stroke volume of the heart
43. Increases ability of blood to carry oxygen
44. Increases blood supply to the muscles
45. Increases HDL cholesterol (the good cholesterol)
46. Lowers heart rate
47. Lowers blood triglycerides
48. Improves glucose tolerance
49. Reduces insulin resistance
50. Makes you feel alive!

An intelligent method of exercising and becoming fit

There are three important components that make what I consider a fit person. In order to achieve physical fitness we have to have **endurance, muscular strength and flexibility**. Let's take each of these components and discuss them separately.

Physical endurance comes from aerobic exercise. Aerobic exercise means that we have to work our heart and respiratory system enough so that their function improves. The remarkable thing about our heart and lungs is that with regular aerobic exercise, they become much stronger and as a result do not have to work as hard for the same load of work. What this means to you is that you don't get winded when you climb that set of stairs and your energy levels and endurance improves. To achieve this is best accomplished by maintaining your pulse or heart rate within a certain range for at least 20 to 30 minutes, three to four times a week. I have included a copy of the exercise formula below that we briefly discussed back in Section 1 of this book. It has been designed to take age into consideration and is a relatively safe method to develop your level of endurance. If you have been inactive for a while, you may want to start with less strenuous activities such as walking or swimming at a comfortable pace. This will allow you to become physically fit without straining your body. Once you are in better shape, you can gradually do more strenuous activity. Remember to always consult your physician when starting any kind of exercise program.

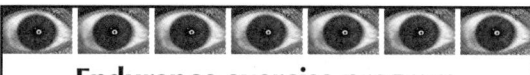

> **Endurance exercise program**
>
> 1. Subtract your age from 220
>
> 2. Take 70 percent of that number (This will be the minimum pulse rate per minute while you exercise)
>
> 3. Take 85 percent of the same number. (This will be your maximum pulse rate per minute while you exercise)
>
> 4. Start exercise and take your pulse after a few minutes
>
> 5. Maintain your pulse rate between the minimum and maximum numbers for at least 20 to 30 minutes, 3 or 4 times a week.

Muscular strength is achieved by resistance training. This means that in order for our muscles to become stronger we need for them to work against a load. Examples of this kind of exercise are cycling, which strengthens legs muscles, swimming, or weight lifting. Exercises such as push-ups or sit-ups use your own body weight as resistance. I would strongly recommend some form of muscular strength exercise in combination with aerobic training. With time our muscles weaken and no longer are able to support our skeletal system such as our back so we become much more prone to injury and accidents. Furthermore improving muscular strength also improves our appearance and assists our veins to pump blood from our legs to our heart. Those of you with low blood pressure need to work the legs. Even 15 minutes of strength training 3 times a week can have enormous benefits. I have put together strength training programs using light weights for the elderly over the age of 70 and even at that age they have shown remarkable increases in strength, in many cases no longer needing their canes or crutches. Ask your fitness consultant for a program that can strengthen the major muscles in your body.

> **Muscular strength exercises**
>
> Swimming or water aerobics (legs, arms, back)
> Cycling (legs)
> Weight training (all body muscles)
> Exercises using your body weight
> Minimum 15 minutes 3 times a week
> Try to exercise all of the major muscle groups

The final major component of physical fitness is **flexibility.** Flexibility is defined as the range of movement we have in a joint. Since attached muscles, connective tissue, tendons and ligaments limit movement around a joint, improvements in flexibility are accomplished by increasing the elasticity of these soft tissues. Stretching the muscles offers the best way to improve elasticity of these tissues. Why should we be regularly doing stretching exercises? Because the more flexible we are the less chance of back injury or joint injury. There are a variety of ways to improve flexibility and activities such as stretching exercises, yoga, or the martial arts offer excellent ways to improve this component of physical fitness. If you ever observe a cat when it wakes up from sleep, you will discover that it always stretches its body before any activity. We need to follow this rule, as sudden rapid movements without giving our muscles a chance to warm up will often result in injury. Try to do a few minutes of stretching every morning when you wake up.

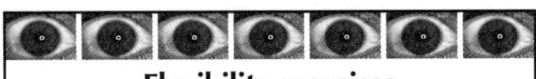

> **Flexibility exercises**
>
> Choose safe stretching exercises that offer flexibility for the neck, shoulders and arms, upper and lower back, the groin, legs and calf.
>
> Do not perform bouncing or bobbing movements, only slow movements.
>
> Hold in position for 15 to 30 seconds.
>
> Repeat more than once.
>
> Perform daily for 15 minutes and always before and after any exercise

I just cannot stress how important exercise is on our health. I have seen what modern medicine calls miracles once an exercise program is adopted. It really is an essential nutrient for the body. When we are young, we engage in sport and physical activity but as we age there is a general tendency to stop being active. This has to change. Our needs for exercise do not stop once we reach middle age, our needs continue well into our final years. Just think of how you could reduce those visits to the doctor or massage therapist if you could maintain a regular exercise program, not to mention decreasing the risks of so many diseases that plague our society. Your body cannot live, function or regenerate well without exercise.

Chapter 19

Eye for an Eye Diet Nutritional Advice Summary

There has been an enormous amount of information discussed so far about all of the major areas that deal with nutrients from the ground all the way up to where food ends up on our plates and in our bodies. I hope that you can appreciate the factors now that affect nutrition and our health. You may feel a little overwhelmed with the amount of work one has to do to stay healthy in the world that we live in. In order to put all the most important issues or advice into perspective, this last chapter of Part 3 serves as a summary for all the major points we have outlined to this point. You will now have the basic nutritional foundation to move on to Part 4. Soon you will be able to construct a nutritional strategy that will support not only your general health but also your specific genetic needs. A brief summary of the most important nutritional advice in Section 3 is discussed below.

Essential "Eye for an Eye Diet" Nutritional Advice
1. Our bodies perform best when we are fed "living food" from soil that is free of chemicals, rich in minerals and cultivated under nature's optimum conditions.
2. The basic unit of life is the cell. The cell is where disease begins, where aging begins, where genetic information is kept and where regeneration takes place. Our cells require adequate ingestion, digestion, absorption, circulation, utilization and detoxification in order to live. If we really want to get to the core of our health problems, we must address what affects our cells.
3. We need to reduce simple and low fiber complex carbohydrates and consume more high-fiber complex carbohydrates that contain fiber preferably in their unprocessed, natural raw form.
4. We need to make sure that we are obtaining quality protein in our diet that includes all the amino acids but not in excessive amounts as found in most Western cultures and to increase our protein intake from fish, nuts and plant sources.
5. Remember that fats are essential in our diet but in order to lower cholesterol and stay lean and healthy, they should not be excessive in our daily intake. Polyunsaturated and mono-unsaturated are best and the intake of saturated and trans fatty acids in the diet should be reduced. Do not waste your time having to count how much fat you take in with your diet.

6. Vitamins are vital components of our diet and are needed for many reactions in the body. Understand their basic functions and in what foods we can find a high concentration of them. Many factors increase the demand for certain vitamins and their deficiency can lead to health problems. Toxic effects of vitamins are usually only found when taking excessive supplements not when ingesting vitamins found in natural food sources. It is always much safer to source these vitamins from the foods we eat. When taking vitamin supplements I recommend that you consult with your natural doctor or therapist.
7. Minerals are micronutrients that are essential to our well-being and play important roles in metabolism as well as in many aspects of function of our cells. While they account for only about four percent of our total human body weight, they are involved in over ninety percent of all bodily functions. Be familiar with their functions in the body, what increases their demand and what effects they have if they are deficient.
8. Water is one of the most important nutrients that we ingest. We cannot live very long without water and the majority of our body is composed of it. Low water intake is associated with many health problems and we need to drink more water especially if we consume coffee, black tea or alcohol. Find natural sources of "live" water or freeze water to activate it, use filters for tap water and store it in glass bottles. Drink a minimum of one unsweetened, un-carbonated glass per day for every 20 pounds or 9 kilograms of body weight. Avoid drinking too much water during a meal or for 30 minutes after eating.
9. Increase your intake of fiber by eating more whole grains, fruits and vegetables. Fiber increases the bulk of the food contents and increases bowel transit time as well as removing cholesterol and fats from the body and slowing down the absorption of sugars. Many health problems are associated with lack of fiber in the diet including constipation, cancer of the colon, hemorrhoids and high blood cholesterol.
10. Follow the "Eye for an Eye Diet" Food Pyramid and the recommended servings from each of the food groups to ensure a well-balanced nutritional diet that supplies adequate protein, carbohydrates, fats, vitamins, minerals and fiber. Ensure that your diet consists of mainly vegetables, whole grains, fruits and berries, some fish, poultry, eggs, nuts and legumes, and minimal milk products, sweets, white flour, potatoes, alcohol and red meat. Include oils such as olive oil but use butter sparingly.
11. There are many factors that affect the quality of our food. They include genetic food engineering, agricultural methods, soil quality, food

ripening, storage and transportation and preparation methods. Our goal should be to retain as much of the natural qualities of food so that when it ends up on our plate it contains a large quantity of the nutrients that we require. Minimize the amount of processed or altered food in your diet and prepare food by reducing cooking time and temperature so that it contains the highest amount of nutritional value. Avoid cooking methods such as frying, grilling or microwaving. Eat at least 60 percent of your dietary fruits and vegetables in the raw form.

12. Food contaminants are considered accidental or non-intentional additions to our foods. In most cases contaminants carry with them chemicals that impose additional burdens on our body's detoxification system and are responsible for many ill health effects. Try to purchase organic produce and free-range eggs and poultry, adequately wash fruits and vegetables, limit canned and processed foods and source clean drinking water.

13. Food additives are intentionally added to our foods and they include colors, preservatives, flavors, sweeteners, modifying agents, bleaching agents, vitamins and minerals. While some are natural, others that are toxic disrupt the natural chemistry in the cells of the body and increase the workload of your detoxification organs. When the blood stream contains toxic additives, the process of regeneration slows down and resistance to disease diminishes. Be aware that many food additives are detrimental to your health and try if at all possible to avoid as many foods that are processed and that contain harmful synthetic additives. You will not only add years to your life but you will also allow your body the best chance to work at optimum capacity for the best of health.

14. Foods that steal are unnatural foods. Foods that steal are those that take more nutrition away than they give to the body. They are what I call "dead" foods. If the proportion of dead foods that we ingest is greater than our body's need for foods that are rich in nutritional value or "alive" then we will succumb to disease and ill health. Avoid excess milk products, margarine, smoked, salty or pickled foods, refined white flour or sugar products, instant and fast foods and excess animal protein. Food items like artificial sweeteners and soft drinks and many condiments have very little or no nutritional value in our diet. Ingestion of many of these foods has been associated with several health problems and I would recommend using them minimally in your diet.

15. We may feel that our bodies need a certain food but often these are what I call food addictions. Common food addictions in our society include alcohol, caffeine, salt, saturated fat, white sugar and chocolate. What they often have in common is that they can cause health problems when in excess and some come with withdrawal symptoms after terminating their consumption. These foods cause imbalances in the body chemistry and cause cravings. Try to avoid or limit these foods in your diet and opt for natural foods that will balance your body's nutritional needs.
16. Although I believe most foods in their natural form have healing abilities, there are some foods that deserve mentioning and should be included in your diet program. These include dark green vegetables and sprouts, fresh fruits and berries, avocado, eggs, figs and dates, nuts and seeds, garlic, fish, olive oil, fresh vegetable juices, grapes and chlorella. These foods have been found to have special healing properties and I recommend using them frequently.
17. There is an incredible amount of misinformation regarding nutrition these days and many nutritional pitfalls that should be avoided. Issues were discussed such as the benefits of breast-feeding over formula feeding, eating regular meals, including raw foods as a source of enzymes in the diet and limiting sugar intake. Other more controversial issues included that eggs may not be bad for you after all, that cholesterol may not be the cause of heart disease and the benefits and disadvantages of eating meat.
18. Nutritional therapy is a method that combines diet, vitamins, minerals and concentrated nutritional supplements which has been successfully used to assist in curing or preventing disease. Often these vitamins and supplements are used in much higher dosages than standard recommended daily dosages set by government health departments. It is therefore recommended that if you are endeavoring to undergo nutritional therapy or take nutritional supplements to first consult your naturopath or doctor who specializes in this therapy and who can advise you on safe dosages. Vitamins and supplements should never replace a good quality diet of fresh food and vegetables, it should as their name implies, only supplement a diet that may often be low in nutritive value. Some nutritional supplements that have been associated with unique health benefits and which I recommend include Lactobacillus acidophilus, enzymes, chlorella, lecithin, omega-3 fatty acids, echinacea, gingko biloba, ginseng, propolis, acerola, vitamin E and bioflavonoids.

19. There are many types of diets that restrict certain foods due to religious, ethical, healthy or moral grounds. These include vegetarians, who generally have a more healthier diet although may sometimes suffer from deficiencies of protein, vitamin B12 and some minerals such as iron, zinc, calcium and vitamin D. It is important to combine vegetable protein foods to achieve all the necessary amino acids and to supplement the diet with B12. For most vegetarians this is not a problem because they usually eat eggs or milk but for some like the vegans, they must be more careful. High protein, no fat, and low calorie diets should be avoided as they bring with them many health risks and do not produce the long-term weight loss results that are often believed. I would recommend if you choose to fast to supplement with plenty of fresh, clean water and limit the duration to only one day. Be aware of the health risks involved with long-term fasting.

20. Finally, exercise is an essential nutrient that your body cannot live without. There are just so many benefits that exercise has on your health that it should never be neglected. Engaging in exercise will prolong your life and protect you from a variety of common diseases. Furthermore it will improve your energy levels, reduce stress and make you feel physically and psychologically healthier. It is important to work on all three components of physical fitness including endurance, muscular strength and flexibility. Follow the guidelines on developing endurance through aerobic activities, increasing muscular strength by regular resistance training and improving the elasticity of the soft tissues by stretching exercises to prevent injury. Your body needs exercise to live, function and regenerate. Any weight loss program or program for preventing or curing disease must include exercise as well as nutritional diet changes.

THE EYE FOR AN EYE DIET

PART 3

The "Eye for an Eye Diet"
Genetic Action Plan:
10 Individual Genetic Eye Constitutions
10 Nutritional Programs

What are Genetic Eye Constitutions?

Chapter 1

Congratulations, you have come with me this far and now I believe that you are ready to embark on discovering or perhaps rediscovering another piece of that jigsaw puzzle we call our health. Part 1 and 2 have given you a backbone on important nutritional principles. We now need to include genetics in our equation of health. As you can remember earlier I mentioned supporting our genetic eye constitution as part of the "Eye for an Eye Diet" Food pyramid. Here in Part 3, we will learn how to identify our genetic eye constitution so that we can understand much more about our own bodies in order to formulate a complete nutritional strategy. In order to be truly healthy not only do we have to follow nature's laws and gain the most from the foods we eat, we also must take our genetics into consideration. We are all individuals and each of us is born with a different set of physical and psychological characteristics. Most of us are born with a set of genes that are probably far from perfect and as we age those weakened organs that we were born with start showing their signs. Some will display their signs or symptoms of disease earlier and others if given the correct nutritional support may never show up. That's right. I truly believe that what we have inherited from our parents and grandparents can to a certain degree be supported. Not only can it be supported, it must be supported otherwise we will certainly succumb to those diseases that result from weakened genetic body organs. Perhaps you have often wondered why you suffer from certain health ailments and why others don't even though you may be eating the same healthy foods. It's all in your genetics. God just did not make us all the same.

The science of Iridology has provided an incredible opportunity to view our genetic make-up by the simple analysis of our eyes and our genetic eye constitution. Many of you may believe that the eyes are the windows to the soul but through iridology we can begin to understand that our eyes reveal sophisticated maps to our body and the condition of our health.

As I have already mentioned, we are all individuals and each of our eyes is unique but through studies of thousands of irises, a number of genetic types or constitutions appear to exist. This does not in any way detract from the fact that our eyes are all different. It only allows classification of types of eyes that are most commonly seen in the world today. Every eye is unique but there are general similarities among many types of eyes.

When we refer to our genetic constitution, we mean, "what we are made of," our genetic strengths and weaknesses or those attributes we have inherited from our parents, grandparents and so on.

Studies in iridology have revealed that there exist a number of constitutions or similar types of eyes each with its own physical and psychological characteristics. Each of us is born with a genetic iris constitution. The type of iris or the colored part of the eye determines your genetic eye constitution. Knowing what type of constitution you have can be very valuable as it identifies weaknesses and permits an understanding of potential health problems. In my studies of thousands of eyes, I have never come across a perfect iris. Each one of us has certain weaknesses, some of which do not become evident until later in life. While we cannot completely change our constitution, we can influence the constitution in a positive or a negative way. This in turn will affect our health throughout our lives as well as the passing on of traits to our offspring.

Some studies on animals have shown that it took three generations of vitamin therapy and quality nutrition to perceive a genetic trait completely disappear. This means that what we inherit may not have to be something that is passed on to our future generations. We need to start improving our lifestyles so that the coming generations are not plagued with rising medical and health problems.

We have already seen that numerous negative influences that can cause a weakened genetic constitution include: inadequate nutrition, too much alcohol, shock, physical or mental trauma, hunger, pollution and smog, drugs, cigarette smoking, depression, stress, radiation, lack of exercise, lack of sunlight, obesity, chemical poisoning and many other factors.

On the other hand, the positive influences that strengthen our genetic constitution include: living in a clean natural environment, quality nutrition, regular exercise, fresh air and sunlight, natural medicine without the use of drugs, good moral behavior, positive thoughts and actions, a balance between friends, family and work, the emotional, spiritual and material, and the ability to accept ourselves as we are.

Remember, our health is influenced by two factors, genotype and phenotype. The phenotype is what we develop during our lives depending on the type of environment, our diet and any physical or emotional events that we experience. Genotype refers to our genetic make-up or constitution, that which we are born with. These are the genetic eye constitutions, which will be described in detail soon in this part of the book. Our phenotype combines with our genotype to make us unique individuals along with unique susceptibilities to illness or health.

I have examined and studied thousands of people's eyes and have come to the conclusion that similar eye types or constitutions exist even though every human eye is always different. I recognize 10 distinct types of genetic eye constitutions. Almost every individual's iris can be placed within one of these constitutional types. Knowing your genetic constitution is a very important step in developing an accurate analysis of your health status. I have found that those with the same genetic type often complain of similar health problems and show similar weaknesses in certain organs and systems of the body. What does this mean for you? If you can identify what type of genetic eye constitution you have you have an excellent chance of finding the cause of your health problems and can then tailor-fit a nutritional strategy that can support those weaknesses so that you can maintain health, body weight and prevent disease.

An understanding of your eye constitution will hopefully inspire or motivate you to make some positive changes for better health.

Brown and Blue Eyes

Chapter 2

Since ancient times we have always been fascinated with the color of eyes. Often when asked what physical features one looks at when choosing a partner, eye color is mentioned. What is it about the color of our eyes that we find so captivating? We interpret a vast amount of information from our eyes and they have always been the center of attention. We use our eyes to communicate our feelings and emotions and often they can reveal our state of health.

How many eye colors are there? Let's take a brief count; blue, green, brown, black, light brown, dark brown, hazel green, gray, light blue, dark blue, yellow green, blue gray, turquoise, and the thousands of shades in between. We use eye color to identify people or criminals but do we really know why there are so many different eye colors? From studying irises and eye colors for many years, I have come to the conclusion that there exist only 2 true basic eye colors, brown and blue. This belief is also shared by a number of iridologists around the world. Many believe that dating back thousands of years, there existed blue-eyed races that migrated to the cooler climates such as Northern Europe and the brown-eyed races migrated to the warmer climates like Africa. As a result of inter-racial mixing over thousands of years we now have the eye colors we see today but they are all a result of blue or brown eyes.

It is important to determine initially whether you are a blue-eye type or a brown eye type. This may not always be an easy task. Even in blue eyes there can appear brown, yellow, white or orange pigments that can often mask your real basic eye color. All green eye, gray and the various shades of blue are considered blue eye types. If you take a close look at your eyes in the mirror or through a magnifying lens and see that there are blue areas of your eyes, even though some areas may exhibit other colors like orange or brown your eyes most likely have a blue base and you are a blue-eye type. If your eyes are solid brown and you do not see any signs of blue, you are a brown-eye type. Brown-eye types usually do not exhibit any blue areas (the one exception being the Mixed type) although yellow, orange or even white pigments may appear.

Blue irises are often associated with fair skin and blonde hair but there are blue-eyed people with dark skin and dark hair. They often suggest a thinner concentration of blood and body fluids. There are some general tendencies of blue-eyed types to have predispositions to tonsillitis, swollen lymphatic glands, respiratory problems, acne or eczema, and arthritic or rheumatic problems in old age.

Brown irises are often associated with dark skin and dark hair although the opposite can also occur. They often suggest a greater concentration of blood and body fluids. Tendencies for brown-eyed people are to develop problems with the liver and circulation, hemorrhoids and thromboses, diabetes, digestive problems, and disturbances of the hormonal system. Often due to poor liver function, cholesterol problems are often seen.

This is not to say that blue eye types will never have liver or cholesterol problems or that brown eye types will always be free of respiratory ailments but there is a greater tendency for these problems to occur in their respective color types.

Make sure you determine what color type your eyes are before moving ahead to the next chapter as you will need this information to assist you in determining your genetic eye constitution. The genetic eye constitutions are divided into blue-eye and brown-eye types. There are a number of different blue-eye genetic eye constitutional types just as there are a number of different brown-eye genetic eye constitutional types. Although in reality there is always some mix of genetic constitutions in every individual, there is usually one dominant type that is present. This is what we will attempt to discover in the next chapter.

Chapter 3

How to identify your Genetic Eye Constitution

I hope by this point you have determined what basic eye color type you have. In this chapter I will run you through a step-by-step analysis of your eyes so that you can find out your true genetic eye constitution. For most of you this will mean having a look in the mirror or having someone else look into your eyes with a magnifying lens. You will first need a quick lesson on zones that are found in the iris of the eye. Every iris (colored part of the eye), whether blue or brown, can be divided into a number of major zones. These include the pupil, the ruff zone (sometimes called the autonomic nerve wreath), which encircles the pupil and the remaining portion of the iris, the ciliary zone. The pupil is the dark opening in the eye that changes in size depending on the amount of light that is present. The ruff zone, so called because of the old English collars or "ruff" that used to be worn is a zone that can be found in every iris. It encircles the pupil and comes in a variety of sizes and shapes. Finally the ciliary zone is the rest of the colored part of the iris of the eye and reaches right to the border of the iris and the sclera (white of the eye). Have a quick look in the mirror or have a look at someone else's eyes with a magnifying lens and try to locate these major zones. Being able to locate these zones will assist you in identifying what genetic eye constitution you have.

The Human Iris

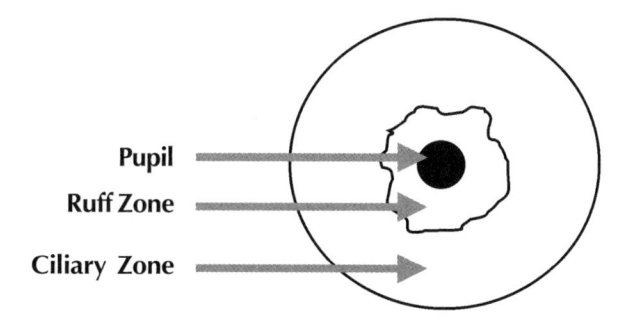

Pupil
Ruff Zone
Ciliary Zone

Another important characteristic to note when looking at your eyes is the density of fibers. If you look closely at the colored part of your eye you will see that fibers radiate outward from the ruff zone through the ciliary zone. If the fibers of the iris are closely packed (high density) your genetic constitution is considered to be strong. If the fibers of the iris are loosely packed (low density) and there exist a number of holes or spaces between the fibers, your genetic constitution is considered to be weak. People with strong genetic constitutions generally have fewer health problems and possess faster healing capabilities. Those with weaker constitutions are plagued with more health problems and have slower healing capabilities and require much more in terms of nutrition to stay healthy.

Strong Genetic Constitution **Weak Genetic Constitution**

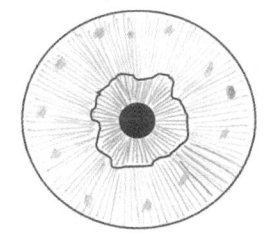

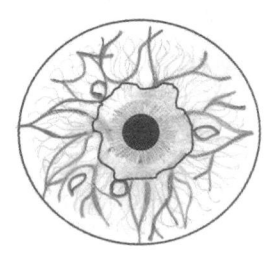

Identifying your Genetic Eye Constitution

Step 1: Determine if your basic eye color is blue or brown.

Step 2: If your basic eye color is blue your genetic eye constitution may be one of the following 7 types of Blue-Eye Genetic Eye Constitutions. If you have brown eyes, go to Step 3.

1. Lymphatic Hyper-active (often seen) Strong genetic constitution

The Lymphatic Hyper-active constitution is a blue-eye type that may appear gray blue with closely compacted fibers. Generally the color of the iris is uniform and other pigment colors are not often seen. Around the outside of the ruff zone you may see a milky white color as well as a light rosary of white clouds on the outer border of the ciliary zone.

2. Lymphatic Hypo-active (most often seen) Weaker genetic constitution

The Lymphatic Hypo-active constitution is a blue-eye type that is probably encountered most often. It appears as a blue to blue-gray iris with other colors often seen in clouds or as pigments, giving the eye a discolored and dull or dirty appearance. Many clouds are found in the outer ring of the ciliary zone and are often connected by spoke-like runners from the border of the ruff zone. These clouds are frequently yellow or brown. The center of the iris around the pupil, the ruff zone, is often a dirty brown color. Because of its looser fiber structure, it is considered a weaker genetic constitution.

3. Kidney Lymphatic (often seen) Weaker genetic constitution

The Kidney Lymphatic constitution is a blue to blue-gray iris with a ring of yellow coloring around the border outside the ruff zone as well as a ring of yellow clouds in the outer area of the ciliary zone. Because of the yellow coloring in the blue iris, the eye appears green. There is often a separation of fibers or weakness signs in the lower part of the ciliary zone at about 5:30 to 6:00 in the right eye or 6:00 to 6:30 in the left eye. This separation of fibers can be found in one or both eyes. Remember your left eye is on the same side as your left hand, right eye on the same side as your right hand.

4. Neuro-Lymphatic (often seen) Strong genetic constitution

The Neuro-lymphatic constitution is a blue to blue-gray iris with the appearance of loose wavy fibers, giving it a cloth-like or weaved appearance. Often you can see a milky white area around the outside of the ruff zone border and sometime fibers that cross against the grain of normal fiber direction. In the outer area of the ciliary zone you can often but not always see what are called nerve rings, which appear as trenches that encircle the iris. Don't be mistaken as these nerve rings can occur in any of the genetic eye constitutions as they indicate a degree of nervous tension or stress. Look primarily for the wavy fibers and the cloth-like appearance.

5. Hydro-Lymphatic (sometimes seen) Weaker genetic constitution

The Hydro-Lymphatic constitution is a blue to blue-gray iris that often appears very light in color. A blurred ring of clouds just outside the ruff zone as well as another ring of well-defined clouds in the outer ring of the ciliary zone identifies this type. These clouds are most often white in color but may sometimes be yellow, orange or brown. In some eyes it may appear that the entire iris is filled with white clouds.

6. Hormonal (rarely seen) Very weak genetic constitution

The Hormonal constitution is rare and appears as a blue iris (in some rare cases it is brown) with many holes or lacunae that encircle and lie close to the ruff zone border. These lacunae can be the same size or varied in size. It indicates a very weak fiber density and weak genetic constitution.

7. Connective Tissue (rarely seen) Very weak genetic constitution

The Connective Tissue constitution appears as a dramatic blue iris (in some rare cases it is brown) with a torn appearance in the fibers. Often there are very large gaping holes reaching the outer areas of the ciliary zone with extremely loose fiber density indicating a very weak genetic constitution.

Step 3: If your basic eye color is brown your genetic eye constitution may be one of the following 3 types of Brown-Eye Genetic Eye Constitutions:

1. Hematogenic (most often seen) Relatively strong genetic constitution

The Hematogenic constitution appears as a brown iris with a velvet sponge-like consistency. Often nerve rings are seen although they can be seen in any of the genetic eye constitutions. Radiating deep dark lines are also often seen which begin in the ruff zone and extend outwards into the ciliary zone. The ruff zone is generally quite small.

2. Plethoric (sometimes seen) Weak genetic constitution

The Plethoric constitution is a brown iris with a generally small pupil. The ruff zone often displays a loose and rough textured appearance and often bulges downward. It is seen occasionally and denotes a weak genetic constitution.

3. Mixed (often seen) Relatively weak constitution

The Mixed constitution appears as a mixed blue and brown iris with brown pigment which overlays onto a base of blue fibers. Commonly the ruff zone appears with brown pigment, and is the darkest area of the iris. This type can sometimes be confused with the Lymphatic Hypoplastic constitution but usually does not have as many clouds in the outer ring of the ciliary zone and does not have spoke-like runners.

Step 4: Determine which genetic eye constitution best resembles that of your eyes by using the information listed above and the color iris slides that are included for each of the genetic eye types in the pages that follow. If you note that your eyes show characteristics of more than one type of constitution, try to find the one that is most dominant.

Step 5: Read all about what your genetic eye constitution reveals in the following chapter.

The Eye for an Eye Diet — Part 3

PHOTOGRAPHS OF INDIVIDUAL GENETIC EYE CONSTITUTIONS

Blue-eye Types

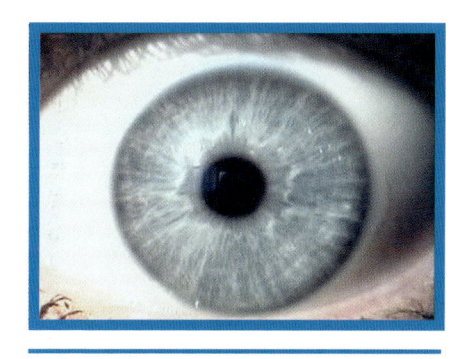

The Eye for an Eye Diet — Part 3

Lymphatic Hyper-active

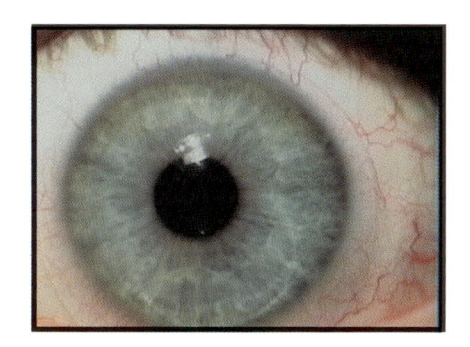

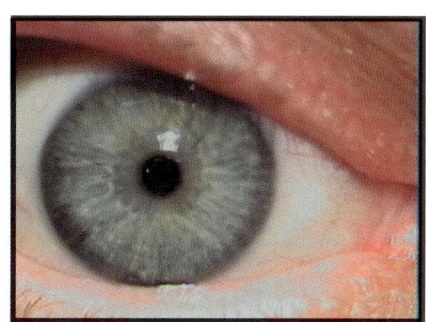

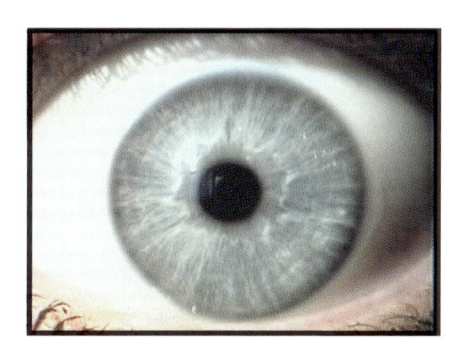

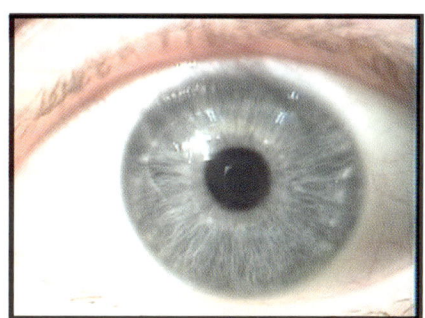

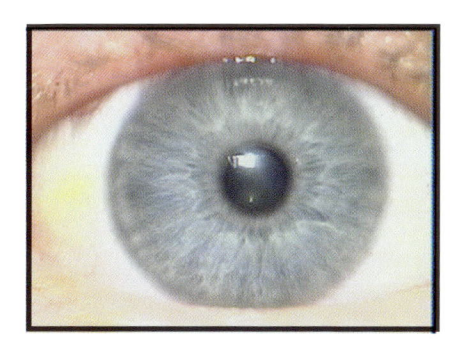

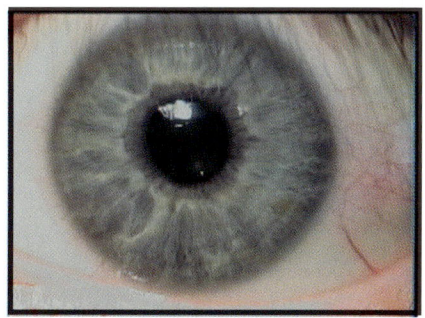

179

Lymphatic Hypo-active

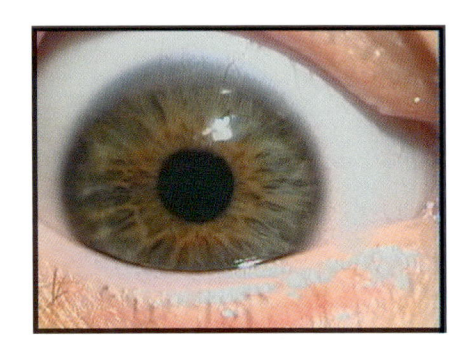

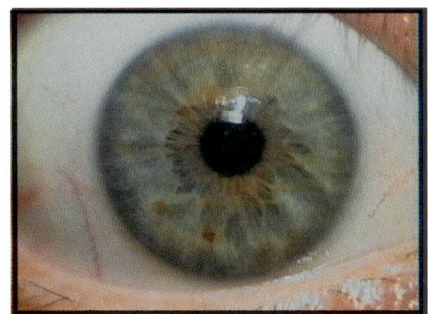

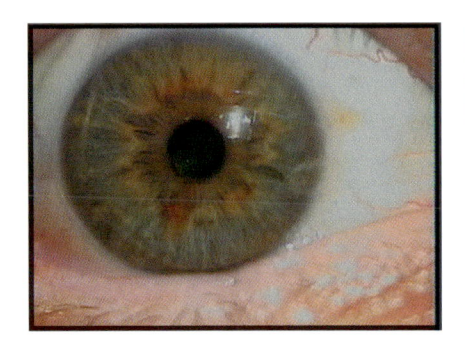

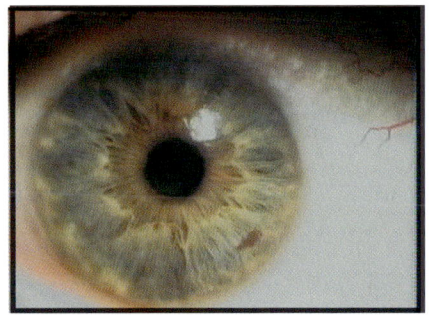

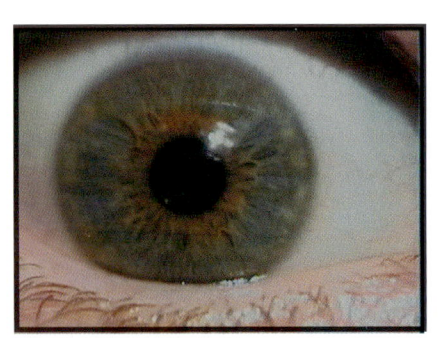

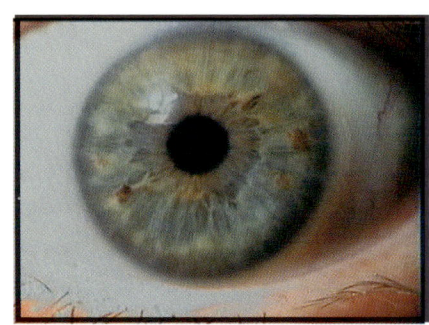

The Eye for an Eye Diet | *Part 3*

Kidney Lymphatic

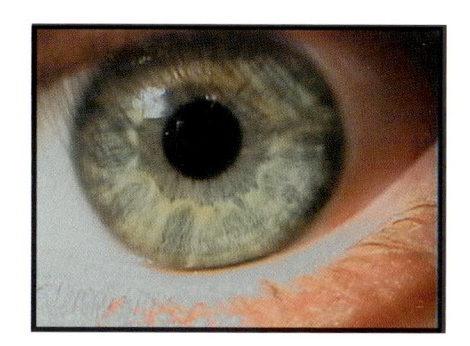

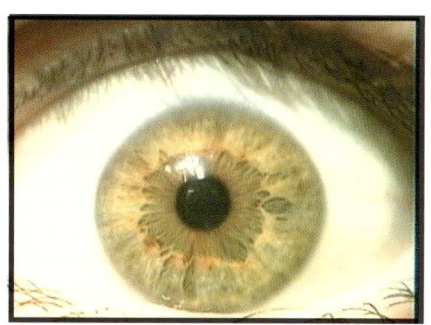

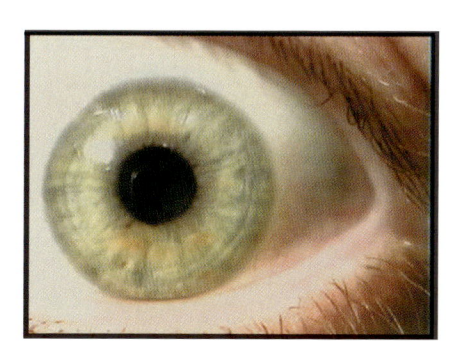

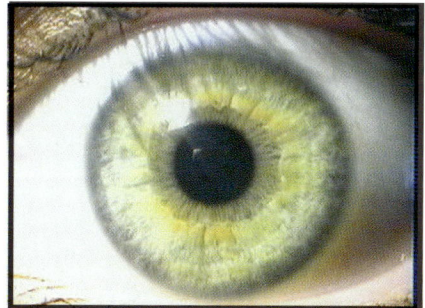

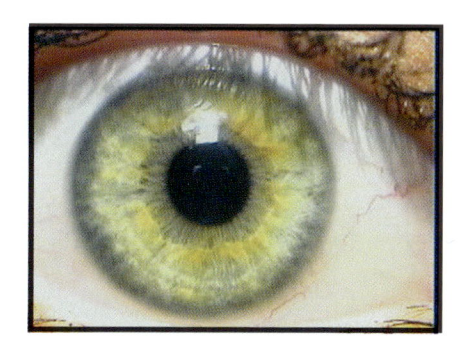

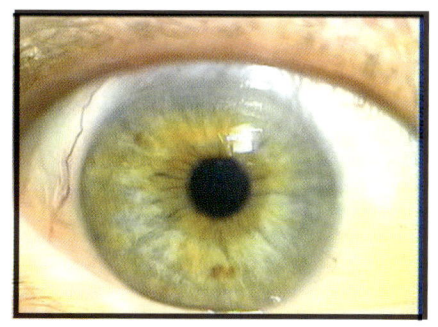

181

Frank Navratil BSc. N.D.

Neurolymphatic

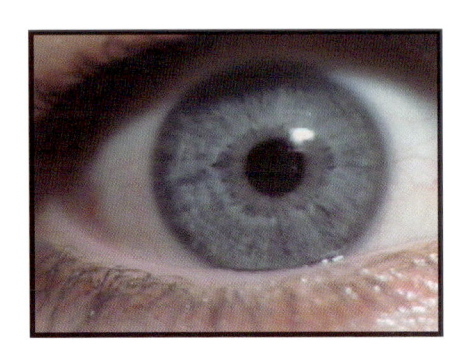

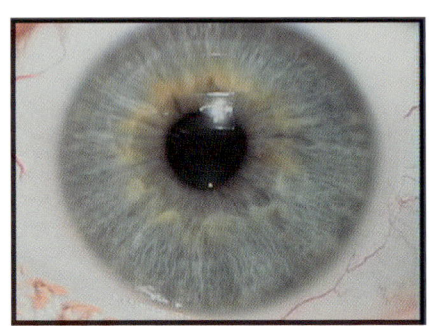

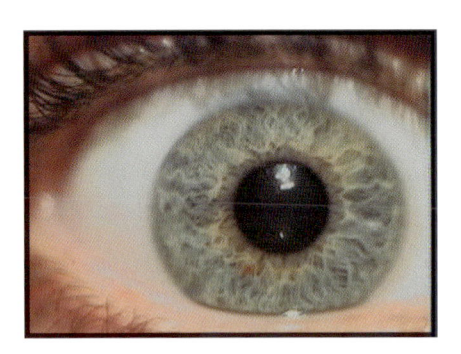

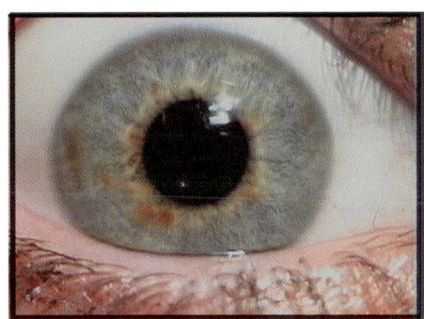

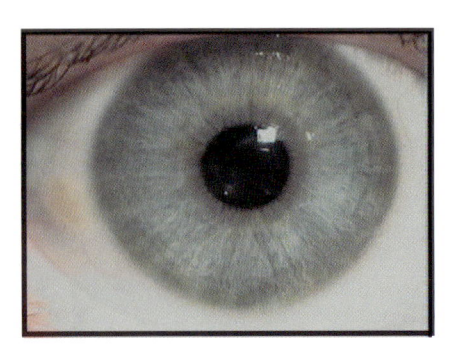

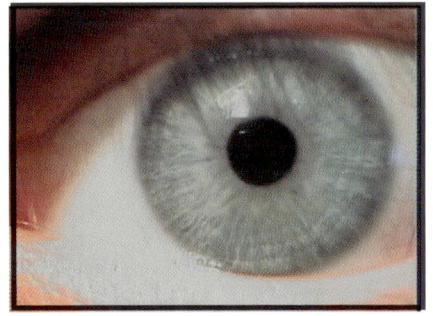

Hydrolymphatic

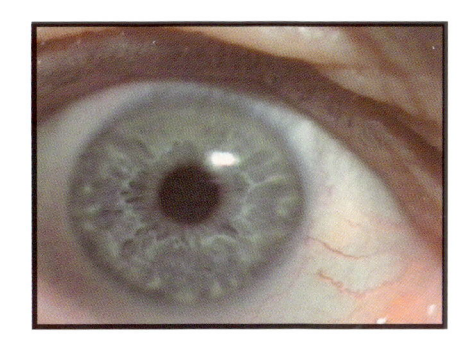

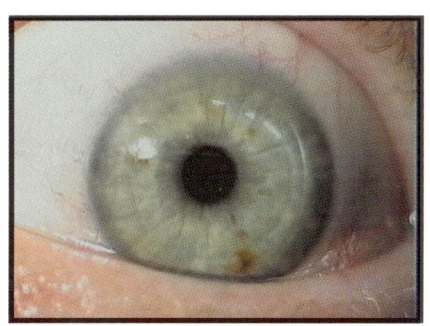

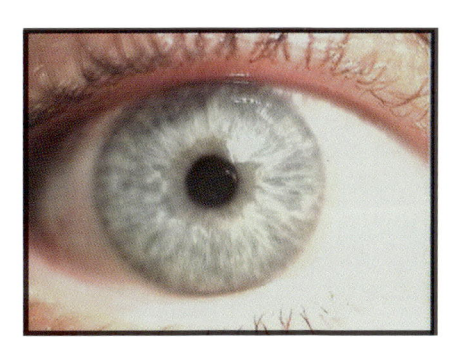

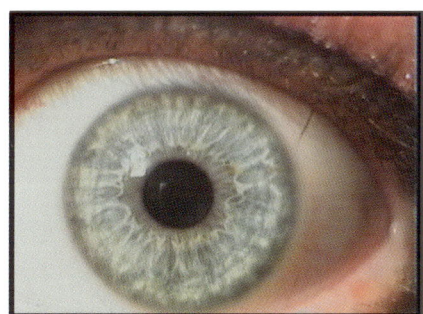

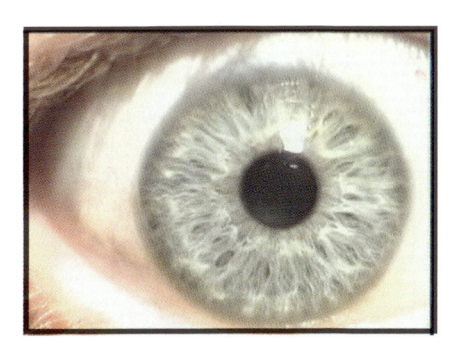

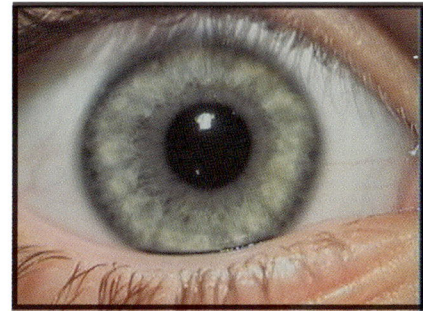

Hormonal

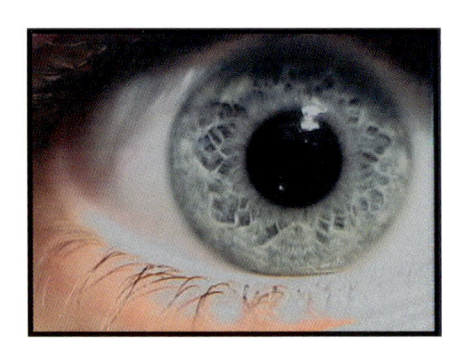

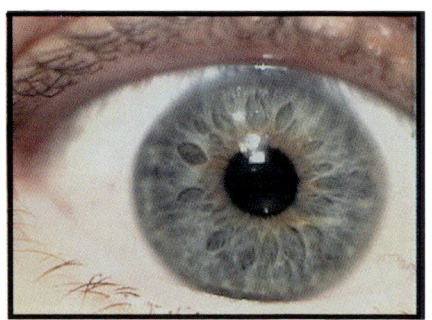

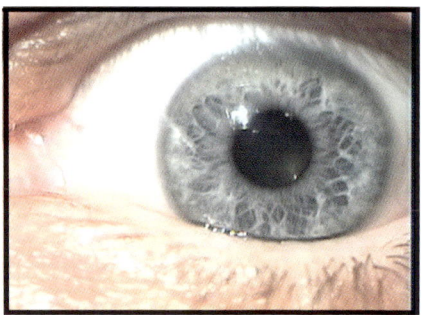

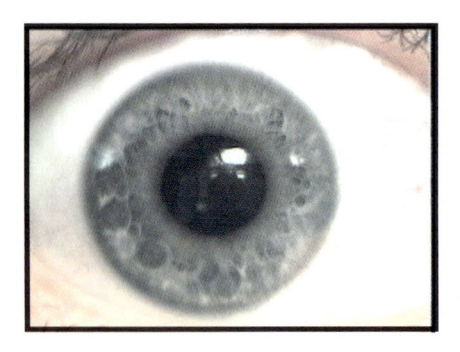

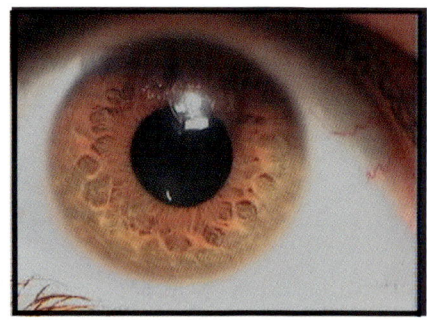

The Eye for an Eye Diet — Part 3

Connective Tissue

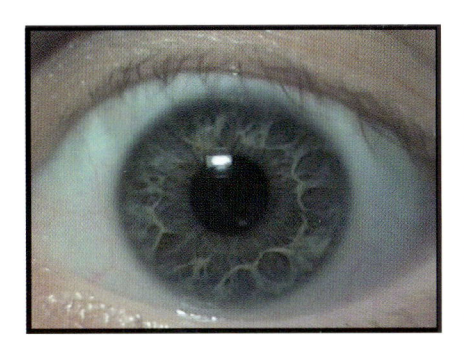

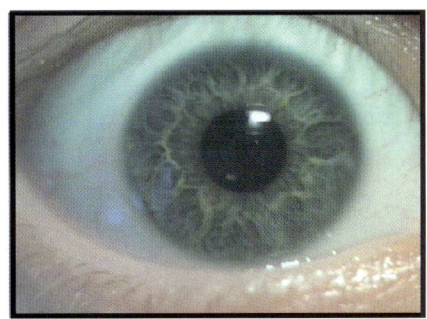

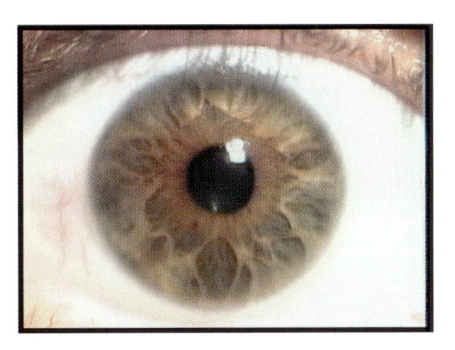

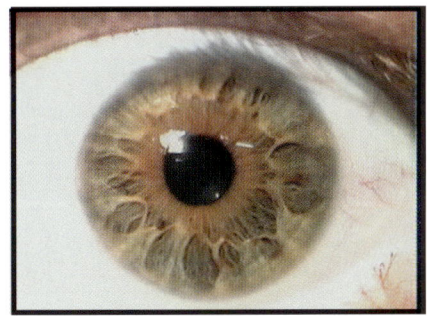

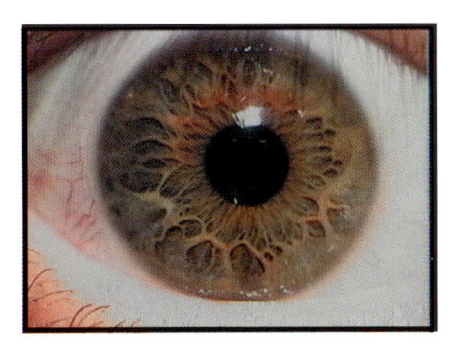

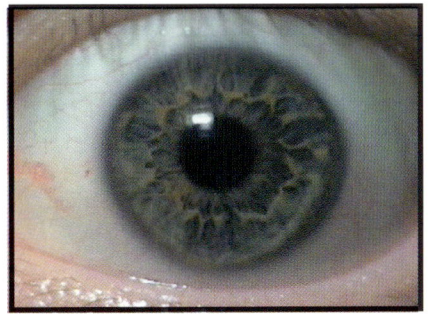

The Eye for an Eye Diet   *Part 3*

Brown-eye Types

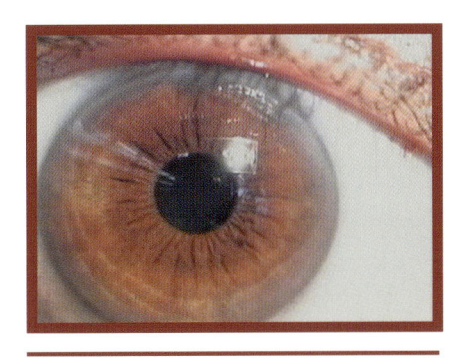

The Eye for an Eye Diet — Part 3

Hematogenic

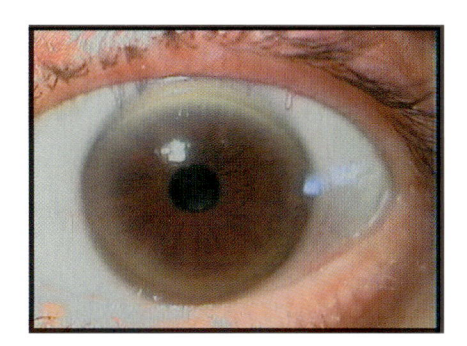

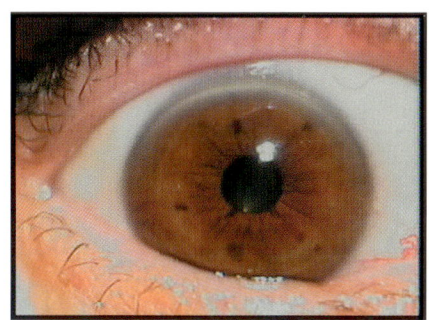

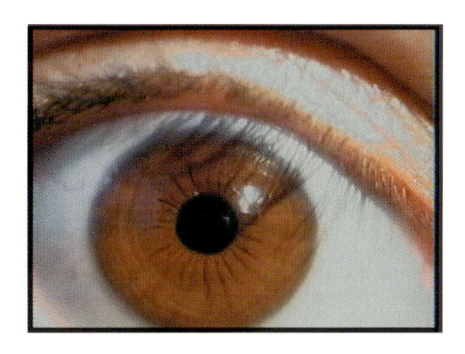

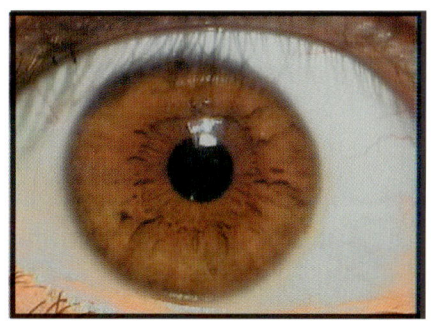

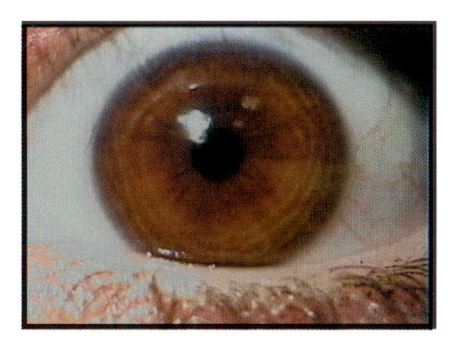

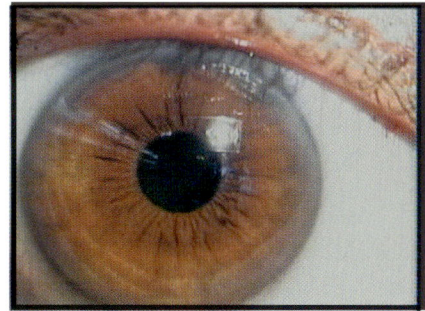

Frank Navratil BSc. N.D.

Plethoric

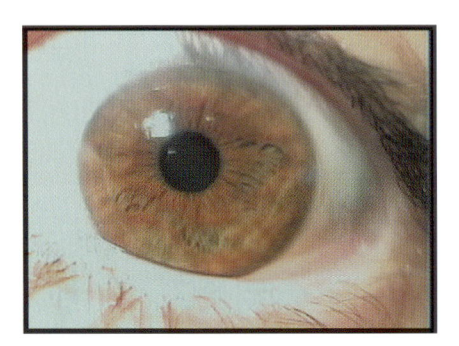

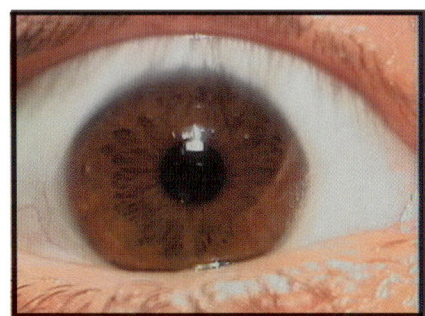

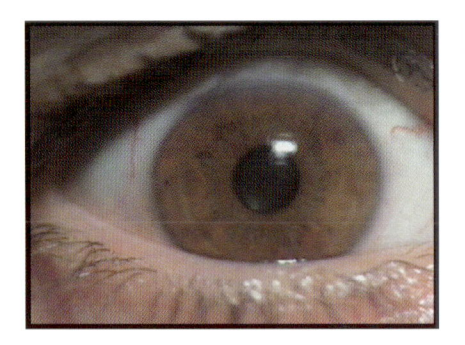

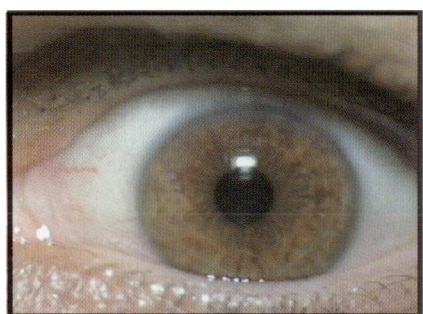

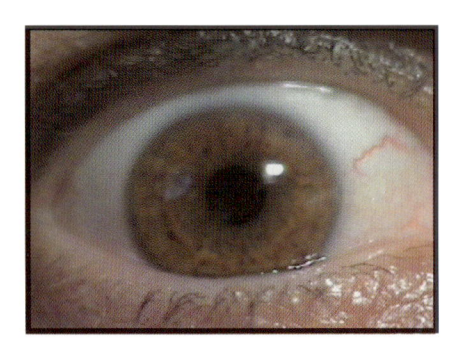

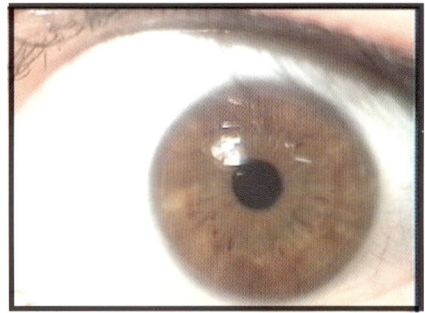

Mixed

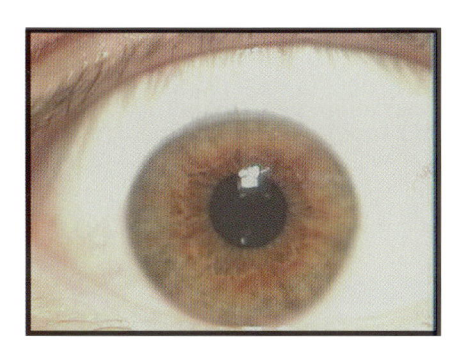

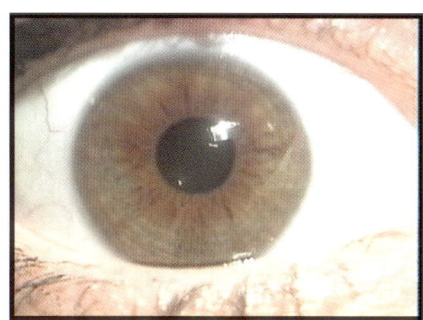

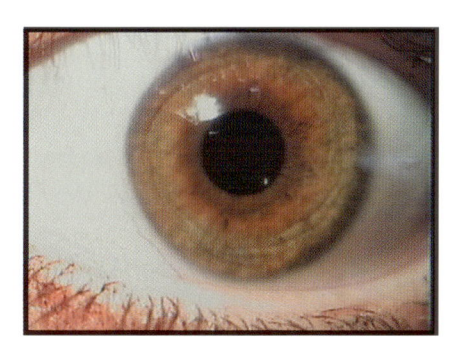

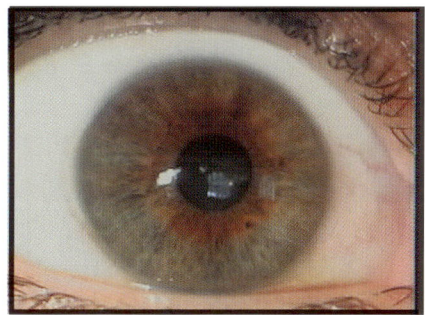

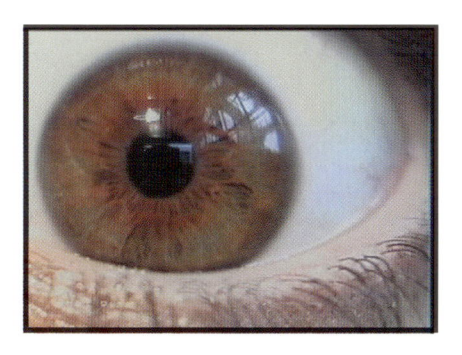

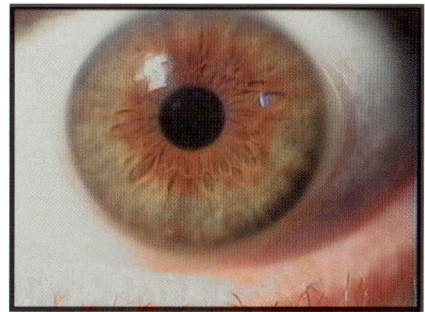

The Ten "Eye for an Eye Diet" Genetic Eye Constitutions

Chapter 4

Now that you have identified your dominant genetic eye constitution you are ready to learn more about your genetic health. Remember if you are still unsure about what genetic constitution you belong to, find the set of characteristics for the constitution described here in this chapter that most closely resembles your health problems. Read through the information on your genetic eye constitutional type and keep in mind that the health problems listed may not be those that you currently perceive or that you have experienced in the past but are those that you are most likely predisposed to and may even show up in later life. Remember it is what you do with what you have that counts. If you have led a healthy life you may have not experienced some of the common complaints that are often observed in people with the same constitutional type that you have. Listed are common general complaints for each of the genetic eye constitutions as well as common complaints in childhood and adulthood. The information provided here forms the basic rationale for the nutritional programs in the following chapters.

The Blue Eye Types

Lymphatic Hyper-active Constitution

General Complaints:
- Enlarged lymph nodes and congested lymphatic circulation
- Sensitive and over-reactive mucous membranes that often produce allergies in the nose, throat, ear, and lung areas
- Allergies to milk lactose are common
- Weakness in the circulation, commonly felt as cold hands and feet.
- All conditions generally improve with warmth.
- Problems in the utilization of some vitamins as well as calcium, magnesium and iron

Common Complaints in Childhood:
- Eczema, skin rashes, hives, acne, and dermatitis
- Ear, nose, throat, tonsil and adenoid inflammation or infection
- Allergies and swollen glands

- Hyper-reactive mucous membranes causing respiratory conditions like bronchitis or asthma

Common Complaints in Adulthood:
- Childhood complaints may become chronic in adulthood
- Excessive mucous production may result in discharges from the nose, ears and throat
- Inflammation of mucous membranes may cause respiratory problems like sinusitis, bronchitis and asthma
- There is often stiffness in the joints and rheumatic and arthritic complaints
- Endocrine problems involving the parathyroid may cause problems like osteoporosis
- Retention of fluids with depletion of energy
- Congested and irritated lymphatic circulation resulting often in swollen and painful glands

Lymphatic Hypo-active Constitution

General Complaints:
- Poor ability to eliminate waste products from the body
- Under-active bowel, kidneys, liver, skin, respiratory organs, and lymphatic circulation
- Poor elimination often leads to long-term stress on the heart and circulation
- Mucous membranes tend to produce inadequate mucus, leading to irritation and inflammation
- Generally slow recovery or regeneration from illness and injury

Common Complaints in Childhood:
- Children with this constitution often look older than their age
- There are often infections of the ear, nose and throat, tonsils, adenoids
- Skin is very sensitive which may result in rashes
- Due to frequent bacterial infections these children are often subjected to high antibiotic use which can lead to a compromised immune system and poor bowel function

Common Complaints in Adulthood:
- Skin problems like eczema, psoriasis, boils, and fungal skin and nail infections are common due to the inability to eliminate waste products efficiently

- Chronic inflammation of the mucous membranes and under-active lymphatic system and hardening of lymph nodes causing conditions like, tonsillitis, nasal congestion, and discharge from the ears and nose
- Breath can be sour and foul body odor is common
- Insufficient functioning of the liver and kidneys
- Water retention leading to edema especially in the legs is common
- Retention of toxins can also cause depression, or mood changes
- Poor circulation in the veins and weaknesses in the heart
- Arthritis due to drying out of tissues
- Reduction in activity of mucous membranes in the digestive system which can lead to reduced absorption and metabolism of vitamins and nutrients from the diet

Kidney Lymphatic Constitution

General Complaints:
- They are born with genetically weakened kidneys which are stressed due to defective metabolism of proteins and foreign toxins often caused by a poor intake of fluids or too much of the wrong kind of fluids
- Dark "kidney bags" under the eyes during times when the kidneys are stressed are often present
- They tend not to feel thirsty and must be trained to drink more fluids.
- Common associated renal problems include, edema, bladder infections, kidney stones and nephritis.
- Sensitive mucous membranes especially around the ear, nose, throat, sinuses, and tonsils which can give rise to tonsillitis, bronchitis, and infections
- Prone to allergies like hay fever
- Skin is very sensitive and prone to skin rashes, itching skin, dry skin, or eczema
- Asthma is common
- Congestion of the lymphatic system
- Prone to headaches or migraines due to retention of fluid or accumulation of toxic substances in the blood
- Due to a predisposition to high levels of uric acid, rheumatoid and arthritic problems are commonly seen in older age
- Disposition to heart and circulation problems due to high levels of nitrogenous wastes in the blood

Common Complaints in Childhood:
- Children may have a very high sensitivity to skin rashes or eczema

- Inflammation of the mucous membranes
- Congestion of the lymphatic circulation
- Tonsillitis is commonly seen

Common Complaints in Adulthood:
- Insufficiency of the kidneys due to nephritis and edema
- Headaches or migraines
- Bladder infections
- Ear and sinus problems and hay fever
- Men often suffer from cramps or colic-type pain
- Liver complaints
- Rheumatoid arthritis and gout in old age due to the accumulation of uric acid
- Diseases of the heart and the circulatory system are often seen
- Great sensitivity to wetness and cold
- General fatigue
- High blood pressure or blood pressure fluctuations

Neurolymphatic Constitution

General Complaints:
- General sensitivity to stress and tendency toward exhaustion caused by over-excitement.
- Sensitivity to weather changes and phases of the moon
- Weakness of the nerves
- Anxiety is common and many suffer from neuroses or variable moods
- Difficulty in overcoming emotional traumas
- Often these people are light sleepers
- May have migraine headaches, or dizziness as the nervous system affects circulation
- Congestion and inflammation of the lymphatic system
- Excessive mucus with a tendency to allergies
- Nervous stress can result in skin conditions, asthma, and nervous stomach or irritable bowel syndromes
- A fast pulse (tachycardia) is common
- Poor utilization of foods due to potent nervous influences

Common Complaints in Childhood:
- Fear, anxiety and high emotional sensitivity
- Very excitable, these types often eat and drink too fast which can result in burping and nervous vomiting
- Very sensitive to changes in the environment

Common Complaints in Adulthood:
- Easily hurt in relationships and highly sensitive to stress
- Often have neuroses and may suffer from nervous breakdown if under a lot of stress
- Often worry unnecessarily over other people's problems
- Due to an overactive nervous system and a poor ability to utilize the B-group vitamins they require B-group vitamins in greater amounts
- Deficiencies in calcium, magnesium, and iron and zinc are commonly seen
- After the fifth decade, there is a tendency to develop muscle weakness, edema, and diabetes
- Nervous stomach, ulcers, and bowel problems
- Headaches or migraines
- Weakening of the adrenal glands
- In women there is a disposition to cancer of the breast and female organs

Hydro-lymphatic Constitution

General Complaints:
- Chronic lymphatic congestion often with persistent infections
- Commonly suffer from asthma, bronchitis, colds and flu
- There are often weaknesses in the heart with high blood pressure or fluctuations in blood pressure
- Predisposition to rheumatoid arthritis
- Depression, mood changes, and impatience are often seen
- Perspire heavily but suffer from heavy fluid retention which can cause edema and weight fluctuations
- Predisposition to diseases of the urinary tract, urinary infections, gallstone and kidney stone formation and varicose veins
- Often these types have minimal endurance

Common Complaints in Childhood:
- Recurrent bronchitis, colds, and flu
- Lymphatic congestion and low immunity to infections
- Prone to allergies

Common Complaints in Adulthood:
- Adults have some tendency to develop a stocky physique with a large abdomen
- Due to fluid problems and edema, they may wake in the morning with a puffy face and eyelids that are swollen
- Cold and damp weather generally worsens their health problems

- These types are more prone to catarrhal problems with heavy mucus secretion like asthma and bronchitis, as well as heart weakness with high blood pressure, rheumatic problems or angina pectoris

Hormonal Constitution

General Complaints:
- The hormonal type experiences functional hormonal problems or congenital degeneration of the hormonal glands
- Hormonal disturbances including the pituitary, thyroid, parathyroid, adrenal, gonads, and pancreas
- Fluctuations in blood sugar and disturbances in mineral economy
- Possible disturbances in basal metabolism and thermo-regulation

Common Complaints in Childhood:
- Disturbances in the growth of bones which includes diseases like rickets
- Frequent inflammation of the tonsils and appendix
- May have growing pains as there tends to be an over production of some of the growth hormones and an accelerated rate of growth
- Teenage girls often have problems during menstruation and malfunction of the thyroid gland
- Tendency to develop puppy fat at an early age

Common Complaints in Adulthood:
- Symptoms are often minor until after the age of 50
- In women there may be irregular or painful menstruation and premature menopause
- In men the adrenal gland suffers leading to blood sugar fluctuations as well as prostate gland and circulation problems in later years
- Weakened pituitary, thyroid, adrenal and pancreas glands
- Thyroid gland problems contribute to fluctuations in body weight and metabolism and weakened hair growth
- Blood pressure fluctuations and dizziness are often complaints after the age of 35
- Fatigue, depression, lack of drive and a greater need for quality sleep
- Constipation and poor digestion
- In old age there is a tendency to develop cancer of the endocrine organs such as the uterus and prostate

Connective Tissue Consitution

General Complaints:
- Connective tissue weakness which often involves the prolapsing or dropping of organs especially in the abdomen
- Weak connective tissues and ligaments may create pain in the long bones and joints of the body as well as frequent injuries to ankles
- Poor and slow recovery and healing of injuries due to a weak immune system
- Insufficient energy and oxygen metabolism leading to poor endurance, constant fatigue and frequent shortness of breath
- Problems generally improve in a warmer climate
- Accumulation of waste products in kidneys and connective tissue creating irritation of muscles and connective tissue and arthritic problems
- Poor posture, weak bones and spinal problems are common
- Weakness in the metabolism of Vitamin C and bioflavonoids which leads to reduced collagen formation
- Connective tissue weakness which can also affect the bowel, glands, nerves, heart, and circulation

Common Complaints in Childhood:
- Children tend to have thin, loose skin which gives them the appearance of being older than their age
- Often there is overstretching of the joints

Common Complaints in Adulthood:
- Hemorrhoids, varicose veins, and hernias
- Weak bones and spinal problems like scoliosis
- Feel tired easily
- Loss of tone and elasticity of the blood vessels leading to circulation problems
- Women often have menstrual problems, abdominal and pelvic difficulties, and infertility due to mild prolapse of the uterus and pelvic organs, which can also put pressure on the bladder and cause irritation
- In older age there may be heart complaints and the face is often heavily wrinkled with loose, hanging skin
- Knee and ankle joint problems
- Organs have a tendency to prolapse especially in the abdominal region

The Brown-Eye Types

Hematogenic Constitution

General Features/Complaints:
- These types often but not always have olive colored skin and dark hair and stem from physically strong genetic backgrounds (Mediterranean, Asian, African)
- A cultural change in diet and lifestyle can greatly influence health in a negative way
- They may display impulsive or hyperactive behavior and have a tendency to be over emotional and easily excited
- The overactive nervous system often causes problems for the heart and circulation, liver and gall bladder
- A rapid circulation, viscous blood and strong pulse often leads to varicose veins
- Asthma is common as well as problems with the thyroid gland

Common Complaints in Childhood:
- May be hyperactive and have difficulty in concentration
- Nervous stomach or cramps may occur
- Skin problems like eczema are likely
- Asthma or other respiratory diseases may be seen

Common Complaints in Adulthood:
- May loose temper easily or be over-emotional
- Digestive problems include slow moving bowels that can result in constipation, hemorrhoids and general toxicity, nervous stomach, dyspepsia or excessive intestinal gas
- Gallstones and kidney stones may form due to high levels of nitrogenous waste and uric acid in the blood
- Skin diseases are often found that develop into boils due to poor liver function
- After the age of 30 there is an greater chance of high cholesterol and angina pectoris
- Arteriosclerosis is often seen in later years as well as memory loss and reduced blood flow to the brain
- Varicose veins

Plethoric Constitution

General Complaints:
- The term "plethora" means an excess amount of blood leading to a slowing down in movement which in this case relates to a sluggish venous flow of blood towards the heart
- Both adults and children are prone to become overweight
- Due to excessive blood in the skin, the complexion is often quite red and acne and skin complaints are frequent
- There are often disturbances in bile flow due to liver congestion which affects digestion
- Excessive production of mucus which can bring on asthma
- May exhibit variable moody or irritable behavior with depression
- Sleepiness, fatigue are often encountered

Common Complaints in Childhood:
- Children of this type are often overweight
- Complexion is red and various skin problems or acne may develop
- Moodiness
- Colds, and sinus problems, and asthma is common

Common Complaints in Adulthood:
- Conditions of blood stagnation and congestion lead to problems like varicose veins, loss of tone in the veins, hemorrhoids and thromboses
- Frequent backaches often due to a blocked congested blood flow and extra weight gain in the abdomen area
- In later years angina pectoris is frequent
- Endocrine weakness especially in the thyroid gland
- High blood cholesterol and arteriosclerosis
- Liver problems with disturbances in bile flow
- Problems in digestion

Mixed Constitution

General Complaints:
- Gastrointestinal problems such as constipation and excessive intestinal gas
- Pancreatic problems in secretion of enzymes and control of blood sugar levels
- Liver and gallbladder complaints which can include problems in bile production and secretion
- Sensitive nervous system

Common Complaints in Childhood and Adulthood:
- Liver problems
- Constipation and/or diarrhea
- Nervous stomach or irritable bowel syndrome
- Flatulence or excessive gas
- Gallstones or gallbladder conditions
- Fluctuating blood sugar levels
- Reduction in digestive enzymes which can lead to insufficient digestion
- Dry skin or acne
- Frequent feelings of nausea
- Nerve weakness

Chapter 5

Specific Nutrition for Genetic Eye Constitutions

Now that you have at least become somewhat familiar with your genetic eye constitution you can probably see how each type is predisposed to a unique set of health problems and organ weaknesses. On average these health problems have a good chance of showing up at some point in your life if you choose to take the path of least effort. I am convinced that if you support the nutritional needs of your genetic eye constitution you will at the very least slow down the natural process of degeneration that is encoded and possibly even prevent those probable diseases from occurring. Moreover, by custom tailoring a nutritional strategy for your genetic weaknesses you may just provide that necessary boost to get to the root of your health problems. By providing your individual body with what it specifically needs you will improve all the seven essential processes of life, you will be able to treat the cause of your health problems, you will make it easier to maintain your ideal weight and you will prevent serious health problems in the future. We can no longer apply one blanket diet for everyone. This would mean that we all have the same identical needs and I hope by now you can understand that this is just not possible as we are all unique individuals. That is why one diet works for some people and for others it has little or no effect. Understanding what your body needs is not an easy task and requires constant learning and experimentation. Genetic eye constitutions will allow you to come closer to understanding these needs. The rest of this chapter deals with specific nutritional strategies custom-tailored for each of the ten genetic eye constitutions. Included are nutrients such as food, vitamins and minerals, supplements and herbs and other valuable nutritional advice that are essential in supporting your genetic make-up to give you the best possible chance of achieving your individualized optimum health.

The Blue Eye Types

Lymphatic Hyper-active Constitution

Beneficial foods that support this genetic eye constitution

As most of the health problems in the Lymphatic Hyper-active constitution result from excessive mucous production and over-reactive mucous membranes as well over-acidity of the body tissues it is important to include alkaline foods and to reduce those foods that are mucous forming.

The alkaline-forming minerals include calcium, potassium, sodium, magnesium and iron. Foods that are high in these minerals should be regularly included in the diet. High calcium foods include almonds, egg yolk, green leafy vegetables, soybeans, sesame seeds, parsley and dried figs. High potassium foods include bananas, apricots, avocado, dates, almonds, cashews, pecans, raisins, sardines, and sunflower seeds. High magnesium foods include nuts, whole grain foods, almonds, cashews, molasses, soybeans, spinach, beets, and broccoli. High sodium foods include celery, liver, olives, peas, tuna and sardines. High iron foods include liver, apricots, oysters, parsley, sesame seeds, soybeans, sunflower seeds and almonds.

As the lymphatic system is prone to congestion, fruits and vegetables that aid in stimulating lymph flow are apples, watermelon, lemon juice, pineapple, blueberries, grapes, celery, garlic and parsley. Some spices such as cayenne pepper, horseradish and ginger also serve to boost a sluggish lymphatic system and are helpful for catarrh conditions. As improvement in lymphatic circulation increases it will allow for better weight control and immunity.

As the congestion of the lymphatic system can lead to lowered immunity, it is important that the digestion and absorption of fats is optimal, which is accomplished by quality bile production from the liver and a healthy intestinal micro floral environment. Liver health can be improved by including foods high in Vitamin C, methionine, choline and inositol. Vitamin C-rich foods include peppers, black currant, broccoli, guava, parsley, pineapple, strawberries, rosehips, raw cabbage, brussel sprouts, and cauliflower. Choline is contained in foods such as beans, egg yolk, lecithin, liver, whole grains and yeast. Inositol containing foods include: beans, corn, nuts, seeds, vegetables, wholegrain cereals and meats. Methionine containing foods include: beans, eggs, garlic, liver, onions, sardines and yogurt. Many children as well as some adults who are Lymphatic Hyper-active types suffer from ear, nose and throat and lung infections and as a result usually undergo several bouts of antibiotics resulting in a disturbed intestinal bacterial environment. Natural yogurt or soured milk products can restore some of the lost beneficial flora.

Beneficial vitamins, minerals, herbs and supplements for this genetic eye constitution

Calcium, potassium, sodium, magnesium and iron are helpful as alkaline-forming minerals. To improve the immune system due to lymphatic congestion, supplements of Vitamin C, E, B-complex, Beta-carotene, Shiitake mushrooms (*Lentinus edodes*), Echinacea, Golden Seal (*Hydrastis canadensis*), Garlic, Ginseng and Zinc are very beneficial. To improve digestion and absorption of fats and to restore digestive function due to antibiotic use include supplements of Lactobacillus acidophilus, Chlorella and Lecithin. Herbs such as Slippery Elm (*Ulmus fulva*) and liquorice root (*Glycyrrhiza glabra*) are useful in repair of the intestinal mucosa. For joint stiffness and arthritis, it is important to assist liver and digestive function and Glucosamine Sulfate and Chondroitin Sulfate can be beneficial in improving the lubrication of joints and regeneration of joint tissue.

Other important advice for this genetic eye constitution

Milk products should be avoided as there are commonly allergies to milk lactose and they can cause an overproduction of mucous which can produce allergies or respiratory problems especially in the nose, throat, ear and lung areas. Other mucous-forming foods that should be avoided are refined grains such as white bread, cakes as well as white sugar. The intake of caffeine, sugar, salt, dairy foods and alcohol also contribute to lymphatic stagnation.

As there are often congested lymphatic glands, regular exercise is particularly recommended for better lymphatic circulation. Swimming is particularly helpful for asthmatic conditions or breathing difficulties. Regular lymphatic massage is recommended to stimulate lymphatic flow.

Avoid too many acid-forming foods such as excess meats, saturated fats and citrus fruits that are picked before they are ripe. This will improve arthritic conditions and osteoporosis.

Avoid cough suppressants as coughing helps get rid of mucous. Practice deep-breathing exercises and avoid smoking and smoky or smoggy environments if you suffer from respiratory conditions such as bronchitis or asthma.

If you are older and suffering from arthritis or respiratory ailments, it may do you well to live in a warmer and dryer climate if possible.

Lymphatic Hypo-active Constitution

Beneficial foods that support this genetic eye constitution

Most health problems in the Lymphatic Hypo-active type result from a poor ability to eliminate waste products from the body due to under-active detoxification organs such as the bowel, kidneys, liver, skin, lungs and lymphatic circulation. It is therefore important to include nutrition that will improve these particular organs and systems in the body.

Water is extremely important for this genetic type to assist in the removal of toxins that are generally slow in being removed from the body by the kidneys. It is important to make sure that drinking water is not chlorinated or fluoridated as this can place an extra load of toxins for the kidneys. Cranberries and blueberries have been known to lower calcium levels in urine and may prevent kidney stones. They also help prevent bacteria from adhering to the walls of the urethra and bladder reducing the risk of infection.

Include plenty of garlic, and green leafy vegetables in the diet. Dried apricots, green leafy vegetables and bananas are rich in potassium, an ample supply of which helps the kidneys excrete the excessive amount of sodium found in a typical western-style diet. Asparagus, celery, parsley, artichokes and black currants should be included regularly as they have gentle diuretic properties that help the kidneys to dispose of body wastes by encouraging urine production. Juices of watermelon, raw beet, cranberry and lemon and teas made from parsley, dandelion or raspberries are excellent for kidney cleansing.

To improve bowel function and to reduce conditions of constipation include plenty of fiber in the diet in foods such as whole wheat bread, apples, bran, dates, bananas, prunes, beans, raw peas, and plenty of vegetables such as broccoli and raw salads that contain live enzymes. Include yogurt or soured milk to improve beneficial intestinal micro flora.

Liver function can be improved by including foods high in Vitamin C, methionine, choline and inositol. Vitamin C-rich foods include peppers, fruits, black currant, broccoli, guava, parsley, pineapple, strawberries, rosehips, raw cabbage, brussel sprouts, and cauliflower. Inositol containing foods include: beans, corn, nuts, seeds, vegetables, wholegrain cereals and meats. Methionine containing foods include: beans, eggs, garlic, liver, onions, sardines and yogurt. Other foods that improve liver and gall bladder function include: apples, avocado, artichokes, blueberries, celery, lettuce, olives, strawberries, free range eggs, broccoli, cauliflower, cabbage, and fish such as sardines, salmon and tuna. Drink plenty of juices from grapes, lemons and carrots to assist in bile formation and liver cleansing.

By assisting the bowel, kidney and liver, skin function will often improve which will benefit conditions like eczema, acne and other skin disorders often seen in the Lymphatic Hypo-active constitution. It is important to include fish in the diet especially salmon and tuna as it is high in Omega-3 fatty acids that can assist many skin conditions. Foods high in the B vitamins (eggs, nuts, whole grains, sprouts, green leafy vegetables, fish) and antioxidants like Vitamin A (green leafy vegetables, carrots), C (fruits, berries, parsley, black currant), E (almonds, vegetable oils and nuts) and Zinc (ginger, sunflower seeds, seafood) are also important to maintain skin function.

The lymphatic system can be assisted by eating fruits and vegetables that aid in stimulating lymph flow and include apples, watermelon, lemon juice, pineapple, blueberries, grapes, celery, garlic and parsley. Some spices such as cayenne pepper, horseradish and ginger boost a sluggish lymphatic system.

The lungs and the respiratory system are also important organs that aid in the removal of wastes particularly carbon dioxide and are also often deficient in the Lymphatic Hypo-active constitution. Eat foods such as broccoli, watercress, apples and ginger and drink plenty of fresh water.

Often the accumulation of toxic substances in the body due to insufficient detoxification organs can cause a strain on the heart and circulation. Make sure to include plenty of antioxidant foods such as fruits and vegetables, nuts and seeds, olive oil, and fish, especially tuna, trout or salmon.

Beneficial vitamins, minerals, herbs and supplements for this genetic eye constitution

Lecithin is beneficial for both the kidneys and liver as it contains choline and assists in fat and cholesterol metabolism. Bioflavonoids such as Rutin or Hesperidin can assist the circulation by improving the strength of the capillary walls. This can benefit the kidneys, heart and other organs in the body. Vitamin C supplements can assist kidney, liver and respiratory function. Antioxidants such as Vitamins C, and E and Beta-carotene can reduce free radical formation caused by the accumulation of toxic substances in the body. Methionine, choline and inositol are beneficial for liver regeneration and function as are herbs such as St. Mary's Thistle (*Silybum marianum*), dandelion (*Taraxacum officinale*), and golden seal (*Hydrastis canadensis*). Coenzyme Q 10 can supply oxygen to the liver and is protective in liver function. Cranberry extract tablets can assist in urinary tract or bladder infections. For the skin, supplements that are beneficial are Evening Primrose oil, B-complex, Omega 3 fatty acids, Zinc supplements, Lactobacillus acidophilus and Chlorella. Herbs such as Gingko biloba are beneficial for circulation especially to the brain area. Herbs such as Echinacea and Garlic are useful to boost the immune system due to a sluggish hypo-active lymphatic system.

Other important advice for this genetic eye constitution

As this constitution has problems in eliminating waste products created normally by metabolism it is important to not increase the toxic load of the body by ingesting harmful food additives such as artificial colors and preservatives. This means that it is particularly important for the Lymphatic Hypoactive type to reduce the amount of processed foods in the diet. Chemical additives and alcohol will put an extra strain on an already weakened liver or kidney. Excess protein often found in eating too much meat, or too much salt and sugar also places an additional load on the kidneys. Healthy lung function should include deep breathing exercises and the avoidance of milk products and smoking or smoggy environments. This will assist the lungs in efficient oxygen exchange and release of carbon dioxide. Relaxation methods to reduce any grief or stress will also assist in a health respiratory system.

Plenty of exercise to the point of sweating (at least 20 minutes, three times per week) is important, as it is necessary for good lymphatic drainage. Maintenance of healthy skin should include skin brushing, wearing breathable natural fabrics and regular exposure to sunlight. Avoid white sugar and refined flour products to keep intestinal micro flora well balanced for an efficient digestive system. Most important of all, drink plenty of clean fresh water to flush out the accumulation of harmful toxins in the body.

Kidney Lymphatic Constitution

Beneficial foods that support this genetic eye constitution

The majority of health problems found in the Kidney Lymphatic constitution are generally due to genetically weakened kidneys. Due to weak kidneys and the result of an excess toxic load in the body there are often associated problems such as migraine headaches, skin problems, water retention, high blood pressure, allergies and infections. Poor kidney function also leads to high levels of uric acid, which commonly leads to rheumatoid and arthritic conditions. Because many of those with this type often tend not to feel thirsty, they need to be trained to drink more water.

Water is probably the most crucial nutrient for this genetic type to assist in the removal of toxins that are generally slow in being removed from the body by the kidneys. Drinking water should not be chlorinated or fluoridated as this can place an extra load of toxins for the kidneys. Cranberries and blueberries are beneficial as they lower calcium levels in urine and may prevent kidney stones. They also help prevent bacteria from adhering to the walls of the urethra and bladder reducing the risk of infection. Alfalfa sprouts are also excellent for bladder infections.

Plenty of vegetables should be included in the diet to combat acidity and garlic is useful as a natural antiseptic. Dried apricots, green leafy vegetables, and bananas are rich in potassium, an ample supply of which helps the kidneys excrete the excessive amount of sodium found in a typical western-style diet of high salt intake. Asparagus, celery, parsley, artichokes and black currants should be included regularly as they have gentle diuretic properties that help the kidneys to dispose of body wastes by encouraging urine production. Juices of watermelon, raw beet, cranberry and lemon and teas made from parsley, dandelion or raspberries are excellent for kidney cleansing. Include foods high in choline such as beans, egg yolk, lecithin, liver, whole grains and yeast which have been found to assist in repairing damaged kidney cells.

Foods high in Vitamin C and the bioflavonoids are beneficial to strengthen the capillary network of blood vessels in the filter of the kidney. These include berries, fruits and the skin of fruits and vegetables. Antioxidant foods high in Vitamin C, E and Beta-carotene will assist in reducing free radical damage to the kidneys. These are found in high amounts in fresh fruits and vegetables, nuts and olive oil.

Eat plenty of wheat germ, bananas, walnuts, red peppers, and cruciferous vegetables, which are high in vitamin B6, and help the body dispose of oxalate harmlessly so that kidney stone formation does not occur. Eat fish such as salmon, tuna and sardines, which are high in Omega-3 fatty acids and will assist heart function due to the high concentration of toxic waste in the blood.

Beneficial vitamins, minerals, herbs and supplements for this genetic eye constitution

Lecithin is a valuable supplement to take for the Kidney Lymphatic type as is Vitamin C and the bioflavonoids such as Rutin and Hesperidin, which will strengthen the capillary network in the kidneys. Antioxidant supplementation in the form of natural Vitamin E and Beta-carotene will assist in protecting from the harmful effect of free radicals. Herbals such as St.Mary's thistle (*Silybum marianum*) and dandelion (*Taraxacum officinale*) will enhance liver function so that less stress or less of a toxic load is imposed on the kidneys. Glucosamine sulfate and Chondroitin sulfate is beneficial for associated arthritic conditions. Omega 3 fatty acid supplements and Natural Vitamin E will help support negative effects on heart function due to build-up of toxic substances in the blood.

Other advice for this genetic eye constitution

Avoid excess meat or protein consumption and sugar, which can place a heavy load on the kidneys and increase the risk of stone formation. Avoid excess salt that can lead to retention of water or high blood pressure. If you suffer from stones, avoid excess intakes of oxalate containing foods such as rhubarb, spinach or black tea. Never resist the need to urinate and don't avoid drinking water just so that you won't have to go so often. Avoid acid-forming foods such as meats, milk products, white sugar and refined grains.

Neurolymphatic Constitution

Beneficial foods that support this genetic eye constitution

The majority of health problems found in those with the Neurolymphatic constitution are due to a genetically over-sensitive nervous system, which can result in a variety of psychological and physical disorders. These individuals have a poor ability to utilize the B-group vitamins and often there are deficiencies in minerals such as calcium, magnesium, iron and zinc. Therefore foods high in these nutrients should be included in the diet to maintain health. There is also a need to support the digestive system so that these vitamins and minerals are absorbed more effectively into the bloodstream. Foods high in Vitamin B include green leafy vegetables, eggs, legumes, nuts and seeds, sprouts, whole grains, organ meats, chicken, fish, yeast and avocado. Calcium-rich foods include almonds, egg yolks, green leafy vegetables, molasses, sardines and soybeans. Magnesium foods include Brewer's yeast, cashews, almonds, parsnips, soybeans and wholegrain cereals. Iron-rich foods include apricots, liver, oysters, soybeans, sunflower and pumpkin seeds, yeast and wheat germ. In order to improve absorption of iron into the bloodstream Vitamin C rich foods such as fruits, berries, peppers, broccoli and parsley should be included with meals as Vitamin C enhances iron absorption. Foods high in zinc include ginger, liver, oysters, whole grains, and yeast and sunflower seeds. Natural yogurt high in beneficial flora or soured milk products can assist digestive function especially if antibiotics have been used. Choline is found in legumes, whole grains, brewer's yeast, soybeans, organ meats, egg yolks, fish and lecithin and is essential for the production of acetylcholine, which is a component of the neurotransmitters in our nervous system.

Beneficial vitamins, minerals, herbs and supplements for this genetic eye constitution

In order for the digestive system to be able to absorb vital minerals and nutrients into the blood stream, there needs to be enough beneficial bacteria in the digestive tract. This also allows for the production of some B vitamins. Supplements of Lactobacillus acidophilus and Chlorella will improve digestive and absorptive functions. Vitamin C supplements with meals can assist in better iron absorption. Vitamin B complex, calcium, magnesium and zinc supplements will all benefit the nervous system. Lecithin supplements contain high amounts of choline needed for neurotransmitters. High stress can exhaust the adrenal glands that can cause blood sugar and blood pressure fluctuations. Herbs such as ginseng and licorice root extract (*Glycyrrhiza glabra*) are helpful to support adrenal function and enhance the resistance to stress as well as aid in proper sugar balance. Other beneficial relaxing herbs are Valerian (*Valeriana officinalis*), which relieves insomnia and chamomile. To improve the microcirculation in the brain and assist in improved oxygenation and therefore better nerve function a popular herb called Gingko biloba is very effective. It also helps migraines, which can sometimes occur in this genetic constitutional type.

Other advice for this genetic eye constitution

Reduce sugar and white flour products, as they are known to feed the acid-forming bacteria in the digestive tract, which leads to inefficient absorption of vital minerals and vitamins. Avoid coffee, tea and alcohol as they all affect nerve function, reduce absorption of nutrients and alcohol depletes some B vitamins. Avoid high sugar intake as the more sugar we eat the more depleted our B vitamins become and B vitamins are necessary for a healthy nervous system. Make sure to engage in regular exercise to relieve stress. Meditation or yoga can reduce anxiety, depression and negative emotions. Avoid mucous and acid- forming foods such as refined sugars and grains, milk products and excess meats. Take the time everyday to relax and try not to unnecessarily stress over things that you cannot change. Be aware that weather changes and phases of the moon may affect moods and behavior as well as health.

Hydro-lymphatic Constitution

Beneficial foods that support this genetic eye constitution

The Hydro-lymphatic constitution is prone to chronic lymphatic congestion and heavy mucus secretion which often lead to low immunity, breathing and heart problems, arthritis and infections.

Again, like the Lymphatic Hyper-active constitution it is important to include alkaline foods and to reduce those foods that are mucous forming.

The alkaline-forming minerals include calcium, potassium, sodium, magnesium and iron. Foods that are high in these minerals should be regularly included in the diet. High calcium foods include almonds, egg yolk, green leafy vegetables, soybeans, sesame seeds, parsley and dried figs. High potassium foods include bananas, apricots, avocado, dates, almonds, cashews, pecans, raisins, sardines, and sunflower seeds. High magnesium foods include nuts, whole grain foods, almonds, cashews, molasses, soybeans, spinach, beets, and broccoli. High sodium foods include celery, liver, olives, peas, tuna and sardines. High iron foods include liver, apricots, oysters, parsley, sesame seeds, soybeans, sunflower seeds and almonds.

Excessive lymphatic congestion found in this type necessitates fruits and vegetables that aid in stimulating lymph flow such as apples, watermelon, lemon juice, pineapple, blueberries, grapes, celery, garlic and parsley. Catarrh conditions can be aided with some spices such as cayenne pepper, horseradish and ginger, which boost a sluggish lymphatic system. As the lymphatic system is improved there will be a reduction in rates of infection.

Congestion of the lymphatic system due to improperly digested fats leads to lowered immunity, which means that it is important for the digestion and absorption of fats to work at an optimal rate. This is accomplished by quality bile production from the liver and a healthy intestinal micro floral environment. Liver health can be improved by including foods high in Vitamin C, methionine, choline and inositol. Vitamin C-rich foods include peppers, black currant, broccoli, guava, parsley, pineapple, strawberries, rosehips, raw cabbage, brussel sprouts, and cauliflower. Choline is contained in foods such as beans, egg yolk, lecithin, liver, whole grains and yeast. Inositol containing foods include: beans, corn, nuts, seeds, vegetables, wholegrain cereals and meats. Methionine containing foods include: beans, eggs, garlic, liver, onions, sardines and yogurt. Natural yogurt or soured milk products can restore some of the lost beneficial flora.

As there are often associated heart and circulatory problems such as angina pectoris and high blood pressure, garlic, foods high in calcium and magnesium such as green vegetables, sesame seeds, and almonds should be used frequently in the diet as well as high potassium foods such as bananas, dates, nuts, sunflower seeds, avocado, raisins and apricots. Ensure that you get a good supply of bioflavonoids, which come from cherries, blueberries, black berries and grape juice. This will strengthen veins and capillaries and improve circulation. Include plenty of fiber foods such as vegetables and whole grains to reduce constipation and pressure on veins. Eat plenty of fish especially salmon, tuna and sardines, as they are high in Omega-3 fatty acids, which have been found to be protective of heart function.

Drink plenty of clean water, which is not chlorinated or fluoridated as this can place an extra load of toxins on the kidneys. Cranberries and blueberries are beneficial as they lower calcium levels in urine and may prevent kidney stones. They also help prevent bacteria from adhering to the walls of the urethra and bladder reducing the risk of infection. Eat plenty of watermelon and include lemon juice to prevent kidney stone formation. Include sources of lecithin such as egg yolks, liver, soybean, wheat germ and cabbage as well as olives and olive oil as they help in the digestion of fats and cholesterol and may prevent gallstones.

Beneficial vitamins, minerals, herbs and supplements for this genetic eye constitution

Calcium, potassium, sodium, magnesium and iron are helpful as alkaline-forming minerals. To improve the immune system due to lymphatic congestion, supplements of Vitamin C, E, B-complex, Beta-carotene, Shiitake mushrooms (*Lentinus edodes*), Echinacea, Golden Seal (not during pregnancy) (*Hydrastis canadensis*), Garlic, Bee pollen, Ginseng and Zinc are very beneficial. To improve digestion and absorption of fats and to restore digestive function due to antibiotic use include supplements of Lactobacillus acidophilus, Chlorella and Lecithin. Herbs such as Slippery Elm (*Ulmus fulva*) and liquorice root (*Glycyrrhiza glabra*) are useful in repair of the intestinal mucosa. For joint stiffness and arthritis, it is important to assist liver and digestive function and Glucosamine Sulfate and Chondroitin Sulfate can be beneficial in improving the lubrication of joints and regeneration of joint tissue. Evening primrose oil, and Omega-3 fish oils also assist arthritic conditions. For high blood pressure and heart conditions, Omega-3 fatty acids, coenzyme Q-10, lysine and Vitamin C, E and bioflavonoids such as rutin or hesperidin are very beneficial. Herbs such as garlic, gingko biloba, ginseng and hawthorn berry (*Crataegus monogyna*) have been known to stabilize blood pressure and improve circulation.

Other important advice for this genetic eye constitution
Milk products should also be avoided as there are commonly allergies to milk lactose and they can cause an overproduction of mucous which can produce allergies or respiratory problems especially in the nose, throat, ear and lung areas. Other mucous-forming foods that should be avoided are refined grains such as white bread, cakes as well as white sugar. The intake of caffeine, sugar, salt, dairy foods and alcohol also contribute to lymphatic stagnation.

As there are often very congested lymphatic glands, regular exercise is particularly recommended for better lymphatic circulation. Swimming is particularly helpful for asthmatic conditions or breathing difficulties. Regular lymphatic massage is recommended to stimulate lymphatic flow.

Avoid too many acid-forming foods such as excess meats, saturated fats and citrus fruits that are picked before they are ripe. This will improve arthritic conditions.

Avoid cough suppressants as coughing helps get rid of mucous. Practice deep-breathing exercises and avoid smoking and smoky or smoggy environments if you suffer from respiratory conditions such as bronchitis or asthma.

Maintain adequate water intake and reduce salt, especially hidden salt found in many processed foods in order to prevent fluid retention in the body.

Hormonal Constitution

Beneficial foods that support this genetic eye constitution
The Hormonal constitution is prone to weaknesses in the hormonal organs especially the pituitary, pineal, thyroid, adrenal and pancreas glands as well as the reproductive organs. It is important to nourish these glands and to protect them from the effects of toxic substances and free radicals so that they can perform their functions of secreting hormones that regulate the numerous processes in the body.

Foods that are beneficial for the pituitary and pineal gland are alfalfa, which is known to balance and nourish, as well as those high in B vitamins such as green leafy vegetables, eggs, legumes, nuts and seeds, sprouts, whole grains, organ meats, chicken, fish, yeast and avocado. Antioxidant foods high in the Vitamins A, C, E and selenium should regularly be included in the diet such as the following: peppers, black currant, broccoli, fruits, guava, parsley, pineapple, strawberries, rosehips, raw cabbage, brussel sprouts, and cauliflower, green leafy vegetables, liver, carrots, apricots, and fish liver oils, almonds, safflower, soybean and sunflower oils, corn, alfalfa, cashews, eggs, fish, garlic, tuna and wholegrain cereals.

For the pancreas, foods high in chromium (egg yolk, grape juice, asparagus, liver, lobster, nuts, oysters, whole grains, raisins, prunes, shrimp, yeast) iron, copper, zinc and chlorine (liver, apricots, parsley, sesame seeds, almonds, sunflower seeds, prunes, brown rice, eggs, ginger, pumpkin seeds, avocado, cabbage, celery, kelp, seaweed and olives) are important as well as the B-vitamin foods listed above for the pituitary. Magnesium and potassium rich foods such as nuts, banana, avocado and soybeans are also important for the pancreas. Eat a good portion of foods in the raw form that contain live enzymes.

The adrenal gland is assisted by potassium rich foods (all vegetables, avocado, banana, dates, nuts, sunflower seeds, raisins, sardines) calcium rich foods (almonds, egg yolk, green leafy vegetables, sesame seeds) magnesium rich foods (soy beans, cashews, whole grains) and sodium rich foods (celery, cheeses, clams, liver, olives, tuna). Foods high in the antioxidants and B vitamin foods listed above for the pituitary gland are also needed, especially the B5 (pantothenic acid) rich foods such as avocado, eggs and beans).

The thyroid gland requires iodine foods (cod, oysters, sunflower seeds, kelp, seaweed) chlorine foods (asparagus, avocado, cabbage, celery, cucumber, oats, olives, pineapple, tomatoes, and turnip) magnesium foods (soy beans, cashews, whole grains), potassium foods (all vegetables, avocado, banana, dates, nuts, sunflower seeds, raisins, sardines), and sodium foods (celery, cheeses, clams, liver, olives, tuna). The B-complex foods listed above for the pituitary as well as the beta-carotene rich foods (carrots, yellow and green vegetables) and Vitamin C rich foods (peppers, black currant, broccoli, guava, parsley, pineapple, strawberries, rosehips, raw cabbage, brussel sprouts, and cauliflower) are also needed.

The liver, which is involved in the metabolism of hormones, should also be taken into consideration so foods high in the liver nutrients, methionine, choline, inositol and Vitamin C should be included in the diet. Vitamin C-rich foods include peppers, black currant, broccoli, guava, parsley, pineapple, strawberries, rosehips, raw cabbage, brussel sprouts, and cauliflower. Choline is contained in foods such as beans, egg yolk, lecithin, liver, whole grains and yeast. Inositol containing foods include: beans, corn, nuts, seeds, vegetables, wholegrain cereals and meats. Methionine containing foods include: beans, eggs, garlic, liver, onions, sardines and yogurt.

A toxic digestive tract is often a source of free radicals that can affect the hormonal glands. Natural yogurt or soured milk products can restore some of the lost beneficial flora and improve digestion.

Beneficial vitamins, minerals, herbs and supplements for this genetic eye constitution

It is extremely important for the digestive tract to be working optimally. Supplements of Lactobacillus acidophilus and Chlorella, as well as Slippery Elm (*Ulmus fulva*) will regenerate the intestinal mucosa and assist in the digestion of vitamins and minerals that are needed by the glandular system. Liver supplements such as methionine, choline, inositol and Vitamin C are recommended as well as herbs like St. Mary's thistle (*Silybum marianum*) and dandelion (*Taraxacum officinale*). B-complex and antioxidant supplements (Vitamins A, C, E, and selenium) will also assist and protect hormonal function. Chromium piccolinate and digestive enzymes will assist pancreatic function. Alfalfa tablets are recommended if there is not enough fresh alfalfa in the diet as is flaxseed oil that is very high in essential fatty acids needed for the hormonal system. Herbs that will assist are barberry (*Berberis vulgaris*), juniper berries (not during pregnancy) (*Juniperus communis*), licorice (minimal use during pregnancy) (*Glycyrrhiza glabra*), ginko biloba and ginseng (especially good for nourishing the pituitary). For women dealing with menopausal difficulties or problems with the ovaries or uterus, black cohosh extract (not during pregnancy) (*Cimifuga racemosa*) (contains natural precursors to estrogen), Wild Yam (*Dioscorea villosa*) which is similar to progesterone and Dong Quai extract (*Angelica sinensis*) have shown some ability to normalize the hormonal system. Vitamin B-complex, Evening Primrose Oil, Vitamin E, ginseng and ginger assist menstrual difficulties. Men should take zinc tablets and ginseng regularly. Kelp tablets will supply necessary iodine that is often deficient in refined foods.

Other advice for this genetic eye constitution

Use whole fruits rather than fruit juices and avoid white sugar and potatoes as they may stress the pancreas too much. Ensure that 60 percent of fruits and vegetables are eaten in the raw form. Eat smaller meals more often and regularly to stabilize blood sugar levels and do not skip breakfast. Avoid excess alcohol, coffee and tea and limit fats. Drink plenty of clean water. Avoid stress and use relaxation methods in order to not overstress the adrenal glands. Avoid refined foods that are often low in many vitamins and minerals such as iodine. Include fiber rich foods to allow blood sugar levels to be raised slowly and avoid sweets. Avoid radiation from microwaves as it can affect the hormonal system. Maintain good posture and spinal health by exercising regularly (at least 3 times a week) to open nerve and circulation channels to the glands. Engaging in yoga is one example of an excellent way to accomplish this. Spend time in nature and perform deep-breathing exercises.

Frank Navratil BSc. N.D.

Connective Tissue Constitution

Beneficial foods that support this genetic eye constitution

The Connective Tissue constitution is prone to connective tissue weakness due to poor metabolism of Vitamin C and the bioflavonoids. This can lead to frequent injuries, back aches, poor wound healing, low immunity and other problems associated with connective tissue weakness. As Vitamin C is necessary for collagen formation, this type requires more of the Vitamin C rich foods some of which include: peppers, black currant, broccoli, guava, parsley, pineapple, strawberries, rosehips, raw cabbage, brussel sprouts, and cauliflower. Bioflavonoid rich foods include citrus fruits, berries and the skins of fruits and vegetables and will assist the immune system, and increase the strength and elasticity of blood vessels reducing the chance of varicose veins, hemorrhoids or bleeding from the gums. Foods rich in zinc (oysters, veal, shrimp, herring, ginger, sunflower seeds, whole grains) are important for increased healing capabilities and recovery from injuries. Ensure that plenty of calcium-rich foods (salmon, sardines, almonds, green vegetables, sesame seeds), magnesium-rich foods (nuts, whole grain foods, almonds, cashews, molasses, soybeans, spinach, beets, broccoli), copper-rich foods (oysters, shellfish, nuts, legumes) and Vitamin D-rich foods (salmon, sardines, eggs) are used frequently in the diet. Ensure the kidneys are protected from accumulation of waste products by drinking plenty of water. Juices of watermelon, raw beet, cranberry and lemon and teas made from parsley, dandelion or raspberries are excellent for kidney cleansing. Include foods high in choline such as beans, egg yolk, lecithin, liver, whole grains and yeast which have been found to assist in repairing damaged kidney cells. Ensure that the digestive tract is in good order by the use of natural yogurts and soured milk products so that absorption of nutrients is improved. Increase the B-vitamin rich foods (green leafy vegetables, eggs, legumes, nuts and seeds, sprouts, whole grains, organ meats, chicken, fish, yeast, and avocado) to improve energy levels and metabolism. Eat plenty of fish such as salmon, tuna or sardines to protect heart function and provide fatty acids for the hormonal system.

Beneficial vitamins, minerals, herbs and supplements for this genetic eye constitution

The most important dietary supplements for this genetic type are Vitamin C and bioflavonoids such as rutin or hesperidin. Acerola is an excellent supplement high in natural vitamin C. This will assist in collagen formation for connective tissue, ligaments and bones.

The immune system can be strengthened by supplements of Echinacea, Bee pollen, Vitamin E, B-complex, Beta-carotene, Shitake mushrooms (*Lentinus edodes*), Golden Seal (*Hydrastis canadensis*), Garlic and Ginseng. To aid the healing and recovery process, supplements of zinc and chlorella are beneficial. It is also important to assist digestion and absorption by supplemental Lactobacillus acidophilus, Chlorella, Digestive enzymes and Slippery elm (Ulmus fulva). Omega-3 capsules are recommended for the heart and hormonal system. Calcium and Magnesium supplements may be required. Glucosamine sulfate can assist in cartilage formation and lecithin and alfalfa supplements for protection of kidney function.

Other advice for this genetic eye constitution
Ensure regular cardiovascular and resistance exercise to increase bone strength and improve circulation to tissues. Avoid smoking, stress and smoggy environments, which can deplete Vitamin C stores in the body. Eat at least 60 percent of all fruits and vegetables in the raw form. Ensure adequate sunlight for Vitamin D formation. Avoid excess alcohol, caffeine, fried foods and sugar. Drink plenty of clean, fresh water.

Hematogenic Constitution

Beneficial foods that support this genetic eye constitution
The majority of health problems in the Hematogenic constitution are due to a genetically weak liver, a sensitive nervous system and viscous blood which can lead to heart and circulatory problems, high cholesterol, skin problems, digestive and gall bladder complaints and arteriosclerosis.

It is crucial to support liver function by including foods high in especially Vitamin C, methionine, choline and inositol. Vitamin C-rich foods include peppers, black currant, broccoli, guava, parsley, pineapple, strawberries, rosehips, raw cabbage, brussel sprouts, and cauliflower. Choline is contained in foods such as beans, egg yolk, lecithin, liver, whole grains and yeast. Inositol containing foods include: beans, corn, nuts, seeds, vegetables, wholegrain cereals and meats. Methionine containing foods include: beans, eggs, garlic, liver, onions, sardines and yogurt. B-complex rich foods are needed which include green leafy vegetables, eggs, legumes, nuts and seeds, sprouts, alfalfa, whole grains, organ meats, chicken, fish, yeast, and avocadoes. For prevention and release of gallstones, olive oil with the juice of lemon can be used as well as plenty of apples, applesauce, fish and beets. Eat plenty of salmon, tuna and sardines that contain Omega-3 fatty acids, which are known to lower serum cholesterol and triglyceride, levels and make the blood less viscous. Prevention of arteriosclerosis and the formation of normal blood clotting factors such as prothrombin are also aided by Vitamin K rich foods such as alfalfa, cabbages, green leafy vegetables, broccoli, eggs, kelp, lettuce, soybeans, spinach, parsley and liver. Foods high in the bioflavonoids such as fruits, berries and skins of fruits and vegetables are important for the veins. To support associated skin problems, the digestive tract should be high in beneficial flora (yogurt and soured milk products) and foods high in zinc should be included in the diet (oysters, veal, shrimp, herring, ginger, sunflower seeds, whole grains). Eat garlic to ensure cholesterol levels are in control. Vitamin E-rich foods (almonds, safflower, soybean and sunflower oils, nuts, egg yolk, corn, liver and green leafy vegetables) will assist in protecting fats from oxidation as well as assisting the heart.

Beneficial vitamins, minerals, herbs and supplements for this genetic eye constitution

Supplements that include methionine, choline, insositol and Vitamin C are helpful along with Vitamin B-complex. Lecithin capsules are beneficial to aid fat digestion, memory loss and the nervous system. Alfalfa tablets are excellent as a liver cleanser. For cholesterol problems use Omega-3 fatty acids and Garlic. To support heart function, use Vitamin C, E, lysine and Coenzyme Q-10. Herbs such as gingko biloba, barberry (*Berberis vulgaris*), milk thistle (*Silybum marianum*), licorice (*Glycyrrhiza glabra*), peppermint (*Mentha piperita*) and dandelion (*Taraxacum officinale*) also assist liver, digestive and circulatory problems. Bioflavonoid supplements of Rutin or Hesperidin strengthen the veins and assist with varicose veins and hemorrhoids. To support digestive function, constipation, and excess gas use Lactobacillus acidophilus, Chlorella, and Slippery Elm (Ulmus fulva). Evening Primrose Oil, Omega-3 fatty acids and Zinc supplements can assist with eczema and other skin conditions. To calm the nervous system, herbals such as Valerian (*Valeriana officinalis*) or chamomile are beneficial.

Other advice for this genetic eye constitution

Avoid milk products, refined carbohydrates, fried foods, spicy foods, margarines, alcohol, coffee, saturated fats and excess intakes of salt and sugar. It is important to be careful of ingesting too many chemical preservatives and artificial colors in foods that can overburden the liver. Ensure plenty of exercise and avoid smoking to assist heart, circulatory and digestive function. Try to stay positive and stay clear of negative emotions such as grief, jealousy and resentment and use relaxation methods to avoid the build-up of stress. Drink plenty of clean, fresh water and herbal teas and ensure adequate fiber to prevent constipation. Ensure that the skin breathes by wearing natural fabrics and brush the skin to stimulate the release of toxins.

Plethoric Constitution

Beneficial foods that support this genetic eye constitution

The Plethoric constitution is prone to an excess of blood in the circulation, which results in a sluggish venous flow towards the heart. This often results in liver congestion, disturbed bile flow, a slow movement through the digestive tract, constipation and heart and circulatory problems such as angina pectoris, varicose veins and hemorrhoids. It is once again important to nutritionally support the liver by including foods high in Vitamin C, methionine, choline and inositol. The Plethoric type should regularly include Vitamin C-rich foods in the diet such as peppers, black currant, broccoli, guava, parsley, pineapple, strawberries, rosehips, raw cabbage, brussel sprouts, and cauliflower. Choline is contained in foods such as beans, egg yolk, lecithin, liver, whole grains and yeast. Inositol containing foods include: beans, corn, nuts, seeds, vegetables, wholegrain cereals and meats. Methionine containing foods include: beans, eggs, garlic, liver, onions, sardines and yogurt. For prevention and release of gallstones, olive oil with the juice of lemon can be used as well as plenty of apples, applesauce, fish and beets. Eat plenty of salmon, tuna and sardines that contain Omega-3 fatty acids, which are known to lower serum cholesterol and triglyceride, levels. Prevention of arteriosclerosis and the formation of normal blood clotting factors are also aided by Vitamin K rich foods such as alfalfa, cabbages, green leafy vegetables, broccoli, eggs, kelp, lettuce, soybeans, spinach, parsley and liver. B-complex rich foods are needed to improve energy levels, which include green leafy vegetables, eggs, legumes, nuts and seeds, sprouts, alfalfa, whole grains, organ meats, chicken, fish, yeast, and avocadoes. Foods high in the bioflavonoids such as fruits, berries and skins of fruits and vegetables are important for the veins to assist and prevent varicose veins and hemorrhoids. To support associated skin problems such as acne, the digestive tract should be high in beneficial flora (yogurt and soured milk products) and foods high in zinc should be included in the diet (oysters, veal, shrimp, herring, ginger, sunflower seeds, whole grains). Eat garlic to ensure cholesterol levels are in control. Vitamin E-rich foods (almonds, safflower, soybean and sunflower oils, nuts, egg yolk, corn, liver and green leafy vegetables) will assist in protecting fats from oxidation as well as assisting the heart. Ensure that there are enough iodine-rich foods (sea fish, shellfish, mushrooms, oysters, kelp, seaweed and sunflower seeds) to support the thyroid gland function. Ensure adequate fiber from foods like whole grains, apples, bran, dates, bananas, prunes, beans, raw peas and broccoli to move food contents through the digestive tract and to prevent constipation.

Beneficial vitamins, minerals, herbs and supplements for this genetic eye constitution

Beneficial supplements include methionine, choline, inositol, Vitamin C and Alfalfa tablets to assist liver function. Lecithin capsules and Digestive enzymes are beneficial to aid fat digestion and Omega-3 fatty acids and Garlic for cholesterol problems. To support heart function and assist in conditions like angina pectoris, use Vitamin C, E, lysine and Coenzyme Q-10. To improve energy levels and metabolism, Vitamin B-complex supplements can be of assistance. Herbs such as gingko biloba, barberry (*Berberis vulgaris*), milk thistle (*Silybum marianum*), licorice (*Glycyrrhiza glabra*), peppermint (*Mentha piperita*) and dandelion (*Taraxacum officinale*) also assist liver, digestive and circulatory problems. Bioflavonoid supplements of Rutin or Hesperidin strengthen the veins and assist with varicose veins and hemorrhoids. To support digestive function and to prevent constipation use Lactobacillus acidophilus, Chlorella, and Slippery Elm *(Ulmus fulva)*. Evening Primrose Oil, Omega-3 fatty acids and Zinc supplements can assist with acne and other skin conditions.

Other advice for this genetic eye constitution

It is very important for this constitution to engage in regular exercise to improve the sluggish flow of venous blood and to prevent obesity. This will reduce backaches and circulatory problems and control cholesterol levels and arteriosclerosis. Be careful of chemicals added to foods and artificial colors that put an extra strain on the liver. Avoid especially alcohol, coffee, saturated fats, fried foods, margarines and excess refined carbohydrates and refined grains. Drink a minimum of two liters of clean fresh water a day. Limit meat consumption and increase fiber to prevent constipation. Milk products should be limited as they cause an increase in mucous, which can bring on asthma or respiratory conditions. Ensure that the skin breathes by wearing natural fabrics and brush the skin to stimulate the release of toxins. Eat plenty of raw fruits and vegetables for their live enzyme content. Perform deep-breathing exercises in nature to ensure a good supply of oxygen.

Mixed Constitution

Beneficial foods that support this genetic eye constitution

The Mixed Constitution type is prone to primarily gastrointestinal problems that often lead to constipation or diarrhea and excess gas. These digestive complaints are often caused by liver or gall bladder weakness, which can affect the production of bile, as well as pancreatic problems that can reduce the amount of digestive enzymes and lead to fluctuations in blood sugar.

Liver function needs to be improved as the liver produces bile and foods high in especially Vitamin C, methionine, choline and inositol are beneficial. Vitamin C-rich foods include peppers, black currant, broccoli, guava, parsley, pineapple, strawberries, rosehips, raw cabbage, brussel sprouts and cauliflower. Choline is contained in foods such as beans, egg yolk, lecithin, liver, whole grains and yeast. Inositol containing foods include: beans, corn, nuts, seeds, vegetables, wholegrain cereals and meats. Methionine containing foods include: beans, eggs, garlic, liver, onions, sardines and yogurt. B-complex rich foods are also needed which include green leafy vegetables, eggs, legumes, nuts and seeds, sprouts, alfalfa, whole grains, organ meats, chicken, fish, yeast, and avocado. For prevention and release of gallstones, olive oil with the juice of lemon can be used as well as plenty of apples, applesauce, fish and beets. Use soured milk products or natural yogurt to ensure adequate supplies of beneficial flora, which will reduce flatulence and diarrhea or constipation. Increase fiber foods such as foods like whole grains, apples, bran, dates, bananas, prunes, beans, raw peas and broccoli to move food contents through the digestive tract and to prevent constipation as well as assist irritable bowel syndrome. Eat raw fruits and vegetables and nuts for their live enzyme content. Eat plenty of foods high in chromium (whole grains, egg yolk, grape juice, asparagus, liver, lobster, nuts, oysters, wheat, raisins, prunes, shrimp and yeast), zinc (oysters, veal, shrimp, herring, ginger, sunflower seeds, whole grains), and Vitamin B-complex (green leafy vegetables, eggs, legumes, nuts and seeds, sprouts, alfalfa, whole grains, organ meats, chicken, fish, yeast, and avocado) to assist in blood glucose regulation.

Beneficial vitamins, minerals, herbs and supplements for this genetic eye constitution

Supplements that include methionine, choline, insositol and Vitamin C are helpful along with Vitamin B-complex. Lecithin capsules are beneficial to aid in fat digestion and assist the nervous system. To ensure that cholesterol problems do not arise due to liver problems use Omega-3 fatty acids and Garlic. Herbs such as barberry (*Berberis vulgaris*), milk thistle (*Silybum marianum*), licorice (*Glycyrrhiza glabra*), peppermint (*Mentha piperita*) and dandelion (*Taraxacum officinale*) also assist liver and digestive function. To prevent constipation, diarrhea or excess gas, use Lactobacillus acidophilus, Chlorella, and Slippery Elm (*Ulmus fulva*). Evening Primrose Oil, Omega-3 fatty acids and Zinc supplements can assist with acne and other skin complaints. To calm the nervous system, herbals such as Valerian (*Valeriana officinalis*) or chamomile are beneficial. Chamomile, ginger and peppermint will also assist digestive disturbances due to stress and nervous tension. If there are gall stones a few tablespoons of olive oil with the juice of a lemon before retiring and upon awakening will stimulate the gall bladder to release them. Chromium piccolinate supplements and Digestive enzymes will assist the pancreas in blood sugar regulation and enzyme production.

Other advice for this genetic eye constitution

Avoid milk products other than natural yogurt or soured milk, refined carbohydrates, fried foods, spicy foods, margarines, alcohol, coffee, saturated fats and excess intakes of salt and sugar. Be careful of ingesting too many chemical preservatives and artificial colors in foods that can overburden the liver. Use relaxation methods to avoid the build-up of stress such as exercise, meditation or yoga. Drink plenty of clean, fresh water and herbal teas and ensure adequate fiber to prevent constipation. Ensure that the skin breathes by wearing natural fabrics and brush the skin to stimulate the release of toxins. Eat small meals five times a day rather than two or three large meals a day to assist the pancreas and digestive system. Do not skip breakfast. Avoid white sugar, fruit juices and potatoes as they can spike blood sugar levels.

The Eye for an Eye Diet and Suggested Healthy Eating Plans by Genetic Eye Constitution

Chapter 6

I have written this chapter to provide some samples of suggested healthy eating plans that will strengthen each genetic constitution. I encourage you to use the foods and nutrients mentioned in the previous chapter for your genetic eye constitution frequently in your diet and to vary the foods so that you can achieve a well-balanced nutritional program. The eating plans suggested here are not designed to be a complete nutritional program. They are just a small sample of the possible variations that you can include in your diet. Make sure to use the nutritional information recommended throughout this book along with the foods, vitamins and supplements listed in the last chapter for your genetic constitution. These samples of eating plans will give you an idea of what you should be aiming for. Feel free to use your creative imagination to think up recipes and food combinations that include the foods and nutrients that your body needs. Refer back to the Eye for an Eye Food Pyramid in Chapter 8 of Part 2 to ensure that you have a healthy balance in all the recommended food groups.

The Blue-Eye Types

Lymphatic Hyper-active Constitution

Suggested Sample Eating Plan

Before breakfast – large glass of water with fresh lemon juice
Breakfast – 1 soft-boiled egg, wholegrain bread (un-toasted) lightly buttered, half a cup of natural yogurt with dates, raisins or fresh blueberries
Before Morning Snack – large glass of water
Morning Snack – Handful of grapes and some nuts and seeds (cashews, pecans, almonds, sunflower seeds, sesame seeds)
Before lunch – large glass of water
Lunch – Fresh large raw salad with olive oil (include avocado, sprouts, parsley, spinach, beets, peas, broccoli, peppers, celery, raw cabbage, corn, onions, olives), tuna fish sandwich on whole grain bread
Before afternoon snack – large glass of water
Afternoon snack – Fruit salad (include apples, apricots, grapes, black currant, blueberries, bananas, watermelon, pineapple - only if fresh)
Before Dinner – large glass of water

Dinner – Salmon or poultry with natural brown rice, steamed broccoli, brussel sprouts and carrots (use garlic or ginger for seasoning), fresh vegetable juice or raw salad, berries with soy milk and honey for dessert
Before After Dinner Snack – large glass of water
After Dinner Snack – dried figs and almonds

Lymphatic Hypo-active Constitution

Suggested Sample Eating Plan

Before breakfast – large glass of water with fresh lemon juice
Breakfast – half a cup of soured milk, wholegrain cereal with soymilk and honey, add some dried apricots, prunes, bran, dates
Before Morning Snack – dandelion herbal tea
Morning Snack – Banana and some nuts and seeds (almonds, sunflower seeds)
Before lunch – raw beet juice / watermelon juice / large glass of water
Lunch – Beans with brown rice, lightly steamed broccoli, raw salad with olive oil (include green leafy vegetables, celery, parsley, raw peas, peppers, cabbage, sprouts, onions, olives, lettuce, garlic)
Before afternoon snack – large glass of water / carrot with ginger juice
Afternoon snack – half an avocado filled with a few shrimp and fresh lemon juice
Before Dinner – large glass of water
Dinner – Large tuna salad (include tuna, olive oil, sprouts, parsley, beets, peas, broccoli, peppers, cucumber, tomatoes, celery, raw cabbage, corn, onions, olives), wholegrain roll, blueberries, black currents and strawberries for dessert
Before After Dinner Snack – large glass of water / watermelon juice
After Dinner Snack – apple /grapes /nuts

Kidney Lymphatic Constitution

Suggested Sample Eating Plan

Before breakfast – large glass of water with fresh lemon juice
Breakfast – Wholegrain cereal with wheat germ, soymilk and honey and a few teaspoons of granulated lecithin
Before Morning Snack – large glass of water / parsley tea
Morning Snack – grapes / half a cup of natural yogurt
Before lunch – unsweetened cranberry juice/ watermelon juice / large glass of water
Lunch – Wholegrain turkey sandwich with alfalfa sprouts, freshly made vegetable soup with no added salt
Before afternoon snack – large glass of water / raspberry tea

Afternoon snack – Dried apricots and walnuts
Before Dinner – large glass of water / unsweetened cranberry juice / fresh vegetable juice
Dinner – Salmon with steamed asparagus or artichokes and natural brown rice, fresh raw salad (include celery, parsley, alfalfa sprouts, beets, green leafy vegetables, red peppers, olives, garlic), blueberries for dessert
Before After Dinner Snack – large glass of water / watermelon juice
After Dinner Snack – apple / grapes / nuts

Neurolymphatic Constitution

Suggested Sample Eating Plan

Before breakfast – large glass of water with fresh lemon juice
Breakfast – poached egg, wholegrain bread lightly buttered, half a cup of natural yogurt with fresh berries
Before Morning Snack – large glass of water
Morning Snack – cashews, almonds, apple
Before lunch – large glass of water / chamomile tea
Lunch – Tofu with raw salad (include parsley, sprouts, peppers, green leafy vegetables), wholegrain roll
Before afternoon snack – large glass of water / ginger tea
Afternoon snack – apricots and pumpkin seeds /sunflower seeds
Before Dinner – large glass of water / fresh vegetable juice
Dinner – Chicken breast or fish with natural brown rice, steamed broccoli, fresh raw salad (include sprouts, green leafy vegetables, peppers, parsley, avocadoes, chick peas, fresh peas) figs and apple for dessert
Before After Dinner Snack – large glass of water / chamomile tea
After Dinner Snack – dates, apple

Hydro-lymphatic Constitution

Suggested Sample Eating Plan

Before breakfast – large glass of water with fresh lemon juice
Breakfast – Fresh fruit salad (include apples, watermelon, pineapple, grapes, bananas, blackberries) with natural yogurt
Before Morning Snack – large glass of water
Morning Snack – raisins, sunflower seeds, almonds
Before lunch – large glass of water
Lunch – sardines, wholegrain roll, fresh raw salad (include parsley, celery, sesame seeds, fresh peas, olives, spinach, beets, peppers, corn, onions, garlic, olive oil, cayenne pepper)

Before afternoon snack – large glass of water / grape juice
Afternoon snack – dried figs, apricots, celery
Before Dinner – large glass of water / fresh apple and celery juice
Dinner – Slice of turkey with cranberries and brussel sprouts or broccoli, raw salad (include cabbage, peppers, parsley, avocado, celery, cucumber), cherries for dessert
Before After Dinner Snack – large glass of water
After Dinner Snack – dates, grapes

Hormonal Constitution

Suggested Sample Eating Plan

Before breakfast – large glass of water with fresh lemon juice
Breakfast – one soft-boiled egg with lightly buttered wholegrain bread, soymilk and half a cup of natural yogurt
Before Morning Snack – large glass of water
Morning Snack – almonds, raisins, apricots
Before lunch – large glass of water
Lunch – Lightly steamed vegetables (include broccoli, brussel sprouts, carrots, cauliflower, celery, ginger, seaweed, onions, cashews) with natural brown rice
Before afternoon snack – large glass of water / grape juice
Afternoon snack – sunflower seeds, pumpkin seeds, banana
Before Dinner – large glass of water
Dinner – cod fish with asparagus, large raw salad (include alfalfa, corn, peas, sprouts, lettuce, cucumber, tomatoes, avocado, peppers, parsley, olives, raw cabbage, almonds, sunflower oil, garlic, sesame seeds), fresh black currants, pineapple, strawberries for dessert
Before After Dinner Snack – large glass of water
After Dinner Snack – dates, apple

Connective Tissue Constitution

Suggested Sample Eating Plan

Before breakfast – large glass of water with fresh lemon juice
Breakfast – one half cup of natural yogurt with black currants and fresh berries, whole peeled orange or grapefruit with the white skin, wholegrain bread lightly buttered and poached or soft-boiled egg
Before Morning Snack – large glass of water
Morning Snack – banana, dates
Before lunch – large glass of water / watermelon juice

Lunch – fresh raw salad with tuna (include tuna, peppers, beans, broccoli, parsley, tomatoes, raw cabbage, cauliflower, spinach, beets, avocado, sesame seeds, sprouts, onions, olive oil), wholegrain roll
Before afternoon snack – large glass of water / dandelion tea
Afternoon snack – cashews, almonds with berries
Before Dinner – large glass of water / parsley tea
Dinner – Salmon with natural brown rice, lightly steamed broccoli, raw salad (include ginger, peppers, sprouts, lettuce, sunflower seeds, parsley, cucumber, tomatoes), for dessert fresh fruit salad (pineapple, guava, strawberries, kiwi, oranges, fresh berries)
Before After Dinner Snack – large glass of water / raspberry tea
After Dinner Snack – grapes

The Brown-Eye Types

Hematogenic Constitution

Suggested Sample Eating Plan

Before breakfast – large glass of water with fresh lemon juice
Breakfast – wholegrain cereal with soymilk and berries and sprinkled granulated lecithin, wholegrain bread only lightly buttered
Before Morning Snack – large glass of water
Morning Snack – apple
Before lunch – large glass of water
Lunch – Small portion of liver with onions and steamed brussel sprouts, raw salad (include parsley, peppers, onions, sprouts, alfalfa, olives, olive oil)
Before afternoon snack – large glass of water / dandelion tea
Afternoon snack – half a cup of natural yogurt or soured milk, sunflower seeds, almonds
Before Dinner – large glass of water
Dinner – Salmon or tuna with brown rice and lightly steamed broccoli and green beans, raw salad (include parsley, raw cabbage, seaweed, peppers, onions, garlic, corn, sprouts, spinach, lettuce, alfalfa, avocado, olives, olive oil with lemon dressing), applesauce for dessert
Before After Dinner Snack – large glass of water / chamomile tea
After Dinner Snack – dates or figs

Plethoric Constitution

Suggested Sample Eating Plan

Before breakfast – large glass of water with lemon juice

Breakfast – one poached or soft-boiled egg with lightly buttered wholegrain bread, small fruit salad (include berries, black currants, apples, fresh pineapple, bananas and prunes)
Before Morning Snack – large glass of water
Morning Snack – grapes, raisins
Before lunch – large glass of water
Lunch – Fresh vegetable or lentil soup, wholegrain sandwich with beets and alfalfa
Before afternoon snack – large glass of water / dandelion tea
Afternoon snack – apple, almonds
Before Dinner – large glass of water / peppermint tea
Dinner – Tuna with wholegrain pasta, broccoli and garlic, raw salad (include peppers, parsley, corn, onions, olive oil or sunflower oil, lemon, alfalfa, lettuce, sunflower seeds mushrooms, spinach, raw cabbage, avocado, raw peas, seaweed), dates for dessert
Before After Dinner Snack – large glass of water
After Dinner Snack – applesauce

Mixed Constitution

Suggested Sample Eating Plan

Before breakfast – large glass of water with lemon juice
Breakfast – half a cup of natural yogurt, dates, prunes, bran
Before Morning Snack – large glass of water
Morning Snack – raisins and almonds
Before lunch – large glass of water
Lunch – Lightly steamed vegetables (broccoli, spinach, green beans, tofu, carrots, sprouts, ginger) with brown rice
Before afternoon snack – large glass of water / dandelion tea
Afternoon snack – banana, sunflower seeds
Before Dinner – large glass of water / peppermint tea
Dinner – Fish or chicken with raw salad (include peppers, parsley, onions, garlic, alfalfa, avocado, raw peas, olive oil and lemon juice), applesauce for dessert
Before After Dinner Snack – large glass of water
After Dinner Snack – dates or figs

THE EYE FOR AN EYE DIET

PART 4

The "Eye for an Eye Diet"
For Specific Health Problems

Chapter 1

The Eye for an Eye Diet for Weight loss or Gain

Achieving your ideal weight is often the greatest challenge that you may be facing and pressures in society just don't make it any easier. As you know, we are constantly bombarded with beautiful people on television and in magazines that advertise anything from diet pills, weight loss drinks or quick crash diet plans that promise rapid results. This kind of advertising is very effective and is making thousands of companies very rich. It is also creating the false perception that results are possible overnight and without any hard work. These desperate measures have resulted in a growing number of calorie counting, crash dieters who religiously follow the newest diet trend even though they may often be depriving their bodies of essential nutrients, just to lose weight. Many of us I am sure have been guilty of crash-dieting a few weeks before summer so that we look good in our swimsuits! Is this an intelligent approach? You know the answer to this by now. Don't waste your time searching for yet another quick weight loss plan. Sooner or later you will have to come to the realization that you will have to do some nutritional work, change some lifestyle habits and start exercising because as much as I hate to disappoint you, this is the only way. This is the only way that nature has intended.

Our bodies are very intelligent. If we drastically deprive them of food they go into a survival mode and learn to slow down our metabolism so less calories are burned. When we start eating again we find that we put on weight much faster, so we apply a crash diet again and the cycle repeats itself. In the end we are no further ahead and often gain even more weight. Our bodies as a result are constantly being stressed and this results in a very poor system of organs that just cannot do their jobs effectively. Our health is jeopardized and the metabolism of fats, carbohydrates, proteins and other nutrients becomes less efficient.

The pressures of society have also created a growing number of people who are seriously underweight and literally starve their bodies in order to achieve that ideal weight that we see advertised in the media. I am seeing an alarming increase in anorexia nervosa and bulimia cases these days. The stress of achieving perfection and unrealistic expectations is taking its toll.

It is important to realize that being considerably underweight or considerably overweight has much more important consequences than just aesthetic or cosmetic changes in appearance. Outlined below are some health consequences of being obese and too underweight.

Possible health consequences of obesity

Increased risk of heart disease and high blood pressure
High cholesterol
Strokes
Increased risk of gallstones and gallbladder disease
Menstrual problems in women including amenorrhoea or excessive bleeding
Increased risk of colon, rectal and prostate cancer in men
Increased risk of cancers of the breast, ovary, uterus, endometrium and cervix in women
Osteoarthritis of weight-bearing joints
Increased risk of diabetes
Poor wound healing
Constipation
Varicose veins
Liver problems
Breathing difficulties
Social discrimination

Possible health consequences of being too underweight

Disturbances in the hormonal system and menstrual cycles
Amenorrhoea (absence of menstrual periods)
Cold hands and feet and poor regulation of body temperature
Heart irregularities and arrhythmias
Digestive problems
Poor nutritional status
Infertility
Osteoporosis
Low blood pressure
Hair loss
Anemia
Impaired kidney function
Fatigue

Let's take a look at some of the causes of why we become overweight or underweight. We need to look at several factors to get at the root of the problem. For every individual there will be a different set of factors because we each have a different make-up.

Reasons why you may be overweight

1. Too much food intake or too little exercise

In general terms, in order to become obese, energy has to be consumed at a greater rate than it is expended. Whatever is in surplus, gets stored mainly as fat. This means that either these people eat too much for the amount of exercise that they partake in or they just don't exercise enough. Usually for most it is a combination of the above that leads to excess weight. Both the number and the size of the fat cells is what reflect the amount of fat on an individual's body. When energy intake exceeds expenditure, fat cells can increase in size. These cells may also divide upon reaching their maximum size. So when an individual's fat cells increase in size and or number, obesity occurs. These same fat cells will shrink in size but will not decrease in number with weight loss. That is one of the reasons why a person who has lost weight can regain it rapidly.

It is also important to understand that people do not have to be obese just because they eat too much. They may just not be active enough in burning those accumulated calories. It only takes a very small amount of daily excess to lead to significant weight gains when accumulated over 10-20 years. Affluent societies have much higher rates of obesity than in other cultures. This is not surprising as there is much easier access to snack foods and less energy needed to expend to get them (cars, elevators, drive thru's, home delivery, escalators etc.)

2. Hormonal factors

Hypothyroidism (lack of thyroid gland hormones) leads to a lowered metabolic rate, which means that in hypothyroid individuals a normal food intake will result in fat storage from the surplus energy. People who have Cushing's syndrome (excessive secretion of cortisol from the adrenal cortex of the adrenal gland) have a tendency to be obese. During pregnancy there are considerable changes in maternal hormonal levels and metabolic changes that are responsible for the increase in body weight, some of which is normal and some of which can be in excess. Also, people who are obese often have disturbances in the metabolism of the sex steroid hormones. Many conditions that result from problems with estrogen and progesterone metabolism and regulation are also associated with the development of obesity. Removal of the ovaries can sometimes be accompanied by weight gain and even the use of the oral contraceptive pill can cause some women to put on weight. In males, castration often leads to an increase in body weight.

3. Stress and unhappiness

When you are under stress there is often a tendency to eat too much of the wrong foods.

When there is not a balance in your life, health begins to degenerate. Refer back to the 4th Eye for an Eye Diet Principle back in Part 1 and review those holistic influences that may be contributing to unhappiness in your life and leading to your weight problems.

4. Some drugs

The effects of several commonly used drugs often cause weight gain including corticosteroids such as antidepressants as well as other drugs used to treat psychiatric disorders. Hormone replacement therapy and oral contraceptives containing estrogen can cause fluid retention and increased appetite.

5. Kidney, Heart or Liver Disease

Disease in these organs can cause fluid retention, which appears as general puffiness all over the body, especially the eyes and ankles.

6. Essential Fatty Acid Deficiency

Essential fatty acids, such as found in flaxseed oil, corn oil, evening primrose oil, Omega 3 oil, tuna, salmon, seaweed, sunflower oil, tofu or wheat germ oil are good fats that are needed by the body to make hormones and maintain the body's metabolic rate. A deficiency has been known to cause cravings, particularly for fatty foods. The first signs of deficiency are often dandruff, dry hair and dry scaly skin and may also be associated with arthritis, eczema, heart disease, diabetes and premenstrual syndrome.

7. When you stop smoking

Nicotine suppresses the appetite and causes the liver to release glycogen, which raises the blood sugar level slightly. When you stop smoking and nicotine is out of your system, you may feel hungry more often. Smoking also elevates the heart rate and increases metabolism. When you stop smoking, your body has to readjust to a lower metabolic rate. Your body will end up using less and storing more of the food as fat. Smoking also dulls the taste buds. Food begins to taste better when you stop smoking so food intake may increase.

8. Genetic Factors – Genetic Eye constitutions

An important component to determining a person's body weight and composition has to do with genetics. It is also genetics that may determine the tendency to gain more weight than others. While it is very important to analyze the factors listed above and make some diet and lifestyle changes, understanding your Genetic Eye Constitution will further assist you to support those genetic weaknesses that may be contributing to your weight problems. Obesity can occur in any of the genetic eye constitutional types but often the causes may be different.

Lymphatic Hyper-active types: A congested lymphatic system and endocrine problems are often at the root of weight problems.

Lymphatic Hypo-active types: Poor functioning liver, kidneys and a congested lymphatic system contribute to being overweight in this genetic type.

Kidney Lymphatic types: Kidney problems may be causing fluid retention as well as toxins in the blood that can affect the hormonal system.

Neurolymphatic types: Anxiety and stress play important roles as well as possible B-vitamin deficiency that can affect the metabolism of sugar and fats in the body.

Hydro-lymphatic types: Heavy fluid retention, kidney problems and chronic lymphatic congestion are often contributors to weight fluctuations and gains.

Hormonal types: Weaknesses in the hormonal glands such as the thyroid, adrenal and disturbances in the regulation of sex hormones often contribute to obesity in this case.

Connective tissue types: Connective tissue weakness that often affects glands, nerves and the heart and insufficient oxygen metabolism are important factors in the onset of obesity in these people.

Hematogenic types: Liver problems that can affect various metabolic reactions as well as heart and circulation problems present the greatest challenges in weight control.

Plethoric types: Liver congestion, sluggish venous flow and thyroid gland weakness can affect weight in these individuals. Both adults and children have a greater tendency to become overweight.

Mixed types: Genetic problems with the liver, pancreas and digestive system are the most likely contributors to becoming overweight.

Reasons why you may be underweight

1. Too little food intake or excessive exercise

Poor nutritional practice, not enough protein, carbohydrate and fats, vitamins or minerals will disrupt the energy equation and leave the body in a deficit situation. Excessive exercise with inadequate intake of nutrients will also stress the body and result in a loss of weight accompanied by other health problems. Anorexia and bulimia are examples of eating disorders that result in too little food and nutrient intake. It is important to understand that being too thin just as being too fat leads to a far from optimum state of health.

2. Hormonal factors

Hyperthyroidism (excess thyroid gland hormones) can increase the metabolic rate and cause loss of weight.

3. Stress and unhappiness

Stress can influence the basal metabolic rate, which can result in weight loss. When there is not a balance in your life, health begins to degenerate. Refer back to the 4th Eye for an Eye Diet Principle back in Part 1 and review those holistic influences that may be contributing to unhappiness in your life and leading to your problems with maintaining a healthy weight.

4. Problems with the absorption of nutrients

Several digestive disorders such as Crohn's syndrome, Colitis, chronic diarrhea, food allergies or others can decrease the absorption of nutrients and may lead to significant weight losses.

5. Excessive coffee intake or smoking

Drinking too much coffee or smoking may increase the metabolic rate, which can lead to some weight loss. Coffee can also block the absorption of some nutrients. Nicotine in cigarettes has been found to suppress the appetite.

6. Genetic factors – Genetic Eye Constitutions

Lymphatic Hyper-active types: Allergies to milk lactose or problems in the utilization of some nutrients may contribute to inability to gain weight.

Lymphatic Hypo-active types: Poorly functioning detoxification organs including poor digestion can lead to inefficient absorption and utilization of nutrients in the body.

Kidney Lymphatic types: Loss of minerals and nutrients in the urine due to poor kidney function and poor regulation of water balance.

Neurolymphatic types: Prone to stress and anxiety which may lead to weight loss and poor eating habits. A fast pulse (tachycardia) is also quite common indicating an increased heart rate. Due to nervous influences there is poor utilization of foods.

Hydro-lymphatic types: They do not usually suffer from being underweight but kidney problems and fluid retention can lead to weight fluctuations.

Hormonal types: Excess production of thyroid hormones by the thyroid gland will lead to weight loss in these people.

Connective tissue types: Weak bones and connective tissue due to poor metabolism of Vitamin C and the bioflavonoids may lead to weight loss.

Hematogenic types: The over-active nervous system and hyperactive behavior and strong pulse can lead to weight loss in some cases. Digestive problems and nervous stomach can affect the absorption of nutrients.

Plethoric types: They do not usually suffer from being underweight but the opposite, however problems in the thyroid gland or digestive system can lead to weight loss in some cases.

Mixed types: Problems with the pancreas and disturbances in blood sugar regulation as well as nervous stomach and digestive disorders can lead to weight loss.

Eye for an Eye Diet Guidelines for maintaining your ideal weight

1. Follow the recommendations in this book with regards to the intake of proteins, carbohydrates, fats, vitamins and minerals.
2. Drink plenty of water.
3. Ensure that adequate fiber is included in your diet.
4. Follow the Eye for an Eye Diet Food Pyramid to ensure adequate nutrients from all the important food groups.
5. Avoid excessive or inadequate food intake.
6. Avoid excess alcohol.
7. Exercise regularly and in healthy moderation.
8. Eat smaller meals more often.
9. Reduce stress and apply the holistic principles.
10. Ensure adequate digestion and absorption.
11. Avoid drugs, hormone replacement therapy and the oral contraceptive pill.
12. Avoid diet pills as they may cause high blood pressure or heart problems.
13. Avoid any rapid crash weight loss or weight gain programs.
14. Avoid starvation diets.
15. Do not count calories; change your diet and lifestyle habits for good.
16. Do not opt for liposuction to reduce fat, follow nature's principles.
17. Do not fall for fad diets.
18. Be happy with who you are and try to be the best that you can be.
19. Ask yourself why you are overweight or underweight and apply the holistic principles.
20. Ensure a healthy liver, heart and kidneys.
21. Ensure adequate essential fatty acids to support the hormonal system.
22. Stop smoking and drinking coffee.
23. Provide nutritional support for your genetic eye constitution as described in Part 3 of this book.

The Eye for an Eye Diet for Diseases of Modern Civilization

Chapter 2

After reading through this book it should be apparent that poor nutritional and lifestyle habits are at the root of most health problems that we see today. Despite this, modern medicine continues in its relentless efforts to find miraculous drugs and chemical cures that attempt to alleviate our ailments without taking into consideration its effects on the whole body. I urge you not to fall prey to this kind of primitive treatment as it leads to one of the greatest illusions of mankind, that we can fool our bodies with chemical drugs. We cannot fool our bodies we can only fool ourselves. Remember that in order to cure your disease (as opposed to only treating the symptoms) you must get at the core of the health problem and apply only natural methods. There is no other way. There is no short cut. It is only the way that nature has intended.

If you are not convinced take a look at the success rate. We have not yet cured cancer nor diabetes, asthma, eczema, allergies, arthritis, osteoporosis, heart disease or high blood pressure, yet modern science boasts about its technological advances. Take a look at these diseases. These are most of the diseases that we suffer from and most of them have no cure yet there is a handy set of drugs for each one of them. We are not moving any further ahead. If we want to survive as a society that is free of disease in the future we need to change the way we have been doing things for the past few hundred years. It is time to get back to the basics. It is time to begin to respect nature's laws again. We seem to have forgotten this in our hectic concrete worlds that we live in. Every once in a while I see an article like "New discovery- Cancer may be caused by poor nutrition" Is this really such a ground-shaking discovery. How could we ever have thought that nutrition does not affect our health? We have become so used to being dependant on our doctors and on drugs to cure us that we have forgotten that we hold the power in our hands to heal ourselves. Nutrition and lifestyle changes are the keys. Open the door and open your eyes and you will enter a new world, a new way of thinking and a new perspective on health that will change the way you may have seen things in the past. You have the ability to change your life and your health for the better.

Every disease of modern civilization has an underlying cause and it is not always just physical. Our mental health is of utmost importance as well and it influences our physical health and vice versa. I have never been a believer that we inherit the diseases that we have, only the weakness in our organs that lead to these diseases. Start thinking about disease as a set of conditions or symptoms that are alerting you of weaknesses in your body organs that need to be strengthened not as something that you might catch or inherit and need to liquidate by drugs or operations. Every one of us is born with a unique set of genetic factors that predispose us to certain diseases. We need to strengthen these weaknesses in order to maintain our health throughout our lives.

Listed below are some of the most common diseases that plague our modern civilization. Although any genetic constitution can succumb to these diseases there are some types that are particularly prone to certain ones and are indicated. Possible causes are discussed for each of the diseases and specific nutrition is recommended. I advise that you consult your naturopath, herbalist or naturopathic doctor before engaging in any of the recommended treatment advice.

Acne

Acne is a common skin condition characterized by blackheads, whiteheads and pimples. The condition usually first appears in adolescence, when an increase in hormones causes sebaceous (oil) glands in the skin to increase in size and in oil production. If these glands become blocked, whiteheads and blackheads can develop. These may become infected by bacteria and cause the condition's characteristic inflammation and pimples. Acne typically appears on the, back, shoulders, face and chest. The condition may be superficial or sometimes deep, which can lead to scarring. In general, most cases of acne clear up after adolescence, although in some persons it may continue or may even begin in adulthood. In my opinion acne is an external sign of an internal imbalance that is going on in the body.

Genetic eye constitutions at greatest risk:

Lymphatic hyper-active, Lymphatic hypo-active, Kidney lymphatic, Neurolymphatic, Hematogenic, Mixed, Plethoric and the Hormonal types are predisposed to acne but it can occur in any of the genetic types.

Possible causes that contribute to this disease:

Hormonal changes during adolescence, menstruation or pregnancy
Ingestion of poor quality fats (saturated fats, trans fatty acids)
Over stimulation of androgens (hormones that cause the sebaceous glands to enlarge and produce extra sebum/oil) which increases the chance of clogging, bacterial inflammation and acne
Accumulation of excess toxins in the blood
Hypothyroidism
Corticosteroid use, antibiotics and other drugs
Poor liver or kidney function
Congested lymphatic system

Greasy face creams and cosmetics
Allergies to lotions, soaps or makeup
High sugar and refined food diet and low fiber intake
Food allergies
A toxic bowel and poor digestion
Excess alcohol
Stress

Eye for an Eye Diet nutrition and lifestyle advice:

Follow the nutritional advice in this book and target specific nutrition to strengthen your genetic eye constitution as explained in Part 3.

Ensure healthy sources of fats including olive oil, avocado, fish oil or flaxseed oil.

Avoid high cholesterol foods, saturated fats and trans fatty acids.

Include plenty of vegetables, high fiber foods, seaweeds, fish (salmon, sardines, tuna), whole grains, sprouts and fruits in the diet.

Include foods high in Vitamin A or beta-carotene such as carrots, yams, apricots and cantaloupe, as well as green vegetables like parsley, liver and spinach.

Include foods high in Vitamin E such as almonds, sunflower seeds, broccoli, wheat germ and vegetable oils.

Avoid fried foods, refined flour, dairy products, processed foods, junk food, alcohol, sugar, chocolate, margarine, nut butters, citrus fruits (except lemon juice) and caffeine.

Drink at least two liters of fresh clean water daily to allow for removal of toxins from the body.

Supplements that can assist acne conditions include Brewer's yeast, Lactobacillus acidophilus, chlorella, digestive enzymes, chromium, Evening primrose oil, Omega-3 fatty acids, flaxseed oil, selenium, Vitamin A (beta carotene), Vitamin B-complex, Vitamin C, Vitamin E and zinc.

Herbs that can help to purify the blood, boost the immune system and cleanse the liver include: burdock (*Arctium lappa*), echinacea, dandelion (*Taraxacum officinale*), Goldenseal (*Hydrastis canadensis*) and milk thistle (*Silybum marianum*).

Tea tree oil or eucalyptus oil can be applied directly to the pimple as an effective skin disinfectant and Valerian (*Valeriana officinalis*) relaxes the nervous system.

Allow the skin to breathe, take barefoot walks and wear natural clothing.

Avoid exposure to oils and greases.

Avoid antibiotics, corticosteroids, drugs, chemical acne medications and hormone therapy.

Perform skin brushing to stimulate skin function and improve circulation.

Lymphatic drainage massage can be helpful for lymphatic congestion that can affect skin function.

Use proper hygiene and avoid touching the face with your hands as they often transmit bacteria.

Avoid smoking.

Avoid stress, intense negative emotions and make sure you relax for some time each day.

Allow adequate oxygen by performing deep-breathing exercises daily and ensure plenty of sunlight and exposure to fresh air and nature.

Exercise regularly and allow the skin to sweat.

Allergies

An Allergy is a hypersensitivity to foreign substances which are normally harmless but which produce a violent reaction in the allergy sufferer. Allergies are generally the body's effort to eliminate something it considers unsuitable. Typical allergic reactions include hay fever, migraine, asthma, digestive disturbances, coeliac disease (allergy to gluten), rhinitis, conjunctivitis, eczema, tinnitus, hyperactivity in children, sinusitis and ear infections. In a certain percentage of people the histamine or anaphylactic reaction can cause muscle cramps, disorientation, unconsciousness and even death from suffocation or shock. Almost any substance can be an allergen for an individual. Common allergens include certain foods, especially milk, wheat and eggs, pollens, cosmetics, food additives, dust or moulds.

Genetic eye constitutions at greatest risk:

Lymphatic hyper-active, Lymphatic hypo-active, Kidney lymphatic, Neurolymphatic and Hydro-lymphatic types are most susceptible but allergies can occur in any of the genetic types.

Possible causes that contribute to this disease:

The most common cause of multiple food allergies, in my opinion, is having increased intestinal permeability or what is commonly called the "leaky gut syndrome." This refers to small openings which occur in the lining of the intestine that allow large molecules of undigested or incompletely digested food particles to enter the bloodstream. If the quantity is too great for the liver to clear immediately, the immune system has a chance to recognize these molecules as being foreign to the body and produces antibodies against them. When the food is eaten again and passes into the bloodstream undigested or only partially digested, the antibodies bind with the food. These antibody-food complexes then travel to any location in the body through the bloodstream where they can cause problems. Several factors can cause the "leaky gut syndrome."

Toxins that include alcohol, nonsteroidal anti-inflammatory drugs (aspirin, ibuprofen, arthritis medications), drugs used to treat cancer, corticosteroid drugs, radiation therapy and especially antibiotics can all increase intestinal permeability. Finally "unfriendly "organisms present in the digestive tract which involve parasites, yeasts such as Candida albicans, salmonella bacteria and many others can also cause increased intestinal permeability.

Formula feeding infants and not breast-feeding can cause allergies as babies have a higher intestinal permeability than older children or adults. Cow's milk is highly allergenic and should not be given to babies.

Nutritional deficiencies contribute to allergies.

Bowel and liver diseases are contributors.

Eye for an Eye Diet nutrition and lifestyle advice:

Follow the nutritional advice in this book and target specific nutrition to strengthen your genetic eye constitution as explained in Part 3.

Support the liver's ability to deal with allergens by including foods high in methionine, choline, inositol and Vitamin C.

Avoid preservatives, artificial colors and flavors and other harmful additives in foods. Foods that you are allergic or sensitive to should be avoided.

Eliminate sugar and refined flour from the diet.

Avoid anti-inflammatory drugs and medications for allergies.

Avoid smoky environments or smog and take frequent walks in nature. Minimize contact with respiratory irritants, such as smoke, dust, molds and volatile chemicals. Consider moving if the air is generally bad where you live.

Avoid all cows milk products including milk, cheese, ice cream, chocolate and cream. Milk protein increases mucous secretion in the respiratory passages and may also contribute to the allergic component of asthma. Not only does this mean avoiding these products, it also means reading labels to be sure that other food products do not contain any milk. Bread for instance, often includes nonfat dry milk as an ingredient. Be careful of possible food sensitivities to peanuts, shellfish, egg whites, caffeine, cheese, citrus fruits and wheat.

Drink plenty of "live" water free of chlorine and fluoride to keep the respiratory tract secretions fluid.

Vegetables (dark green leafy variety are best) and fruits should make up a large part of your diet because of the vitamins, minerals and fiber they contain. Essential fatty acids are important to intestinal integrity, and are especially high in fatty fish, such as salmon and mackerel, as well as cold pressed oils such as flaxseed oil.

Include plenty of foods high in bioflavonoids as they have been found to inhibit both histamine release and the allergic response to allergens.

Supplements that can assist allergies include Lactobacillus acidophilus, Chlorella and Slippery Elm (*Ulmus fulva*) for the digestive tract. Methionine, choline (Lecithin) and inositol supplements will assist liver function. Digestive enzymes help to break down food into smaller less allergenic molecules, which can decrease your reaction to the foods you eat. Omega-3 fatty acid supplements can reduce allergic symptoms as can Vitamin C. Quercetin, one of the bioflavonoids can inhibit the release of histamine and other mediators of inflammation in allergies. Vitamin B-complex provides nutritional support for stress and support for the adrenal gland, which is necessary for production of cortisol, the body's natural anti-inflammatory hormone. Herbs such as Licorice (*Glycyrrhiza glabra*) nourish the adrenal glands, Echinacea and Garlic boost the immune system, Milk thistle (*Silybum marianum*) protects the liver and ginger reduces the inflammation caused by allergic reactions.

Arthritis

There are two main types of arthritis, rheumatoid arthritis, a chronic inflammatory condition that affects not just the joints but also the entire body and osteoarthritis, the most common type where the weight-bearing joints and the joints of the hand are most commonly affected. Symptoms of osteoarthritis include formation of large bone spurs in the joint margins and cartilage destruction that result in deformity, pain and limited movement of the joint. In my opinion, most medical intervention promotes the progression of the disease and drug treatments with aspirin, anti-inflammatory drugs and corticosteroids have serious side effects including gastrointestinal upsets, headaches, tinnitus and dizziness. It is interesting to note that arthritis is not commonly found in societies with a primitive diet.

Genetic eye constitutions at greatest risk:

Lymphatic hyper-active, Lymphatic hypo-active, Kidney lymphatic, Hydrolymphatic and the Connective tissue types often are predisposed to arthritis although it can occur in any of the genetic types.

Possible causes that contribute to this disease

High acidity in the body
Liver disease or congestion
Kidney problems
Sedentary lifestyle
Food allergies
Leaky gut syndrome (increased intestinal permeability)
High meat, sugar and white flour diet
Low water intake
Insufficient Vitamin C

Eye for an Eye Diet nutrition and lifestyle advice:
Follow the nutritional advice in this book and target specific nutrition to strengthen your genetic eye constitution as explained in Part 3.

Ensure beneficial foods for arthritis sufferers such as alkaline foods that include plenty of vegetables, seaweed, parsley, carrots, almonds, blackberries, olive oil, sesame seeds, celery, bananas, avocado, alfalfa sprouts, kelp, brown rice, seeds, garlic, onions, figs and cherries.

Eat plenty of salmon, tuna, mackerel and sardines, as they are rich sources of beneficial fats that decrease inflammation and tissue destruction.

Include foods high in antioxidants, especially those high in beta-carotene, Vitamin C and E. and in the liver and kidney nutrients, methionine, choline and inositol.

Drink celery and carrot juice.

Avoid acid-producing foods such as sugar, white flour, meat, refined carbohydrates and saturated fats.

Avoid milk products other than soured milk or natural yogurt.

Reduce meat intake as meat has a high phosphorus-to-calcium ratio that can have negative effects on the body if taken in excess and it increases acidity.

Avoid salt, coffee, alcohol, vinegar and citrus fruits (except lemons)

Be careful of artificial flavors, colors and preservatives in the foods that you eat.

Drink plenty of "live" water free of chlorine and fluoride.

Avoid using aspirin or other anti-inflammatory drugs.

Supplements such as Lactobacillus acidophilus, Chlorela and Slippery Elm bark (*Ulmus fulva*) assist the Leaky gut syndrome and reduce free radical formation, lecithin and milk thistle (*Silybum marianum*) for the kidney and liver, and Cod liver supplements, Yucca, B-complex, Omega-3 fatty acids, Vitamin C, E, Glucosamine sulfate, chondroitin sulfate and Evening Primrose oil have all been found to benefit regeneration of tissue and reduce inflammation in the arthritic patient.

Some anti-inflammatory herbs that can assist with inflammation and pain are Angelica (*Angelica archangelica*), Black Cohosh (*Cimicifuga racemosa*), Feverfew (*Chrysanthemum parthenium*), Ginger (*Zingiber officinale*), Bromelain, a chemical in pineapple and Wild Yam (*Dioscorea villosa*)

Engage in regular exercise preferably swimming as it places the least strain on the joints.

Asthma

Asthma is a chronic inflammatory condition of the airways of the lungs. It affects millions of children and adults around the world. When the sensitive airways of these people are exposed to certain "triggers" (cigarette smoke, emotional stress, colds and flu, exercise, inhaled allergens such as pollen, animal hair or dust mites, some foods, food preservatives, colors or certain drugs), their airways narrow, making it hard for them to breathe. As a result the inside lining of the airways is often red and swollen, the muscle around the airway tightens and extra mucus is often produced. No one knows really why asthma occurs and its causes vary from individual to individual. Most medical treatments of asthma involve the use of bronchial dilating drugs that only treat the symptoms and not the cause.

Genetic eye constitutions at greatest risk:

Lymphatic hyper-active, Kidney lymphatic, Hydro-lymphatic, Hematogenic and Plethoric types are at greatest risk but asthma can occur in any genetic type.

Possible causes that contribute to this disease:

Food sensitivities: peanuts, nuts, shellfish, fish, and egg, citrus, wheat (due to gluten which is hard to digest), chocolate and milk (which promote the formation of mucous within the body).

Diet: Excess sweets, dairy products and meat.

Hypochlorhydria: Lack of hydrochloric acid in the stomach results in improper digestion, which may create food allergies and food sensitivities.

Food Additives: Artificial dyes, colors and preservatives or monosodium glutamate widely used in foods, beverages and drugs can contribute to cause asthma attacks in some individuals.

Spinal problems can cause a diminished nerve supply to the lungs and bronchi.

Emotional stress can bring on asthmatic attacks.

Vitamin and mineral deficiencies: Selenium and Magnesium. Selenium is very important in a biochemical pathway that is responsible for reducing bronchial constriction. Magnesium controls smooth muscle tone and has been found to cause relaxation of bronchial smooth muscle in both acute and chronic asthma cases. Other common deficiencies associated with asthma are Vitamin B especially B12 and B6, C and Vitamin E.

Eye for an Eye Diet nutrition and lifestyle advice:

Follow the nutritional advice in this book and target specific nutrition to strengthen your genetic eye constitution as explained in Part 3.

Avoid all cows milk products including milk, cheese, ice cream, chocolate and cream. Milk protein increases mucous secretion in the respiratory passages and may also contribute to the allergic component of asthma. Not only does this mean avoiding these products, it also means reading labels to be sure that other food products do not contain any milk. Bread often includes nonfat dry milk as an ingredient. Be careful of possible food sensitivities to peanuts, shellfish, egg whites, caffeine, cheese, citrus fruits and wheat.

Eat a predominantly vegetarian diet that include beets, broccoli, brussel sprouts, lentils, peas, onions, garlic and asparagus as well as plenty of sea fish like salmon and tuna. Eat plenty of almonds, soybeans, legumes and green leafy vegetables, as they are high in magnesium. Include foods high in selenium such as alfalfa, cashews, garlic and tuna. Include antioxidant foods high in Vitamin A, C, E to defend against free radicals, which can cause irritation and inflammation in asthmatics. Sources are fresh fruits and vegetables, seeds and nuts.

Eliminate sugar and refined flour from the diet and avoid preservatives, colors and artificial flavors in foods.

Some nutritional supplements that can provide some assistance include: Vitamin B-complex, C, E, beta-carotene, magnesium, selenium and the bioflavonoids. To restore stomach and digestion function, supplements of Lactobacillus acidophilus, Chlorella and digestive enzymes that include betaine HCL and pepsin can offer assistance. Fish oil capsules have an anti-inflammatory effect. Peppermint tea can provide some relief.

Drink plenty of "live" water free of chlorine and fluoride to keep the respiratory tract secretions fluid.

Perform deep breathing exercises daily.

Avoid smoky environments or smog and take frequent walks in nature. Minimize contact with respiratory irritants, such as smoke, dust, molds and volatile chemicals. Consider moving if the air is generally bad where you live.

Engage in regular exercise (be careful if exercise triggers your asthma) especially swimming to clear mucus from the airway.

Have some manipulative therapy done on the chest and back such as Bowen therapy, which can be very effective for asthmatic conditions.

Avoid becoming dependent on drugs such as bronchial dilators or corticosteroids.

Engage in meditation or other relaxation methods to reduce stress or anxiety.

Cancer

The incidence of this disease is rising in alarming proportions and modern medicine seems to have only a handful of methods to deal with cancer such as radiation therapy, chemotherapy and removal of tumors by operation. Unfortunately all of these drastic measures tax the immune system and introduce harmful toxic substances into a body that is in desperate need of detoxification. Removing a tumor or liquidating cancer cells is just superficial treatment. Look for the root of the problem and the possible reasons why cancer has started in the first place.

Genetic eye constitutions at greatest risk:
I have found the Lymphatic Hypo-active, Neurolymphatic, Plethoric and Hormonal types are at greatest risk but cancer can occur in any of the genetic types.

Possible causes that contribute to this disease:
Genetic weaknesses in the detoxification organs like the liver, kidneys, digestive tract, skin, lungs or lymphatic system
Ingestion of artificial chemicals, preservatives, hormones and colors in food and water supply
Drugs
Radiation
Periods of intense stress, psychological trauma, unhappiness, grief, resentment, depression or dissatisfaction
Nutritional deficits and ingestion of refined or processed foods
Poor lifestyle habits
Lack of exercise
Lack of contact with nature

Eye for an Eye Diet nutrition and lifestyle advice:
Follow the nutritional advice in this book and target specific nutrition to strengthen your genetic eye constitution as explained in Part 3.

The body is in need of detoxification and the removal of toxins from the body should be first on the list of priorities. This means watching out for artificial chemicals, colors and preservatives in foods that can tax the detoxification organs such as the liver. Eating organic food helps reduce exposure to herbicides, pesticides and hormones, which may increase cancer risk. Protect the liver by herbs such as milk thistle (*Silybum marianum*) and strengthen the liver by foods high in methionine, choline, inositol and Vitamin C. Improve digestion and absorption by supplements of lactobacillus acidophilus and Chlorella. Other vitamins and supplements that can assist are the antioxidants Vitamins A, C, E and selenium, zinc, B complex, Beta-carotene, Omega 3 fatty acids and Evening Primrose oil.

Eat fresh, unrefined, unprocessed foods free of hormones. Include fruits, vegetables, whole grains, soy, legumes, cold-water fish (salmon, tuna, sardine and mackerel), olive oil, green tea, garlic, onions, tomatoes, shitake mushrooms, almonds, ginger, nonfat yogurt, seaweed and fiber. Drink a few glasses of freshly squeezed vegetable juice daily. Proper nutrition supports the immune system, starves cancer cells, and provides macro and micronutrients that the body requires.

Avoid sugar, dairy products, refined foods, fried foods, junk foods, caffeine, alcohol, nitrates and limit high-fat foods high in saturated and trans fats, particularly meat and margarines, which have been implicated in colon, rectal, prostate and endometrial cancers. Also avoid smoked, pickled and salt-cured foods due to their nitrosamine content.

Drink plenty of clean fresh "live" water daily without chlorine and fluoride.

Get plenty of sleep. If you are having trouble sleeping use herbs like Valerian (*Valeriana officinalis*).

Skin brushing helps to detoxify the body by improving circulation of the lymph and blood. After bathing, stroke the skin with a brush toward the heart.

Engage in massage therapy, which will reduce pain, relieve stress, promote blood and lymph flow and stimulate the nervous system. One of the best methods I know and have used for many years is Bowen therapy massage developed originally in Australia.

Exercise regularly to reduce stress and to increase energy, vitality, circulation and waste product removal. Barefoot walks in nature are recommended.

Psychological counseling, support groups and even psychotherapy make up a critically important aspect of therapy for this disease. Often a traumatic psychological event in a person's life or a prolonged period of intense stress may trigger the appearance of cancer one to two years later.

Chronic fatigue

Chronic fatigue syndrome, often known as myalgic encephalomyelitis seems to be a mysterious disease, which has been growing in incidence over the past decade. No clear cause has been found yet and sufferers appear healthy and frequently have normal blood test results. Their main symptom is a feeling of severe fatigue, which is often debilitating, affecting physical and mental function and persisting for six months or more. There are often muscle aches, mood and sleep disturbances, a recurrent sore throat, enlarged glands in the neck and a slightly high temperature. It seems most likely that chronic fatigue syndrome represents not one disease but a combination of symptoms that may be caused by several different diseases. A number of infectious and immunological causes have been proposed, but the cause or causes of CFS to date remain unknown.

Genetic eye constitutions at greatest risk:

Lymphatic hypo-active, Kidney lymphatic, Neurolymphatic, Hydro-lymphatic, Plethoric, Hormonal and the Connective tissue types often suffer from chronic fatigue although it can occur in any of the genetic types.

Possible causes that contribute to this disease:

Weakness in the detoxification organs of the body (liver, kidney, digestive tract, lymphatic system, skin, lungs)

Viruses: mononucleosis (Epstien barr virus EBV), Herpes virus, Cytomegalovirus and others
Yeasts, moulds: Candida albicans and others
Bacteria (Chlamydia), Parasites
A large proportion of people with CFS have been shown to have defective mitochondria (the power producers) in their cells.
Reduced blood flow and circulation problems
Neuroendocrine dysfunction
Disturbances in the immune system
Hormonal abnormalities (adrenal and thyroid glands)
Diet, food allergies and intolerances
Environmental toxins and excess toxicity in the body
Excessive stress
Mercury amalgam fillings

Eye for an Eye Diet nutrition and lifestyle advice:

Follow the nutritional advice in this book and target specific nutrition to strengthen your genetic eye constitution as explained in Part 3.

Ensure that you support all the detoxification organs of the body. Include foods high in methionine, choline and inositol and Vitamin C for the liver and the kidneys and assist bowel function with natural yogurt or soured milk products.

Supplements that will assist in detoxification of the body include Lactobacillus acidophilus, Chlorella and Slippery Elm bark (*Ulmus fulva*) to aid in digestion and absorption as well as lecithin for the liver, kidneys and nervous system. The antioxidant vitamins C, E, beta-carotene and selenium can counteract free radical formation.

Assist the immune system and liver function by including supplements of Echinacea, dandelion (*Taraxacum officinale*), milk thistle (*Silybum marianum*) Golden Seal (not during pregnancy), Shiitake (*Lentinus edodes*) and Maitake mushrooms (*Grifola frondosa*) and Garlic.

Herbs such as Gingko biloba are beneficial for circulation especially to the brain area and bioflavonoids (rutin or hesperidin) found in skins of fruits and vegetables and berries or as supplements will assist in strengthening the capillaries.

To improve energy levels ensure foods high in Vitamin B-complex, Vitamin C, Iron, magnesium and beta-carotene. Supplements of Coenzyme Q-10 can also assist.

Eat smaller meals five times a day.

Ensure adequate rest and moderate exercise, but not to the point of exhaustion.

Perform five minutes of deep breathing exercises every day.

Reduce stress in your daily life and do not push yourself too hard.

Do not smoke.
Have your amalgam fillings removed by a specialist who knows what they are doing.

Constipation or diarrhea

The incidence of constipation and diarrhea in our society is in epidemic proportions. Just take a look how many laxative products there are on the market. The majority of problems with constipation and diarrhea stem from diet and lifestyle factors. Often we view constipation and diarrhea as diseases yet they are generally only symptoms that are alerting us of something that is not right in the body.

Genetic eye constitutions at greatest risk:

Lymphatic hypo-active, Neurolymphatic, Hematogenic, Plethoric, Hormonal and the Connective Tissue types are at greatest risk but constipation or diarrhea can occur in any of the genetic types.

Possible causes that contribute to these conditions:

Insufficient water intake
Disturbances in the micro floral environment of the intestines
Lack of fiber in the diet
Diet high in meat and animal fat and refined sugar
Irritable bowel syndrome and digestive diseases
Lack of exercise and weak abdominal muscles
Liver, pancreas or gall bladder problems
Emotional stress
Viral or bacterial Infection /parasites
Food allergies / food intolerance / lactose intolerance
Certain drugs (pain medications, antacids, antidepressants, iron supplements)
Abuse of laxatives interferes with the colon's natural ability to contract.
Under active thyroid gland and other hormonal disturbances
Changes in life such as aging or pregnancy may cause constipation
Nerve damage to the intestine
Specific diseases such as multiple sclerosis, diabetes and lupus can cause constipation
Traveling long distances
Excess coffee, alcohol or black tea
Overuse of sweeteners such as sorbitol
Irregular eating habits, overeating or not chewing food thoroughly
Not going to the toilet when nature calls
Intestinal obstruction or diverticulosis

Eye for an Eye Diet nutrition and lifestyle advice:

Follow the nutritional advice in this book and target specific nutrition to strengthen your genetic eye constitution as explained in Part 3.

Drink at least two liters of fresh clean water daily.

Ensure that you have 1 to 3 bowel movements a day and always go to the toilet when nature calls.

Eat regular meals and chew food thoroughly.

Ensure plenty of fruits and vegetables in the diet.

Ensure adequate fiber in the diet by including foods such as whole grains, dates, bananas, broccoli and beans.

Reduce high meat intake, sugar, white flour products and milk products other than soured milk or natural yogurt.

For constipation include foods that have natural laxative properties such as almonds, apricots, avocado, dates, figs, flaxseed, grapes, mangos, olives, papayas, parsley, pineapple, prunes, rhubarb, soybeans, pears, turnips and walnuts. Juices such as prune and apple-pear are excellent as natural laxatives as well.

Supplements that can assist are psyllium husks, Bromelain, Lactobacillus acidophilus, Chlorella, pectin, slippery elm (*Ulmus fulva*), chamomile, Betaine hydrochloride to assist the digestion of proteins in the stomach for constipation and Vitamin C. Goldenseal (*Hydrastis canadensis*) is particularly helpful in diarrhea caused by bacterial agents.

Strengthen the liver and bile production by eating foods high in methionine, choline and inositol, using herbs such as dandelion (*Taraxacum officinale*) and milk thistle (*Silybum marianum*) and being careful of chemical preservatives, artificial colors and flavors.

Engage in regular exercise and do sit ups or crunches to strengthen abdominal muscles.

Avoid chemical laxatives, drugs and medications.

Avoid, coffee, black tea, and sweeteners such as sorbitol.

Reduce stress by relaxation methods

Depression

Clinical depression, one of the most common psychiatric disorders, affects the mind, body, behavior and mood and can strike at any age, although it is most common in early middle age and among the elderly. Women experience depression at roughly twice the rate of men and it is often found in patients with cardiac disease. If untreated it can lead to serious consequences including suicide attempts. Depression has a very dramatic detrimental affect on the immune system and the healing and regenerative capacity of the body. Although depression is a complicated disorder that has yet to be completely understood there are several nutritional and lifestyle factors that often can assist in prevention or even elimination of this common problem in modern society.

Genetic eye constitutions at greatest risk:
Lymphatic hypo-active, Neurolymphatic, Hydro-lymphatic, Plethoric and Hormonal types often suffer from depression but it can affect any of the genetic types.

Possible causes that contribute to this disease:
- Genetic predisposition
- Excessive stress, emotional traumas or life changes (divorce, loss of a loved one)
- Heart and circulatory disorders
- Hormonal imbalances
- Chemical imbalance in the brain that involves the neurotransmitters dopamine, norepinephrine, and serotonin
- Injuries to the head or neurological disorders (Parkinson's, stroke, Alzheimer's)
- Nutritional deficits such as vitamin or mineral deficiencies (especially biotin, folic acid, Vitamin B, Vitamin C, calcium, copper, iron, magnesium or potassium)
- Excess caffeine, sugar or alcohol
- Food allergies
- Toxic digestive tract and Candidiasis
- Weakness in the detoxification organs such as the liver, kidneys and lungs leading to accumulation of toxins in the brain
- Certain medications and drugs (sleeping pills, anti-anxiety medications, heart and blood pressure medications)
- Heavy metal exposure (Lead, cadmium, mercury)
- Lack of exercise
- Lack of sunlight

Eye for an Eye Diet nutrition and lifestyle advice:
Follow the nutritional advice in this book and target specific nutrition to strengthen your genetic eye constitution as explained in Part 3.

Eat plenty of fresh green vegetables, whole grain cereals and beans, seeds, sprouts, alfalfa and soy protein.

Special attention should be paid to avoid foods that may cause allergic reaction, tiredness, heaviness or any other bad feelings.

Assist the heart with foods high in Omega-3 fatty acids such as salmon, tuna and sardines and foods high in Vitamin C (black currant, broccoli, parsley, peppers, fruit) and the bioflavonoids (berries, skins of fruits and vegetables, buckwheat).

Eat foods high in zinc (ginger, sunflower and pumpkin seeds, whole grains, liver), the B-vitamins (legumes, nuts, beans, sprouts, yeast, almonds, green vegetables, liver, salmon), iron (parsley, apricots, soybeans, liver), magnesium (almonds, cashews, whole grains) and potassium (bananas, vegetables, avocado, dates, nuts, raisins), as deficiency in these nutrients has been associated with depression.

Avoid any processed food, artificial colors, preservatives, canned foods, dairy products or white flour products.

Avoid coffee, sugar, alcohol and smoking.

Drink at least two liters of fresh clean water daily to allow for removal of toxins from the body.

Supplements that can assist in depression include: Vitamin B-complex, Vitamin C, Lactobacillus acidophilus, Chlorella, lecithin, Omega-3 fatty acids, a mineral supplement and Evening primrose oil.

Some herbal supplements that can assist include Siberian ginseng, gingko biloba, licorice (*Glycyrrhiza glabra*), Saint-John's wort (*Hypericum perforatum*) which may increase the availability of serotonin in the brain.

Regular physical exercise should be a part of any therapy for depression. Some studies have shown that aerobic exercise performed three times a week can be as effective as psychotherapy in treating depression.

Avoid antidepressants and other drugs and medications unless absolutely necessary.

Ensure plenty of early-morning sun to help lift depression and spend as much time as possible outdoors in nature. Avoid too much time in concrete buildings, at your computer and avoid using microwave ovens or mobile phones.

Remove sources of aluminum and mercury (amalgam dental fillings) and other heavy metals.

Deep breathing exercises, massage or acupressure are excellent in aiding relaxation and promoting good oxygenation of the entire body.

Ensure adequate sleep.

Accept yourself and be accepting of others. Get involved in volunteer work to take your mind off of yourself and your problems.

Diabetes

Diabetes mellitus is a disorder resulting from absolute insulin deficiency or abnormalities in insulin secretion and function. Diabetes can also result from pancreatic disease, hormonal disorders or genetic syndromes. Due to our neglect of nutrition and poor lifestyle habits, it has become one of the fastest growing diseases in modern civilizations. It is however, rare to see in underdeveloped countries.

Insulin, a hormone produced in the pancreas, is essential for the body to metabolize glucose (blood sugar) to maintain the proper level in the blood and help regulate the breakdown of fats.

When glucose is not properly metabolized (broken down), too much remains in the blood and a condition called hyperglycemia results. When this occurs, the body begins to metabolize fat, resulting in increased ketone production and a disruption in the body's acid-alkaline balance. Symptoms of hyperglycemia include excessive urination and thirst, weight loss, blurry vision and fatigue.

Diabetes is classified as type 1 diabetes mellitus (insulin dependent) and type 2 diabetes mellitus (non–insulin dependent).

Type 1 diabetes mellitus usually occurs in adolescence or childhood and is sometimes called juvenile onset diabetes. It is most common in patients under the age of 30 and results from the destruction of insulin-producing cells in the pancreas. Patients diagnosed with type 1 diabetes mellitus must use injected insulin to live but with nutritional strategies the amount of insulin needed may decrease and it may be possible in some cases to be completely free of the need to inject insulin.

Type 2 diabetes mellitus results from impaired insulin secretion and the decreased ability of insulin to function. It occurs most commonly in patients over the age of 30. Patients with type 2 diabetes may use insulin and other drugs to help control their blood sugar, although the condition also can be effectively controlled through proper diet and exercise.

Diabetes mellitus can lead to chronic complications such as cardiovascular disease, circulatory disease in the limbs, retinal disease, cataracts, kidney disease, nerve damage, foot ulcers and an increased risk for infection.

Genetic eye constitutions at greatest risk:

Neurolymphatic, Mixed and the Hormonal types are at the greatest risk but diabetes can occur in any of the genetic types.

Possible causes that contribute to this disease:

The body may not produce enough insulin, insulin receptors may be inadequate or function improperly, or the insulin produced by the body may be defective or destroyed before it can do its job.

Obesity

Excessive consumption of simple carbohydrates such as sugar

Lack of exercise or sedentary lifestyle

Liver or pancreatic disease

Exposure to cow's milk in early life or food-borne chemical toxins

Lack of chromium, B vitamins and some minerals (copper, manganese, magnesium and zinc) in the diet

Low fiber in the diet

Irregular eating patterns
Stress
Some drugs
People who do not get enough sleep on a regular basis may become less sensitive to insulin

Eye for an Eye Diet nutrition and lifestyle advice:

Follow the nutritional advice in this book and target specific nutrition to strengthen your genetic eye constitution as explained in Part 3.

Eat less more often (5 small meals a day) to reduce stress on the pancreas and insulin production.

Eliminate sugar, fructose, glucose, corn syrup, sweet and dried fruits, white bread or white flour products, potatoes, honey, molasses, maple syrup, fruit juice or concentrate as these forms of sugar increase urinary chromium excretion as well as increase requirements for insulin.

Avoid coffee, fatty or fried foods and alcohol.

Beneficial foods include a primarily vegetarian diet with complex carbohydrates, brown rice, tofu, soybeans, legumes, fish, walnuts, sardine oil, vegetables, kelp, sesame seeds and lecithin.

Ensure a high fiber, high complex carbohydrate diet, which may assist diabetics to eventually decrease their insulin medication. Fiber consumption with meals slows glucose absorption and reduces insulin demands. Fiber supplements of Guar gum, psyllium and pectin may be helpful.

Add foods high in the minerals chromium, copper, manganese, magnesium and zinc as they may be deficient and are associated with glucose intolerance and phosphorus and potassium high foods (garlic, nuts, vegetables, seeds) as they are associated with insulin resistance.

Strengthen the liver by foods high in methionine, choline, inositol and Vitamin C.

Ensure foods high in organic chromium such as whole grains, natural rice and brewer's yeast.

Prevent retinopathy associated with diabetes by supplements of Evening primrose oil, vitamin E and bilberry (*Vaccinium myrtillus*).

Strengthen the kidneys by supplements of lecithin and rutin.

Improve circulation by supplements of gingko biloba, grapeseed extract, omega-3 fatty acids, vitamin C and bioflavonoids.

Other supplements that are beneficial are Vitamin C, B-complex, Vanadium, Garlic, Ginseng, fenugreek seeds (*Trigonella foenum-graecum*) and digestive enzymes.

Avoid smoking.

Ensure regular exercise, relaxation and adequate sleep.

Digestive disorders

Digestive disorders are probably one of the most important signs of serious health problems. As we have learned, without effective digestion our cells will not receive the nutrients they require and disease will eventually ensue if the problem is not rectified. Digestive disorders are very common and include inflammatory bowel diseases such as Crohn's disease and ulcerative colitis as well as diverticular disease, intestinal polyps, indigestion, flatulence, ulcers, irritable bowel syndrome, gastritis, leaky gut syndrome, appendicitis, heartburn caused by reflux and lactose intolerance. Associated problems include pancreatitis, liver or gall bladder disease and hemorrhoids. As you can see, this is a very impressive list with an enormous percentage of the population affected and a medical drug available for each one of these conditions. What we often fail to realize is that almost all of these conditions have their root cause in improper diet and lifestyle choices.

Genetic eye constitutions at greatest risk:
Lymphatic hypo-active, Neurolymphatic, Hematogenic, Mixed, Plethoric, Hormonal and the Connective Tissue types often suffer from digestive disorders but they can be seen in any of the genetic types.

Possible causes that contribute to this disease:
Antibiotic use and some drugs
Low fiber diet
Liver, gall bladder or pancreatic disease
Nutritional deficits
Stress
Chemicals ingested with food such as preservatives and artificial colors
Excess fried foods, coffee and alcohol
High sugar and refined carbohydrate diet as well as excess white flour products
Cigarette smoking
Constipation

Eye for an Eye Diet nutrition and lifestyle advice:
Follow the nutritional advice in this book and target specific nutrition to strengthen your genetic eye constitution as explained in Part 3.
Eat preferably five small regular meals a day and chew foods thoroughly.
Eat plenty of fruits and vegetables and raw salads.
Reduce excess meat intake, alcohol and coffee.
Eat your last meal at least 2 or 3 hours before bedtime.
Strengthen the liver and bile production by eating foods high in methionine, choline, inositol and Vitamin C, using herbs such as dandelion (*Taraxacum*

officinale) and milk thistle (*Silybum marianum*) and being careful of chemical preservatives, artificial colors and flavors.

Stop smoking.

Avoid milk products except natural yogurt and soured milk.

Avoid sugar, sweets and white flour products

Avoid the use of laxatives, antacids and other medications for digestive problems.

Ensure that there is more fiber in your diet.

Drink at least two liters of fresh clean water daily and avoid fluids with meals.

Supplements that can assist are Lactobacillus acidophilus, Chlorella, Slippery Elm (*Ulmus fulva*), psyllium, zinc, digestive enzymes and Bromelain (a simple digestive enzyme extracted from pineapple).

Herbals such as chamomile, ginger, peppermint and valerian (*Valerian officinalis*) help soothe the bowel and calm the intestinal tract.

Regular exercise will assist peristalsis, prevent constipation and improve digestion and circulation to the digestive organs.

Relieve stress by ensuring time for relaxation every day.

Eczema (atopic dermatitis)

Eczema is a very common skin disease today and occurs at any age but most often affects infants who normally grow out of it by the age of two. Eczema typically affects the wrists, face, upper chest, back of knees, elbows and ankles. Most drugs that are used in dealing with eczema just take away the symptoms and do not treat the cause and can further suppress the disease. The problem with eczema, as with any other skin problems, lies inside the body and is often due to weakness of the body's detoxification organs.

Genetic eye constitutions at greatest risk:

Lymphatic hyper-active, Lymphatic hypo-active, Kidney lymphatic, Hematogenic and Plethoric types are at greatest risk but it can occur in any of the genetic types.

Possible causes that contribute to this disease:

A toxic bowel or weak liver function

Food allergies to milk products or sugar are common

Hypochlorhydria: Lack of hydrochloric acid in the stomach results in improper digestion, which may create food allergies and food sensitivities

Stress and anxiety

Excess alcohol

Family history of allergies, asthma or hay fever

Lack of sunshine and fresh air
Contact with substances that irritate the skin chemically such detergents, soaps, diesel or engine oils, strong chemicals or cleaners

Eye for an Eye Diet nutrition and lifestyle advice:
Follow the nutritional advice in this book and target specific nutrition to strengthen your genetic eye constitution as explained in Part 3.

Select alkaline foods in the diet such as those high in calcium, potassium, sodium, magnesium and iron. High calcium foods include almonds, egg yolk, green leafy vegetables, soybeans, sesame seeds, parsley and dried figs. High potassium foods include bananas, apricots, avocado, dates, almonds, cashews, pecans, raisins, sardines and sunflower seeds. High magnesium foods include nuts, whole grain foods, almonds, cashews, molasses, soybeans, spinach, beets and broccoli. High sodium foods include celery, liver, olives, peas, tuna and sardines. High iron foods include liver, apricots, oysters, parsley, sesame seeds, soybeans, sunflower seeds and almonds.

Avoid citrus fruits, peanuts, sugar, refined flour, milk products and excess animal fats.

Supplements that can assist include essential fatty acids such as Evening primrose oil supplements, omega 3 supplements, flaxseed oil, Vitamin A (beta carotene), selenium, burdock root (*Arctium lappa*), liquorice and zinc. Methionine, choline and inositol as well as Vitamin C can assist the liver function while Lactobacillus and Chlorella and digestive enzymes can assist bowel function.

Avoid exposure to chemicals and strong detergents.

Allow the skin to breathe. Wear natural fabrics only. Ensure regular exposure of skin to sun and fresh air. Do not allow the skin to sweat under clothing. Topical applications include cod liver oil, cucumber juice, lemon, an oatmeal bath or a chamomile compress to relieve the itch. Avoid long baths and only in lukewarm water. Avoid cortisone creams.

Make sure that newborns are breast-fed not formula fed.

Engage in meditation or other relaxation methods to reduce stress or anxiety.

Heart disease

Heart disease or atherosclerosis is characterized by changes that cause a narrowing of the arteries due to accumulation of fatty deposits that can decrease oxygen and nutrient supply to the heart muscle. It is one of the leading causes of death in our society. While the consequences eventually often show up as angina pectoris or heart attack and result in the administration of drugs such as nitroglycerine pills or procedures such as by-pass surgery, the best way to avoid this disease is prevention by quality nutrition and lifestyle decisions.

Genetic eye constitutions at greatest risk:
Lymphatic hypo-active, Kidney lymphatic, Hydro-lymphatic, Hematogenic, Plethoric and the Connective Tissue types are at greatest risk but heart disease can occur in any of the genetic types.

Possible causes that contribute to this disease:
Genetic heart weaknesses
High cholesterol
Liver or Gall bladder disease
Vitamin C deficiency
High intake of refined carbohydrates like white sugar
High saturated fat intake
Low fiber in the diet
Smoking and high alcohol intake
Excess coffee intake
Sedentary lifestyle
Stress and sadness
Obesity

Eye for an Eye Diet nutrition and lifestyle advice:
Follow the nutritional advice in this book and target specific nutrition to strengthen your genetic eye constitution as explained in Part 3.

Increase your intake of fish especially salmon, tuna and sardines, as they are high in Omega-3 fatty acids that reduce the risk of heart disease.

Increase your intake of fruits and vegetables especially those high in Vitamin C and beta-carotene.

Reduce the amount of saturated fat, which means reducing animal fats from meat, cheese and milk products. Saturated fats increase platelet aggregation (binding together) as well as increasing the chance of embolism, while polyunsaturated fats, particularly lineolic and linolenic acids, have the opposite effect.

Strengthen the liver to assist bile production so that cholesterol metabolism in the body is improved. Include foods high in methionine, choline, inositol and Vitamin C and use olive oil regularly. Include herbs such as Milk thistle (*Silybum marianum*) and dandelion (*Taraxacum officinale*) to improve liver function.

Other supplements that can assist in heart disease are: Garlic, Omega-3 fatty acids, Vitamin C, Natural Vitamin E, lysine, chromium, magnesium, potassium, gingko biloba, psyllium, soy lecithin, Co-enzyme Q-10 and Vitamin B-complex.

Eliminate sugar and refined flour from the diet and avoid preservatives, colors and artificial flavors in foods.

Avoid trans fatty acids that are found in hydrogenated vegetable oils such as margarines and vegetable shortenings. Avoid fried foods.

Ensure complex carbohydrates and adequate fiber in the diet.

Drink plenty of "live" water free of chlorine and fluoride and avoid coffee.

Include garlic, onions, ginger and alfalfa regularly in the diet as they can inhibit clot formation and reduce cholesterol deposits.

Engage in regular exercise to strengthen the cardiovascular system and to prevent obesity.

Avoid smoking and excess alcohol, which have been found to be significant risk factors for heart disease.

Avoid excess salt and watch out for hidden salt found in most processed foods.

Use relaxation methods to deal with the build-up of stress, which can have negative effects on the heart.

High blood pressure (Hypertension)

Blood pressure is the force of blood against the walls of arteries. Blood pressure has two components, systolic pressure (the force that blood exerts on the artery walls when the heart is pumping) over the diastolic pressure (the force that remains when the heart relaxes between beats). The measurement is written one above the other, with the systolic number on top and the diastolic number on the bottom. For example, a blood pressure measurement of 120/80 mm Hg (millimeters of mercury) is expressed verbally as "120 over 80." Blood pressure varies from person to person and by age as well as from left arm to right arm. High blood pressure is usually termed as higher than 135/90. The problem when blood pressure gets too high is that it can damage the heart, blood vessels, kidneys and other organs.

Genetic eye constitutions at greatest risk:

Lymphatic hypo-active, Kidney lymphatic, Hydro-lymphatic, Hematogenic, Plethoric, and the Hormonal types are at greatest risk but high blood pressure can occur in any of the genetic types.

Possible causes that contribute to this disease:

High salt intake
Arteriosclerosis
Weakness in the veins and arteries
Liver and kidney disease
Some drugs
Excess blood
Stress
Excess caffeine

Smoking
Low fiber intake
High saturated fat diet
High intake of sugar and refined carbohydrates
Obesity
Heavy metals and toxic chemicals
Diabetes

Eye for an Eye Diet nutrition and lifestyle advice:

Follow the nutritional advice in this book and target specific nutrition to strengthen your genetic eye constitution as explained in Part 3.

Ensure foods high in potassium as they assist to prevent and control blood pressure. Some good sources are apricots, bananas, avocado, dates, nuts, raisins and sunflower seeds.

Magnesium deficiency has been implicated in high blood pressure so ensure plenty of green leafy vegetables, whole grains, legumes, soymilk, tofu, almonds and broccoli.

Calcium has a blood pressure lowering effect and good sources of calcium are yogurt, broccoli, salmon, almonds, avocado and green leafy vegetables.

Restrict salt, especially hidden sources that are in most processed foods.

Drink at least two liters of fresh clean water daily.

Use garlic, celery and onions regularly.

Include plenty of fish high in Omega-3 fatty acids such as salmon, tuna and sardines.

Strengthen veins and arteries by including foods high in Vitamin C and the bioflavonoids such as black currant, broccoli, fruits, parsley, buckwheat, berries and skins of fruits and vegetables.

Include plenty of fiber and include raw vegetables and salads.

Avoid sugar, refined flour, excess meat, milk products or processed foods.

Restrict alcohol, smoking and caffeine (coffee, cocoa, chocolate)

Exercise regularly and relax often to relieve stress and spend time with animals and pets.

Some supplements and herbs that can benefit high blood pressure are Valerian (*Valeriana officinalis*) Hawthorn (*Crataegus oxyacantha*), Mistletoe (Viscum album), garlic, Omega-3 fatty acids, Evening primrose oil, Vitamin C and bioflavonoids (rutin, hesperidin), Co-enzyme Q-10, Dandelion (*Taraxacum officinale*) and Chlorella.

Infertility / Problems during pregnancy

The survival of the human race is dependant on a healthy reproductive system and fertility. There is a growing incidence of infertility both in females and in males, and what was commonly thought of as a female problem is now seen as a problem of both sexes as almost half the cases involve male infertility. The sperm count is generally considered to be declining over the past fifty years and there is a greater occurrence of miscarriages and couples that just cannot have children. I strongly believe that diet and lifestyle factors are behind many of these alarming statistics. It is a team effort in order to ensure a safe and healthy pregnancy.

Genetic eye constitutions at greatest risk:
Neurolymphatic, Lymphatic hypo-active, Hormonal and Connective Tissue types are at greatest risk but infertility or problems during pregnancy can occur in any of the genetic types.

Possible causes that contribute to this condition:
Nutritional deficits including vitamin, mineral and protein deficiencies
Caffeine, alcohol, drugs and smoking
Excess intake of chemical additives in foods and the water supply including pesticides, monosodium glutamate, colors and flavors
Stress
Liver disease
Hormonal problems and thyroid disease
Endometriosis
Polycystic ovarian syndrome
Low sperm count or abnormal shape of sperm in males
Sexually transmitted infections
Testicular injury
Ovulation disorders or poor egg quality
Anatomical problems with reproductive organs
Disorders or blockages of the fallopian tubes
Male tube blockages
Long-term use of the contraceptive pill
History of abortions

Eye for an Eye Diet nutrition and lifestyle advice for infertility:
Follow the nutritional advice in this book and target specific nutrition to strengthen your genetic eye constitution as explained in Part 3.

Include foods high in zinc (ginger, herring, liver, sunflower and pumpkin seeds) and foods high in magnesium (almonds, Brewer's yeast, cashew, whole grains), as they are fundamental for hormonal production, sperm count and motility as well as roles in the production of follicle-stimulating hormone (FSH) and estrogen.

Ensure foods high in Vitamin E (almonds, nuts, sunflower, wheat germ, green leafy vegetables) as they help to normalize hormone production by rejuvenating the endocrine system.

Eat preferably organic fruits and vegetables grown without the use of potentially toxic chemical pesticides. Include kelp and alfalfa.

Include the intake of essential fatty acids as they stimulate the production of sex hormones. Excellent sources are oily fish, fish liver oils, seeds, nuts, beans and unrefined vegetable oils.

Avoid saturated fats and hydrogenated oils (e.g., margarine); use olive oil.

Do not smoke, as it has been associated with low sperm count, poor sperm motility and abnormal sperm. Smoking is also seen as reducing blood flow to the cervix and inhibiting the action of cilia, the tiny hairs in the fallopian tubes that guide the egg toward the uterus.

Supplements and herbs that assist female infertility include, Zinc, Evening primrose oil, linseed oil, Omega 3 fatty acids, Black cohosh (not during pregnancy), Licorice (*Glycyrrhiza glabra*) (aids adrenal glands), Dandelion (*Taraxacum officinale*) (to cleanse the liver), Vitamin B-complex with folic acid, Vitamin C and bioflavonoids (assists to prevent miscarriages and strengthens the capillary vessels of the uterus), ginseng, Vitamin E, selenium and beta-carotene. Assist digestive function and a healthy micro floral environment by including supplements of Lactobacillus acidophilus and Chlorella.

Supplements and herbs that assist male infertility include, Zinc, wheat germ oil, antioxidants (Vitamins C, E, beta-carotene, selenium and bioflavonoids protect the sperm from free radical damage), Co-enzyme Q-10, Vitamin B-complex and folic acid, ginseng, Dandelion (*Taraxacum officinale*), Astragalus (*Astragalus membranaceus*) and Royal Jelly. Assist digestive function and a healthy micro floral environment by including supplements of Lactobacillus acidophilus and Chlorella.

Avoid the contraceptive pill.

High body temperature can kill sperm in testicles so do not take a hot bath before sexual intercourse, as sperm need cool temperatures to survive.

Drink at least two liters of fresh clean water daily to allow for removal of toxins from the body and ensure that it is free of chlorine and fluoride.

Avoid caffeine (coffee, black tea, colas, chocolate) and restrict alcohol

Avoid excess sugar, red meat and white flour products.

Ensure regular exercise but make sure it is not excessive.

Assist stress by relaxation methods like deep breathing exercises, acupressure, yoga or meditation.

Eye for an Eye Diet nutrition and lifestyle advice during pregnancy

Ensure adequate calcium (almonds, alfalfa sprouts, avocado, sesame seeds, green vegetables, sardines), folic acid (brocolli, beans, eggs, lentils, whole grains, spinach), protein (fish, soy products, nuts, beans, lentils, eggs), Vitamin C (fresh fruits, vegetables and berries), Vitamin B especially B6 and B12 (liver, fish, brewer's yeast), iron (liver, tuna, parsley, sunflower seeds, dried apricots) and zinc (ginger, herring, liver, sunflower and pumpkin seeds).

Ensure adequate fiber (wholegrains, nuts, fruits and vegetables, berries, brown rice) to prevent constipation, which is common.

Drink plenty of clean, fresh water daily.

Avoid any artificial sweeteners.

Avoid sugar and refined foods.

Avoid processed foods with preservatives, artificial colors and flavors.

Avoid caffeine containing foods and beverages (coffee, tea, cocao, chocolate, cola) as they can interfere with the absorption of calcium and iron.

Eat smaller meals more often, eat slowly and relax after meals.

Ensure adequate exposure to sun for Vitamin D.

Avoid alcohol or smoking due to the risk of potential birth defects.

Do not diet or attempt to lose weight during pregnancy.

Engage in regular gentle exercise such as swimming.

Cravings for foods can indicate a lack of minerals especially iron and zinc.

Stay away from negative emotions, avoid stress and relax with deep-breathing exercises daily.

Kidney disease

The kidneys perform a vital function for the human body. They cleanse the blood, maintain the correct balance of various body chemicals and help regulate blood pressure. When the kidneys become diseased or damaged, they can suddenly or gradually lose their ability to perform these vital functions. Waste products and excess fluid then build up inside the body, causing a variety of symptoms from chronic fatigue, migraines, high blood pressure or skin diseases. Associated problems include kidney stones, bladder or urinary tract infections and edema.

Genetic eye constitutions at greatest risk:

Lymphatic hypo-active, Kidney lymphatic, Hydro-lymphatic, Hematogenic and the Connective Tissue types are predisposed to kidney problems but it can occur in any of the genetic types.

Possible causes that contribute to this disease:

    Genetically weak kidneys
    Insufficient fluid intake
    Infections
    Diabetes

High saturated fat and cholesterol diet
High blood pressure
Drugs or heavy metals
Excess salt in the diet
Nutritional deficits

Eye for an Eye Diet nutrition and lifestyle advice:

Follow the nutritional advice in this book and target specific nutrition to strengthen your genetic eye constitution as explained in Part 3.

Drink at least two liters of fresh clean water daily.

Avoid sugar, salt, alcohol and caffeine.

Avoid drugs and medications.

A low acid diet, which is rich in vegetables, should be the foundation of the diet. Avoid acid-forming foods such as meats, milk products, white sugar and refined grains.

Include dried apricots, green leafy vegetables, and bananas, as they are rich in potassium, which helps the kidneys excrete the excessive amount of sodium found in a typical western-style diet of high salt intake.

Avoid excess protein especially excess meat, cheese and milk products.

Increase fiber in the diet.

Never resist the need to urinate and don't avoid drinking water just so that you won't have to go so often.

Limit foods high in oxalic acid such as beans, cocoa, chocolate, instant coffee, rhubarb, spinach and tea.

For bladder and urinary tract infections include cranberries or cranberry juice (with no added sugar).

Natural diuretics beneficial for the kidney include celery, parsley, watermelon and dandelion leaves.

Juices of watermelon, raw beet, cranberry and lemon and teas made from parsley, dandelion or raspberries are excellent for kidney cleansing.

Other useful supplements and herbs to improve kidney function and circulation include lecithin, garlic, bioflavonoids (rutin and hesperidin), Vitamin C, artichoke and juniper berries (*Juniperus communis*).

Liver and Gall bladder disease

One of the numerous functions of the liver is to detoxify and excrete a variety of substances consumed in the diet and waste products of our body's metabolism. The liver also produces proteins necessary for the clotting of the blood as well as bile, which is necessary for digestion of fats and regulation of cholesterol. The gall bladder stores and concentrates bile. If the liver is sick and insufficient poor quality bile is produced it may lead to the formation of gallstones, a frequent problem in today's society and often resulting in the removal of the gall bladder. Through nutrition we can improve liver function and often prevent the occurrence of gallstones.

Genetic eye constitutions at greatest risk:
Lymphatic hypo-active, Kidney lymphatic, Hydro-lymphatic, Hematogenic, Mixed and the Plethoric types are at greatest risk although liver or gallbladder disease can occur in any of the genetic types.

Possible causes that contribute to this disease:
- Genetic weaknesses in the liver or gall bladder
- Nutritional deficits
- Viral infections
- Diabetes
- Excess alcohol
- Medications and drugs
- Use of the contraceptive pill and hormone therapy
- Excess intake of saturated fats and cholesterol
- High intake of refined and processed foods
- Stress and intense negative emotions like anger, resentment and bitterness
- Ingestion of artificial additives in foods
- Obesity and lack of physical activity

Eye for an Eye Diet nutrition and lifestyle advice:
Follow the nutritional advice in this book and target specific nutrition to strengthen your genetic eye constitution as explained in Part 3.

Increase dietary fiber and eat plenty of vegetables.

Reduce excess meat intake as well as milk products other than soured milk or natural yogurt.

Foods that are beneficial for the liver and gall bladder include apples, applesauce, alfalfa, artichoke, blueberries, carrots, celery, grape juice, lemon, olive oil, broccoli, sprouts, cauliflower, cabbage, salmon, sardines and tuna.

Include foods high in especially Vitamin C, methionine, choline and inositol. Vitamin C-rich foods include peppers, black currant, broccoli, guava, parsley, pineapple, strawberries, rosehips, raw cabbage, brussel sprouts and cauliflower. Choline is contained in foods such as beans, egg yolk, lecithin, liver, whole grains and yeast. Inositol containing foods include: beans, corn, nuts, seeds, vegetables, wholegrain cereals and meats. Methionine containing foods include: beans, eggs, garlic, liver, onions, sardines and yogurt. B-complex rich foods are also needed which include green leafy vegetables, eggs, legumes, nuts and seeds, sprouts, alfalfa, whole grains, organ meats, chicken, fish, yeast and avocado.

Formation of normal blood clotting factors such as prothrombin are also aided by Vitamin K rich foods such as alfalfa, cabbages, green leafy vegetables, broccoli, eggs, kelp, lettuce, soybeans, spinach, parsley and liver.

For natural removal of gallstones use a few tablespoons of extra virgin cold pressed olive oil with the juice of a lemon before retiring and upon awakening but ensure that you have strengthened the liver at least a couple of months before you do this in order to improve the condition of the bile so that existing stones will soften and not cause pain on release.

Beneficial supplements include methionine, choline, insositol and Vitamin C, Vitamin B-complex, lecithin (to aid fat digestion) and alfalfa tablets (excellent as a liver cleanser). For associated cholesterol problems use Omega-3 fatty acids and Garlic. Herbs such as milk thistle (*Silybum marianum*) and dandelion (*Taraxacum officinale*) also assist liver function.

Drink at least two liters of fresh clean water daily and avoid fluids with meals.

Eliminate alcohol, drugs, use of the contraceptive pill and other medications.

Avoid processed foods and be very careful of ingesting artificial chemical food additives.

Get out in fresh air often.

Ensure regular exercise.

Do not skip breakfast.

Avoid stress and negative emotions.

Menstrual difficulties and Menopausal symptoms

The experience of menstruation varies from woman to woman. Problems such as pain and irregularity are usually the result of natural hormonal changes, and do not necessarily signify illness. Some common menstrual problems include painful periods (Dysmenorrhoea), lack of periods (Amenorrhoea), heavy periods (Menorrhagia), Pre-menstrual syndrome and menstrual migraines.

Menopause is a natural process and the time at "mid-life" when a woman has her last period. It happens when the ovaries stop releasing eggs and is usually a gradual process. During that time a woman's hormones are affected and common problems such as hot flashes and osteoporosis are often encountered.

Genetic eye constitutions at greatest risk:
Neurolymphatic, Plethoric, Hormonal and Connective tissue types are at the greatest risk but these conditions can occur in any of the genetic types.

Possible causes that contribute to this disease:
Weakness in the pituitary, ovaries or adrenal glands and hormonal imbalances

The Eye for an Eye Diet   Part 4

    Weight loss or anorexia
    Obesity
    Thyroid problems may affect menstruation
    Weak liver function
    Excess sugar and saturated fats in the diet
    Lack of essential fatty acids
    Use of the contraceptive pill
    Infections
    Nutritional deficits and mineral deficiencies
    Lack of exercise

Eye for an Eye Diet nutrition and lifestyle advice:

Follow the nutritional advice in this book and target specific nutrition to strengthen your genetic eye constitution as explained in Part 3.

Consume greater amounts of fresh fruit and vegetables and include alfalfa for hormonal glands like the pituitary.

Eat a mixed assortment of seeds such as sunflower, sesame, pumpkin and linseed.

Include iron rich foods such as parsley, apricots, liver, soybeans, sunflower and pumpkin seeds.

Eat foods high in essential fatty acids such as salmon, trout, tuna and sardines.

Increase soy in your diet e.g. tofu, soy milk, or take soy capsules. Soy helps to balance hormones.

Avoid foods high in sugar, salt, fat, alcohol and caffeine (cola, coffee, chocolate) as well as saturated fats including dairy products and red meats.

Avoid processed foods that contain artificial colors, additives and preservatives and foods that contain hormones such as commonly found in chicken, beef and dairy products.

Eat 5 small meals per day.

Avoid hormone treatment or hormone replacement therapy, as there are possible increased risks of breast and endometrial cancer, gall bladder disease and heart disease.

If you suffer from hot flashes, increase foods high in Vitamin E (almonds, egg yolk, nuts and wheat germ) and soy foods (tofu, soy milk, soy beans)

Follow the dietary guidelines for osteoporosis in this section especially if going through menopause.

Supplements that can assist menstrual problems and menopause include Vitamin B-complex, Vitamin C, iron, lecithin, Vitamin E, bioflavonoids, Zinc, Evening primrose oil, Omega-3 fatty acids, and herbs such as Wild Yam (*Dioscorea villosa*) which contains a natural form of progesterone, Black cohosh

(*Cimifuga racemosa*) (for relief of menopausal symptoms but should not be taken during pregnancy), Unicorn root (*Aletris farinosa*), valerian (*Valeriana officinalis*), ginger and chamomile.

Herbs such as dandelion (*Taraxacum officinale*) and milk thistle (*Silybum marianum*) will improve liver function to maintain normal hormonal balance.

Engage in regular exercise as it often relieves menstrual and menopausal problems and helps to naturally regulate the hormonal system.

Reduce stress and ensure that you give yourself relaxation time everyday.

Avoid the use of birth control pills as they can contribute to menstrual problems and abnormal hormonal fluctuations.

Migraine headaches

The amount of pharmaceutical preparations for headaches and migraines is a testimonial to the increasing prevalence of this condition we see today in society. For many the pain from migraine headaches is unbearable and is responsible for many sick days from work for many people throughout the year. Often they are accompanied by visual disturbance or gastrointestinal upset. There is no cure according to modern medicine and the causes or triggers are different for each individual. More women complain of migraines than men.

Genetic eye constitutions at greatest risk:

Lymphatic Hypo-active, Kidney lymphatic, Neurolymphatic and Hematogenic types are at greatest risk but migraines can occur in any of the genetic types.

Possible causes that contribute to this disease:

Foods known to precipitate migraine attacks include aged cheeses, oranges and citrus fruits, alcohol (especially red wine, brandy or whisky), beer, eggs, canned meats, salami and sausages, chocolate, vinegar and pickled foods, smoked foods, dairy products, nuts, wheat, caffeine (tea, coffee, cola, chocolate), avocado, tomato, foods containing nitrates and nitrites (hot dogs, salami, sausage), foods containing monosodium glutamate and artificial sugar substitutes.

Smoking

Stress or excitement: often some time after the stress is experienced

Exhaustion

Posture and spinal misalignment: a bad back, shoulders or neck can contribute to migraines

Sleep: too much or too little sleep can trigger a migraine attack

Environmental factors: sensitivity to bright light, office buildings with no fresh air, fluorescent lighting.

Irregular eating habits and fluctuating blood sugar levels can bring on migraine headaches.
Fluctuations in hormone levels during menstruation or ovulation
Allergies
Some drugs and antidepressants
Liver or kidney disease
Constipation
Lack of exercise
Poor circulation

Eye for an Eye Diet nutrition and lifestyle advice:

Follow the nutritional advice in this book and target specific nutrition to strengthen your genetic eye constitution as explained in Part 3.

Eat foods high in magnesium such as almonds, soybeans and whole grains. Magnesium relaxes the constriction of blood vessels and helps to lower blood pressure and in this way may relieve migraines.

Ensure a healthy liver by including foods high in methionine, choline, inositol and Vitamin C as well as foods that will assist the kidneys such as beans, egg yolk, lecithin, liver, whole grains and vegetables. Eat a minimum amount of meat and include foods high in Vitamin C and the bioflavonoids to strengthen the capillary network of blood vessels in the filter of the kidney. These include berries, fruits and the skin of fruits and vegetables.

Ensure effective digestion by including supplements of Lactobacillus acidophilus and Chlorella.

Other supplements and herbs that are effective for migraines include feverfew (*Chrysanthemum parthenium*) that has been found to stop the blood platelets from releasing an excessive amount of serotonin which tends to lead to migraine headaches, gingko biloba which improves the microcirculation in the head and Valerian (*Valeriana officinalis*) which relieves stress and assists sleep. Vitamin B-complex, Omega 3 fatty acids, ginger, bioflavonoids and Vitamin C supplements may also reduce the frequency and severity of migraine headaches.

Drink plenty of "live" water free of chlorine and fluoride to prevent constipation, and to assist kidney function.

Avoid coffee, black tea, chocolate, cocoa and cola drinks.

Avoid preservatives, artificial colors and flavors and other harmful additives in foods like monosodium glutamate. Foods that you are allergic or sensitive to should also be avoided.

Eat meals regularly and more frequently to avoid blood sugar fluctuations that may trigger migraines.

Engage in regular exercise to improve circulation.

Monitor and avoid those foods listed that may trigger migraine attacks.
Stop smoking
Engage in meditation or other relaxation methods to reduce stress, anxiety or intense emotions such as anger.
Use physical therapy or cervical manipulation to assist in reducing pain. Bowen therapy has been very successful in relieving pain from migraines.

Osteoporosis

Osteoporosis is a condition of decreased bone mass where bone density and structural quality deteriorate, leading to weakness and increased risk of fracture. Common sites to fracture are the wrist, hip, spine, pelvis and upper arm. Although Osteoporosis primarily affects postmenopausal women due to hormonal changes it can occur at any age or gender.

I believe that osteoporosis is more of a calcium-loss disease than a calcium deficiency. This means that if your diet and lifestyle are not healthy you will lose more calcium than you take in with your diet.

Genetic eye constitutions at greatest risk:
Lymphatic hyper-active, Neurolymphatic, Hormonal, and Connective Tissue types are at greater risk but osteoporosis can occur in any of the genetic types.

Possible causes that contribute to this disease:
Lack of weight-bearing exercise
High intake of carbonated drinks
High intake of sugar
Milk products
High intake of meat and protein
Lack of weight-bearing exercise
Ingestion of fluoride
High aluminum intake
Some prescription drugs
Menopause and hormonal problems
Vitamin D deficiency due to lack of sunlight

Eye for an Eye Diet nutrition and lifestyle advice:
Follow the nutritional advice in this book and target specific nutrition to strengthen your genetic eye constitution as explained in Part 3.

Eat plenty of foods high in calcium and magnesium and include fresh green vegetables, soy products and whole grains, almonds, avocado, broccoli, figs, bananas, natural yogurt, sesame seeds, apricots, blueberries, raspberries, cabbage and alfalfa sprouts.

Eat foods that build collagen including those high in Vitamin C, A (beta-carotene) and zinc.

Avoid milk products other than natural yogurt or soured milk as well as sugar, excess meat and white flour products.

Avoid carbonated beverages and meat as they are high in phosphorus and result in calcium loss.

Avoid all kinds of fluoride including what is in tap water, mouthwash and toothpaste.

Avoid antacids that contain aluminum or deodorants with aluminum and do not use aluminum cooking pots as they can create a negative calcium balance.

Avoid hormone replacement therapy.

Avoid prescription drugs that cause bone loss, such as diuretics and synthetic cortisones.

Improve calcium absorption by supplements such as betaine hydrochloride, Lactobacillus acidophilus, Chlorella and Slippery Elm bark (*Ulmus fulva*).

Take a calcium/magnesium supplement.

Stop smoking, as it is one of the highest risk factors with osteoporosis.

Ensure adequate sunlight to get enough Vitamin D as a deficiency can cause calcium loss.

Eliminate coffee and alcohol and excess salt.

Engage in weight-bearing exercise such as swimming, cycling, brisk walking or light weight training (even in old age) as it increases bone density.

Stress

The impact of stress on our health is seriously underestimated. As a result of our modern hectic lifestyles the majority of us feel the effects of this condition, often daily. Stress affects every system in our body including the nervous, circulatory, digestive, reproductive, hormonal and immune systems.

It can result in anything from skin problems, menstrual difficulties and asthma to cancer and for this it has often been termed the "silent killer." We need to really understand that prolonged stress is detrimental to health and that psychological well-being is closely related to our physical well-being. Stress is personal and individual and affects each one of us in different ways.

Genetic eye constitutions at greatest risk:
Neurolymphatic, Lymphatic Hypo-active, Hydro-lymphatic, Hematogenic, Mixed and the Plethoric types are most sensitive to stress but stress can affect any of the genetic types.

Possible causes that contribute to this disease:
Nutritional deficits

Psychological trauma
Major life changes (career change, financial problems, death of spouse, moving, divorce, injury etc.)
Inner conflicts
Excess toxic chemicals in the body
Lack of sleep or relaxation
Excess caffeine (Coffee, tea, chocolate, cola) stimulates the release of adrenalin, which increases stress
Excess alcohol
Excess sugar, salt, meat and saturated fat
Lack of exercise and a sedentary lifestyle
Unbalance in working life and personal life

Eye for an Eye Diet nutrition and lifestyle advice:

Follow the nutritional advice in this book and target specific nutrition to strengthen your genetic eye constitution as explained in Part 3.

Eat unprocessed foods free of artificial preservatives, colors or flavors.

Assist the liver and kidneys to cleanse the body. Refer to Eye for an Eye recommended nutritional advice for Kidney disease and Liver disease.

Stay away from coffee, tea, chocolate and cola as it causes nervousness and inhibits sleep.

Avoid alcohol as it depletes Vitamin B, which is important in coping with stress.

Ensure that you include foods high in Vitamin B-complex such as whole grains, yeast, sprouts, eggs, almonds, salmon, seeds, avocado, Brewer's yeast and liver.

Ensure foods high in Vitamin C as this vitamin is also quickly depleted when under stress.

Avoid sugar intake.

Supplements and herbs that assist stress include Vitamin B-complex, Siberian ginseng, Vitamin C, beta-carotene, chamomile and valerian (*Valeriana officinalis*)

Ensure adequate sleep.

Perform deep breathing exercises every day.

Spend as much time as you can with animals as they have a magical calming effect.

Accept who you are and that life has its ups and downs.

Take the time to do the things that you enjoy.

Exercise regularly and practice yoga and meditation.

Take frequent walks in nature.

Listen to music, as it is a significant mood-changer and reliever of stress

Avoid negative emotions like anger, grief, distrust and resentment.

Tinnitus

Tinnitus is a common condition in which there is an abnormal ringing, buzzing or whistling in the ears and affects millions of people around the world. Many people find it very difficult to live with it and it often becomes a very debilitating condition with psychological effects. The noise can be intermittent or continuous and may be caused by many factors. Tinnitus should be seen as a symptom of an underlying medical condition, not a disease.

Genetic eye constitutions at greatest risk:

Lymphatic hypo-active, Kidney lymphatic, Neurolymphatic and the Hematogenic types are at greatest risk of tinnitus but it can occur in any of the genetic types.

Possible causes that contribute to this condition:

Excess toxins in the body
Drugs (such as antibiotics, aspirin or chemotherapy) and heavy metal poisoning
Stress
Prolonged exposure to loud sounds or explosions
Head injury
Ear infection or nerve damage
Blocked ear canal or Eustachian tube or hearing loss
Hypertension
Hypothyroidism
Circulatory disorders
Smoking
Mercury in amalgam dental fillings
Excessive alcohol or caffeine
Carbon monoxide from gasoline fumes
Jarring from high impact exercise
Meniere's disease (disorder of the inner ear)
Disorders or misalignments of the neck, jaw or tempomandibular joint
An abundance of animal protein, especially red meat, refined flours and sugars and processed foods which can constrict the arteries
Food allergies
Aging

Eye for an Eye Diet nutrition and lifestyle advice:

Follow the nutritional advice in this book and target specific nutrition to strengthen your genetic eye constitution as explained in Part 3.

Reduce the intake of saturated fats and cholesterol as they may reduce the flow of oxygen and nutrients to the inner ear.

Eat fish (salmon, tuna and sardines), foods high in Vitamin C as well as garlic to keep blood pressure at safe levels.

Increase dietary magnesium and potassium (good sources are apricots, baked potatoes, bananas, beets, leafy greens and nuts).

Drink at least two liters of fresh clean water daily.

Avoid excess meat, sugar and refined flour intake.

Avoid the intake of all toxic substances including artificial food additives, drugs (especially aspirin, antibiotics) as well as exposure to environmental pollutants such as automobile exhaust.

Avoid alcohol.

Avoid caffeine and smoking, as they constrict blood vessels.

Cut down on salt in your diet as it can cause fluid to build up in your ears, worsening tinnitus.

Avoid loud noises and wear earplugs when there is any loud noise around.

Engage in regular exercise to improve circulation and perform leg exercises to increase blood circulation to head area.

Bowen therapy or Acupressure are often effective for relieving tinnitus from causes due to spinal or jaw misalignments.

Perform five minutes of deep breathing exercises everyday.

Enhance the immune system and prevent infections by supplementing with Vitamin C, bioflavonoids and Echinacea.

Other supplements or herbs that can benefit tinnitus are kelp, Lactobacillus acidophilus, Chlorella, gingko biloba, garlic, Omega-3 fatty acids, B-complex, hawthorn (*Crataegus oxyacantha*), Vitamin A (beta carotene), Vitamin E, lecithin and zinc.

Chapter 3
The Eye for an Eye Diet as we Age and Change

As we approach the end of our journey through the study of nutrition and genetics, we are often reminded that our bodies are living organisms that change with time. Along with changes in our bodies come changes in our needs for nutrition. Requirements for food and nutrients are different but just as important when we are growing, during adolescence, during pregnancy, in adulthood and old age. They vary according to our genetics, our activity level and the variety of stresses that we encouter. To maintain health and be free of disease during these times, we need to take these factors into consideration. It is not only important to support our genetic weaknesses but to adapt to the body's needs as we age and change.

The majority of us do not look forward to that day when we can really say that we are old. Being old is considered a handicap for most and unfortunately due to a lifetime of bad nutritional and lifestyle habits it often carries with it several doctor and hospital visits, operations and medications. As we age, we may grow wiser but our organ systems diminish in function and this varies from individual to individual. Everyone would like to find a miraculous method or "fountain of youth" that would allow us to stay young and slow down the aging process but as we should realize by now, there are no quick-sure miracles. How we age depends on our genetics, our diet and lifestyle choices that we have made throughout our lives and the amount and types of stresses we have encountered that have taxed the body over the years.

For many, the golden age does not have to mean countless doctor and hospital visits but an active and productive time of life. The process of aging does not just have to mean the physical changes that occur but attitude and society norms play a great part in the psychological aging process. We have people who are 50 that believe they are old, act old and feel old, while some who are over 80 and active have completely different and opposite attitudes. A lot depends on how we view our elderly. In most Western cultures the elderly are considered a nuisance and are locked away somewhere in old age homes. There are other cultures that respect the elderly, learn from them and allow them to share their wealth of a lifetime of experiences. It does not matter at what age we are, we all need to feel that we are contributing in some way to society. Once we feel that we are no longer needed, both psychological and physical health quickly degenerate. I believe we need to aim to value the elderly as many have accumulated a vast amount of knowledge and experience that can help us in our future. Remember, as I have mentioned before, the only way I truly believe we can learn the truth about health and nutrition is to learn from experience and from the old and wise. If you believe that some young arrogant executive for a leading food company has the knowledge and experience to preach the health virtues of their product, you may find that you will be sadly disappointed. Learn and value the time with the elderly population, as I believe the rewards are immeasurable and remember you too will one day be old.

Before we learn about the specific nutritional requirements of the elderly it is important to first understand some of the degenerative changes that commonly occur as we age. Some general features of the aging body include loss of height, wrinkles, thinning gray hair and diminished balance and coordination. Some features of body systems as they age are included below.

Body systems as we age

Skin, Nails and Hair

Common changes in skin include the appearance of wrinkles, loss of elasticity, age spots, lines, dryness and fragility. Due to a decreased activity of the oil and sweat glands, thinning of the skin and loss of subcutaneous fat can cause the skin to lose some degree of its ability to act as a barrier against dehydration. Nails become dry and brittle while the hair loses its pigmentation and begins to thin. In women there is often an increase in facial hair with loss of pubic and axillary hair while in aging males there is an increase in hair growth in the ears and nose.

Sensory function (Eyesight, Hearing, Smell, Taste and Touch)

Eyesight often becomes worse and eyes will produce less moisturizing tears. Changes to the lens due to the accumulation of insoluble proteins often result in diseases such as cataracts. The lens of the eye may become less elastic leading to presbyopia. The incidence of glaucoma increases with age and accounts for one of the highest causes of blindness.

Ear bones will become hardened and production of earwax will increase as well as the incidence of hearing problems. Elderly people who are hard of hearing are particularly sensitive to high-pitched sounds. The sense of balance will be affected as the inner ear will also degenerate and falls are more common. There is a greater incidence of tinnitus or ringing in the ears.

Both the sense of smell and the number of taste buds are decreased in the elderly.

The sense of touch is often decreased and loss of tactile sensation may predispose the elderly to burns and minor injuries.

Digestive function

The elderly often suffer from digestive disturbances due to a thinning of the stomach mucosa as well as decreased hydrochloric acid and enzyme production. There is a higher incidence of peptic ulcers, biliary tract disease, intestinal obstructions and hiatus hernia. They also often have a poor appetite due to loss of taste buds and decreased sense of smell. This often leads to a variety of nutrient deficiencies. It is common to find constipation contributed by lack of exercise, low fluid intake and low fiber diets. The aging population also has a higher percent of colon cancer. Loose and worn teeth and dentures can cause difficulties in chewing food.

Cardiovascular function

With aging there is decreased elasticity and degeneration of the blood vessels and often there is increased blood pressure and greater incidence of atherosclerosis leading to angina or heart attacks. There is diminished arterial circulation to all organs including the heart, kidney and brain.

Respiratory function

The aging process results in loss of elasticity of the lungs and a decrease in lung capacity, resulting in lower gaseous exchange in the alveoli and a lower concentration of oxygen in the arteries. Older people generally breathe more shallow and frequently and often due to the effects of environmental pollutants or smoking, suffer from decreased ciliary action, increased mucous production and poor elasticity of the lungs.

Nervous function

The elderly are often predisposed to depression and sleep disturbances due to many causes including a reduction of neurotransmitters. Coordination and balance are decreased along with problems in retrieving information as the number of neurons is reduced due to degeneration of the central nervous system. Deficiencies in mental acuity and sensory interpretation occur as well as mood changes. Elderly people commonly have decreased memory power and often find it more difficult to learn new things or to change behaviors.

Genitourinary function

With age there is a loss of nephrons, the functional units in the kidney. The mass, volume and filtering capacity of the kidney is reduced which result in decreased kidney function and ability to concentrate urine. Incontinence and/or frequency of urination may result due to loss of sphincter tone, changes in bladder reflexes, decreased muscle tone or an enlarged prostate in the male.

Musculoskeletal function

With aging comes a thinning of the vertebra and intervertebral discs and increased curvature of the spine, which can cause a stooped posture and tilted head. The body composition of the elderly often changes, as there is a reduction in lean muscle mass and increased abdominal fat. It is common to see a decrease in bone mineral mass, weight loss, osteoarthritis, rheumatoid arthritis and osteoporosis that can lead to fractures, degeneration of the joints, restricted movement and a higher risk of falling. Muscles shrink with old age causing a general loss of muscle strength.

Factors that affect health in the elderly

A. Malnutrition

It is common to find that a large percentage of the elderly suffer from nutritional deficiencies. There are several reasons why they are at particular risk. Often they do not eat a wide enough variety of foods, eat too little of the wrong kinds of foods or mishandle the storage or preparation of food. They may also lose the motivation to eat properly due to psychological factors such as social isolation, loneliness, depression and the loss of a spouse. They may not have the desire to eat due to anorexia from diseases such as cancer, emphysema or cirrhosis, gastrointestinal disease, stroke, dementia, Parkinson's disease or use of medications. Poor dentition and loss of taste buds and sensory capabilities may also contribute to cases of malnutrition. Finally the elderly may just not be aware of nutrition or due to economics may choose to save money for rent or other essentials rather that purchase quality food.

B. Inadequate absorption and utilization

We have seen how absorption and utilization are critical life processes. Due to the increased incidence of conditions of lack of hydrochloric stomach acid, gastrointestinal diseases, alchoholism and interactions between nutrients and drugs, the elderly often are unable to adequately absorb nutrients into the bloodstream and the cells are unable to utilize those nutrients effectively enough.

C. Increased nutrient requirements

There may be greater requirements for nutrients due to the higher incidence of fever, inflammatory diseases, injuries or surgery, not to mention increased losses of nutrients due to drugs or chronic diseases.

D. Interactions between drugs and food

Drugs certainly affect how the body handles nutrients and it is very common that the elderly often take a variety of medications. Due to this they are at an increased nutritional risk as some drugs including pain medications, antibiotics, aspirin or chemotherapy can suppress the appetite, cause constipation or diarrhea, nausea, vomiting or alter taste so that food can seem bitter or bland. Chronic laxative use can also be harmful as it can cause a loss of nutrients. The liver and kidneys often suffer due to excess medications. Food can also affect the absorption of a drug or how it is metabolized in the body as some drugs are taken on an empty stomach while others are taken with meals. Antacids, especially those containing aluminum, are best avoided because of their interference with calcium absorption, zinc and magnesium and the possibility of aluminum toxicity, which has been implicated in Alzheimer's disease and other types of senility. Many diuretic drugs used by the elderly cause depletion of potassium, zinc, magnesium and other mineral stores as they stimulate the kidneys to clear these minerals. As a result mineral deficiencies can easily result. Antibiotics reduce colon flora, which is a source of production of B vitamins and vitamin K.

E. Problems with Food Handling, Safety and Storage

Elderly people are at greater risk than younger people of becoming seriously ill due to improper handling, cooking and storage of food. Their age-associated deficits in sight, taste, and smell, may causes them to not realize that they are eating stale or contaminated food which can lead to food poisoning and nutrient deficiencies.

F. Obesity

A significant number of the elderly may be overweight to some degree, which is associated with a number of diseases such as diabetes, high blood pressure, heart attacks and strokes. Due to injuries or ailments exercise is often neglected.

G. Stubborness / Apathy

It is quite common to see the elderly be resentful, apathetic or even rebellious when it comes to eating habits. Due to routines, they find it difficult to change these habits and to encourage them to eat better nutritious foods can be often more difficult than with teenagers. As a result of this behaviour they may have a very unbalanced diet that can consist of a limited number of foods. Malnutrition is common with low calorie and protein intakes and many deficiencies of important vitamins and minerals. Many elders eat less because of such reasons as apathy, diminished sense of taste and smell or poor teeth.

Common health problems in the elderly caused by inadequate nutrition or poor eating habits

Insomnia

Anorexia

Obesity

Fatigue

Depression

Poor eyesight and hearing

Fragile bones and osteoporosis

Fractures

Weakened resistance to infections

Cancer

Aging of the skin and wrinkles

Poor digestion and absorption

Constipation

Chronic dehydration

Slow healing ability

Arthritis

Common nutrients that are deficient in the Elderly

The diet of the elderly is often deficient in several essential nutrients. Even though there is a lower need of protein for tissue production in old age due to poor assimilation and absorption, just as much protein is needed to be ingested as before to provide the body with its needs and to enable tissue repair. Enough calories also need to be consumed and this is often a problem for the elderly as we have discussed earlier. Fiber is a nutrient that is crucial in colon health, the reduction of colon cancer and constipation, all of which are common health problems in the elderly. As throughout all our life, water intake is necessary for clearing impurities and for waste elimination. It improves skin function and prevents dehydration, which is commonly seen in the elderly population.

Several vitamin and mineral deficiencies are also evident due to poor intake of fresh nutrient-rich foods. Vitamin A deficiency can lead to poor vision, weakened immunity and dry skin. Several of the B vitamins are often deficient which can reduce energy levels, regeneration and affect skin function. A great percentage of the elderly have been found to be deficient in Vitamin C which affects health of tissues, healing ability and resistance to disease.

Poor digestion and lack of hydrochloric acid and digestive enzymes can also affect absorption of many minerals. Calcium intake is one of the biggest concerns. Calcium deficiency is more common in elderly women than in men. Low-calcium foods, lack of exercise, low hydrochloric acid and poor digestion in the elderly lessen calcium availability. Magnesium in the diet may also be low, while phosphorus intake is often normal or elevated and excess phosphorus may allow even more bone loss when calcium is deficient. Imbalances among calcium, phosphorus, magnesium and even low levels of vitamin D also affect calcium bone metabolism. Zinc, a mineral vital for immune function, acid-base balance, tissue healing and the prevention of aging, is often inadequate in the diet. Low immune function due to zinc deficiency is frequently a factor in infections, cancer and cardiovascular problems. Potassium may also be deficient because of low intake of vegetables and higher intake of salt. Sodium, chloride and potassium are important electrolytes that help balance acid-base chemistry and fluid movement. With weakened kidney function, which is not uncommon in the elderly, electrolyte imbalances occur. Another common mineral that is often deficient is chromium, which is often poorly absorbed. Chromium is important to blood sugar regulation, the glucose tolerance factor and insulin function. Iron may be low as well, but fortunately there is less need for it in the aging population although in some cases it can lead to anemia. Finally, copper is often deficient and important for many energy and enzyme systems in the body.

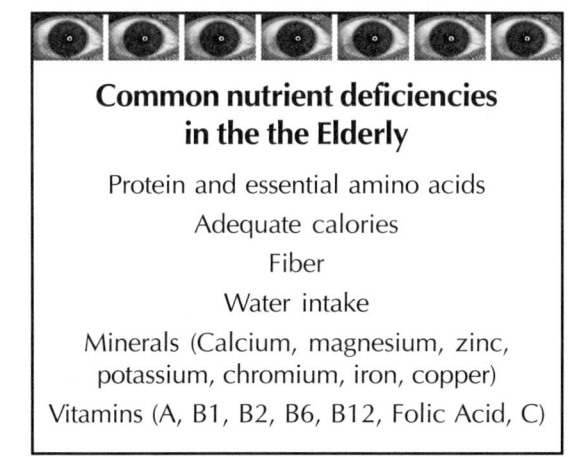

Common nutrient deficiencies in the the Elderly

Protein and essential amino acids

Adequate calories

Fiber

Water intake

Minerals (Calcium, magnesium, zinc, potassium, chromium, iron, copper)

Vitamins (A, B1, B2, B6, B12, Folic Acid, C)

What speeds up the aging process?

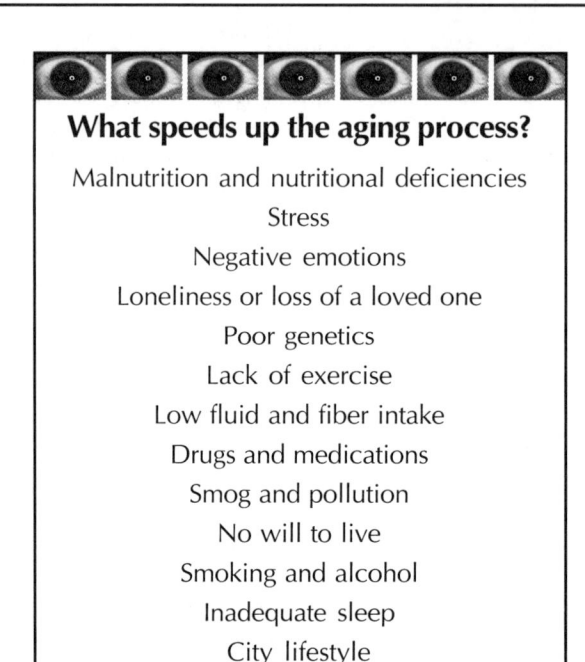

Malnutrition and nutritional deficiencies
Stress
Negative emotions
Loneliness or loss of a loved one
Poor genetics
Lack of exercise
Low fluid and fiber intake
Drugs and medications
Smog and pollution
No will to live
Smoking and alcohol
Inadequate sleep
City lifestyle

Recommended Eye for an Eye Diet diet and lifestyle advice for the elderly and how to prevent premature aging

General nutritional and lifestyle advice

Include plenty of fresh fruit and vegetables in the diet.

Include adequate fiber, which is available in vegetables, whole grains and bran to assist bowel function and reduce the incidence of constipation.

Include prune juice and some bran as common laxative foods to help keep elimination regular and avoid constipation. A morning or evening drink made with prune juice, water, lemon juice and a few tablespoons of wheat or oat bran can be beneficial.

Ensure foods high in Vitamin B such as green leafy vegetables, eggs, legumes, nuts and seeds, sprouts, whole grains, organ meats, chicken, fish, yeast and avocado.

Ensure foods high in chromium: egg yolk, grape juice, asparagus, liver, lobster, nuts, oysters, whole grains, raisins, prunes, shrimp and Brewer's yeast.

Ensure food sources high in copper: almonds, pecans, sunflower seeds, beans, mushrooms, oysters, prunes, whole grains, brown rice and eggs.

Include foods high in zinc: ginger, liver, oysters, whole grains, and yeast and sunflower seeds.

Ensure magnesium-rich foods, as are nuts, whole grain foods, almonds, cashews, molasses, soybeans, spinach, beets and broccoli.

Include potassium-rich foods like bananas, apricots, avocado, dates, almonds, cashews, pecans, raisins, sardines and sunflower seeds.

Ensure that you include high iron foods like liver, apricots, oysters, parsley, sesame seeds, soybeans, sunflower seeds and almonds.

Include vitamin C-rich foods such as peppers, black currant, broccoli, guava, parsley, pineapple, strawberries, rosehips, raw cabbage, brussel sprouts, and cauliflower.

Ensure that plenty of calcium-rich foods such as salmon, sardines, almonds, green vegetables, sesame seeds, natural yogurt or soured milk are included regularly in the diet for bone health.

Nutritional supplements that can be beneficial in old age include vitamin C, E, beta-carotene, selenium, psyllium, B-complex, digestive enzymes, Chlorella, lactobacillus acidophilus, chromium, brewer's yeast, lecithin, Omega-3 fatty acids, calcium, magnesium and mineral supplements.

Herbs that can be beneficial in old age include ginseng and gingko biloba. Ginseng is known as the "longevity" herb and is used regularly by elderly Chinese men and women to slow the aging process. Gingko biloba can help with circulatory problems, senility, tinnitus, poor memory and hearing disorders.

For prostate health herbs such as saw palmetto, parsley, ginger, marshmallow and juniper berries can assist.

Reduce salt intake.

Avoid refined flour products and the intake of sugar.

Avoid processed foods, especially that contain harmful food additives.

Avoid excessive fat intake.

Avoid both aluminum cookware and the storage or heating of foods in aluminum foil.

Drink adequate water, herbal teas and nutritious soups.

Ensure enough calories are consumed and all the essential amino acids are included.

Include a variety of foods.

If whole foods are a problem to eat due to state of health of the teeth, include fresh vegetable juices or pureed foods.

Avoid overeating and underactivity. Exercise as we know is an essential nutrient at every age. It will improve appetite, prevent osteoporosis, reduce the chance of constipation and improve digestive and circulatory function. Make sure to include exercises that will improve endurance, muscular strength as well as flexibility.

Do not stay inside and become antisocial even if you have lost your life partner. It is important to have hobbies and spend time with friends or make new friends.

Spend time in nature and ensure plenty of fresh air. Perform breathing exercises to increase oxygen uptake.

Get plenty of sleep each night.

Avoid or minimize the use of unnecessary pharmaceutical medications such as laxatives, antacids and antibiotics and other drugs such as nicotine, caffeine and alcohol.

Think young, enjoy life the best you can and avoid any negative emotions.

Specific concerns for the elderly by Genetic Eye Constitution

Ensure that you support your Genetic Eye Constitution by utilizing the advice given back in Chapter 5 of Part 3. Included here are specific health concerns that particularly affect the elderly for each Genetic type.

Lymphatic Hyper-active types: There is often stiffness in the joints and rheumatic and arthritic complaints as one ages. Endocrine problems may arise involving the parathyroid and can cause problems like osteoporosis.

Lymphatic Hypo-active types: These individuals often look older than their age. Kidney and liver weakness can lead to several chronic health problems. It is common to see edema or water retention in the legs. Due to excess toxins in the body and brain, depression or mood changes may be more frequent. Arthritis is commonly seen due to drying out of tissues. Reduced absorption and metabolism of vitamins and nutrients is common due to reduction of activity of mucous membranses in the digestive system.

Kidney Lymphatic types: Due to insufficiency of the kidneys, problems like kidney disease or even kidney failure can occur as one ages. Poor kidney function often causes electrolyte imbalances, blood pressure problems and fatigue. Due to the accumulation of uric acid, rheumatoid arthritis and gout are also common.

Neurolymphatic types: Deficiencies in calcium, magnesium, and iron and zinc are commonly seen as well as the B vitamins. Long-term stress can exaust the adrenal glands and affect blood pressure and blood sugar. After the fifth decade, there is a tendency to develop muscle weakness, edema, and diabetes. In women as they age there may be a predisposition to cancer of the breast or female organs.

Hydro-lymphatic types: As one ages, there is a greater frequency of infections and a significant decrease in immune function. Fluid problems and edema is common and there is a predisposition to catarrhal problems with heavy mucus secretion like asthma and bronchitis. High blood pressure is also very common along with rheumatic problems and angina pectoris.

Hormonal types: Symptoms of this genetic type often begin after the age of 50. There is often a higher incidence of blood pressure fluctuations, fatigue, constipation, digestive problems, depression and a greater need for quality sleep. In women there may be premature menopause and in older men there are often problems with circulation and the prostate gland. There is a tendency to develop cancer of the endocrine organs such as the uterus and prostate in old age.

Connective tissue types: Osteoporosis, weak bones and spinal problems are common in old age. Circulation problems including hemorrhoids, varicose veins and a loss of elasticity of the blood vessels are common. In older age there may be heart complaints and the face is often heavily wrinkled with loose, hanging skin due to a rapid loss of collagen. The abdominal organs have a tendency to prolapse that may cause extra problems for the prostate gland or uterus and bladder.

Hematogenic types: As one ages, there is a higher frequency of digestive problems including slow moving bowels that often result in constipation. Gallstones or kidney stones are common and skin diseases due to poor liver function. Arteriosclerosis, angina pectoris and high cholesterol as well as memory loss and a reduced blood flow to the brain are particular concerns for this type in old age.

Plethoric types: Due to conditions of blood stagnation and congestion, problems like varicose veins, loss of tone in the veins, hemorrhoids and thromboses are common in old age. Angina pectoris or arteriosclerosis is frequent as well as thyroid and digestive problems caused by disturbances in bile flow.

Mixed types: Constipation and insufficient digestion due to reduction of digestive enzymes are very common as one reaches old age. Liver problems often affect bile production and can result in gallstones and gallbladder conditions. Pancreatic disease can also result in blood sugar fluctuations and diabetes.

What can slow down the aging process?

Adequate nutrition for the individual

Adequate nutrition that supports genetic weaknesses

Adequate nutrition for periods of stress that tax the body

Foods high in antioxidants

Daily relaxation and meditation

No smoking and limited alcohol

Positive thinking and emotions

Regular exercise

Adequate water intake

No drugs or medications

Clean air

Hobbies and interests

Friends and loved ones

Adequate sleep

Living close to nature

THE EYE FOR AN EYE DIET

MY CONCLUSION AND YOUR NEW BEGINNING

Frank Navratil BSc. N.D.

My Conclusion and Your New Beginning

I waited several months before I finally gained the necessary inspiration to write this conclusion. That time remarkably came during the massive floods that occurred here in the Czech Republic in August of 2002, those that the country had not seen in over 100 years and that even left some cities in surrounding countries like Germany and Austria in ruins. As I watched the accounts of all the massive devastation I couldn't help but think how we are all at mercy to the forces of nature.

However, from the end or conclusion of all natural disasters and often buried beneath the rubble emerges a chance for a new beginning, a new light that gives us strength once again to go on and rebuild what has been destroyed.

It is always heart breaking to see so much of what mankind has built be shattered within a very short time but I believe there is always some good to come from it and a valuable lesson to be learned.

We often have the naive impression that we have complete power over this world of ours and yes we have made great advances in technology, in transportation and in many other areas of science, but I believe we have forgotton one fundamental premise. The human race is part of a giant ecosystem, a living, breathing complex association of millions of elements in symbiosis. Every living organism has its vital place in this diverse ecosystem and must adhere to laws that are governed by nature. We cannot escape that basic fact. The power of nature is an incredible force and we cannot rule over it. For every negative action against nature, there is an equal and opposite reaction. Nature often strikes back when we cross the line. Hence, global warming, holes in the ozone layer, increasing incidence of catastrophes, strange weather patterns, floods, droughts and other examples of imbalances which are possibly only reactions to mankind's abuse of nature's laws.

The deterioration of our soil with chemical fertilizers and inefficient cultivation, the contamination of our water supply with pollutants and industrial chemicals, the destruction of trees, the laying down of pavement over millions of miles across this planet, has rendered useless a large part of our natural enviroment. All of these actions have an affect on the delicate balance of nature. How will nature respond to all this abuse? We really don't know for sure but perhaps we are already seeing it happen around us.

There are some like the Hunza or other native cultures that have not forgotten and who still respect the power of nature. They have learned to live in symbiosis, not in a world that comprises futile industrial attempts to control nature. They are the old and the wise and we need to learn from them but they too are gradually dwindling as modern civilization with its self-destructing technology rapidly encroaches and destroys everything we have ever known as natural in its presence.

Just as we are suppressing the power of nature beneath sheets of pavement, concrete jungles and industrial pollutants, we are doing the same with our bodies when we ingest chemical drugs, when we crash diet, when we ingest chemical additives with our foods, when we ignore our need for sleep or any other time we try to do what I call, fool our bodies. As we have come across time and time again in this book, the end result is that we only fool ourselves. The piece of machinery we call our body is a component of nature and it too has its delicate balance. The minute we disrupt that balance it fights back, this time through escalating rates of cancer, diabetes, obesity, digestive disorders and kidney and liver disease among many other health problems.

The wonderful gift or ability that we have been given is that our bodies are not like machines. Unlike machines, our bodies can regenerate. If it were not for this essential life process, this whole book would have absolutely no significance whatsoever. The fact that it is possible for our cells to regenerate is the last great hope that we can really cure the health or weight problems that we commonly suffer from.

As we mentioned, the cell is where it all happens. It is where our genetic material, our DNA is located and where all those vitamins, minerals, fats, proteins and carbohydrates ultimately end up. There they are utilized for the thousands of reactions that need to occur in our bodies. It is through understanding our nutritional needs that we can really see changes in the body and hence changes in our state of health and often state of mind.

The wonderful method of Iridology has shown us a way in which we can better understand those nutritional needs. It is very important to learn about basic principles of nutrition but we also need to understand our genetic strengths and weaknesses that make us the unique individuals that we are. These genetic traits strongly influence the kind of nutrition our body requires. Identifying your Genetic Eye Constitution is one way in which we can get closer to matching up our genetic weaknesses with specific targeted nutrition.

We also have to take into consideration that our nutritional demands change with the degree of stress we impose on the body. We have seen the various age-related and non age-related factors that can stress the body and place additional demands on nutrition.

At times it may seem that this whole game of nutrition is just too hard or just too complicated but it really comes down to one basic concept:

Give the body what it needs. If the body does not get what it needs, it breaks down and begins to degenerate and all those essential processes of life begin to malfunction. This opens the way for disease to occur.

How do we provide the body with what it needs?
1. Ingest a balanced variety of healthy nutrients as close to their natural form as possible
2. Adopt healthy holistic lifestyle habits
3. Target specific nutrition to support your genetic weaknesses (as seen in your Genetic Eye Constitution)
4. Be prepared to change your nutrition as you change, as you encounter stress and as you age

If you have understood these concepts you now have the key to the Eye for an Eye Diet. Take that key and open a new door and choose the right path. Make an intelligent decision and don't fall prey to unhealthy influences around you. To quote Robert Frost once again,

> *"Two roads diverged in a wood, and I-*
> *I took the one less traveled by,*
> *And that has made all the difference."*

I sincerely hope that whatever unnatural disaster you have subjected your body to, has found or is soon to find its conclusion and that this book has provided you with some natural light at the end of a long dark tunnel. I also hope it inspires you to emerge from old lifestyle and dietary habits to a new method of thinking and caring for your health. Like the aftermath of all great natural disasters, it is time for a new beginning, your new beginning, a time to get out from under the rubble, evaluate the damage done and to start re-building once again.

Thankyou for under-taking this journey with me through the Eye for an Eye Diet.

Yours in natural mind, body and spirit,

Frank Navratil BSc. N.D.

The Eye for an Eye Diet- Quick Reference Genetic Nutrition Table

Lymphatic Hyper-active

Main Common Complaints	Beneficial Foods	Beneficial Vitamins, Minerals, Herbs, Supplements	Other Advice
Lymphatic congestion, allergies-nose, throat ear, lungs, allergies to milk, sinusitis, bronchitis, asthma, arthritis, endocrine problems, swollen and painful lymphatic glands, retention of fluids	Almonds, egg yolk, green leafy vegetables, soybeans, sesame seeds, parsley, dried figs, bananas, apricots, avocado, dates, nuts, raisins, sardines, sunflower seeds, wholegrains, molasses, spinach, beets, broccoli, celery, olives, peas, tuna, apples, watermelon, lemon juice, pineapple, blueberries, grapes, garlic, horseradish, ginger, cayenne pepper, peppers, blackcurrants, guava, strawberries, rosehips, raw cabbage, brussel sprouts, lecithin, yeast, beans, corn, onions, natural yogurt, soured milk	Calcium, Potassium, Sodium, Magnesium, Iron, vitamin C, E, B, Beta-carotene, Shiitake mushrooms (*Lentinus edodes*), Echinacea, Golden Seal (*Hydrastis canadensis*), garlic, Ginseng, zinc, Lactobacillus acidophilus, Chlorella, Lecithin, Slippery Elm (*Ulmus fulva*), liquorice root (*Glycyrrhiza glabra*), Glucosamine Sulfate, Chondroitin Sulfate	Avoid milk products, refined grains, white bread, cakes, white sugar, caffeine, sugar, salt, and alcohol. Regular exercise, especially swimming. Regular lymphatic massage. Avoid excess meats, saturated fats and citrus fruits. Avoid cough suppressants as coughing helps get rid of mucous. Practice deep-breathing exercises and avoid smoking and smoky or smoggy environments. If you are older and suffering from arthritis or respiratory ailments, it may do you well to live in a warmer and dryer climate if possible. Drink plenty of water.

The Eye for an Eye Diet- Quick Reference Genetic Nutrition Table

Lymphatic Hypo-active

Main Common Complaints	Beneficial Foods	Beneficial Vitamins, Minerals, Herbs, Supplements	Other Advice
Slow recovery or regeneration, inability to eliminate waste, skin problems, infections, tonsillitis, nasal congestion inflammation of mucous membranes discharge from ears, nose, hardening of lymph nodes, sour breath, body odor weak liver and kidneys, edema, fatigue, depression, mood changes, reduced absorption, poor circulation and heart weakness	Cranberries, blueberries, garlic, green leafy vegetables, apricots, bananas, asparagus, celery, parsley, artichokes, black currants, juice of watermelon, raw beet, cranberry, lemon and carrot. teas made from parsley, dandelion, and raspberry, wholegrains, apples, bran, dates, prunes, beans, raw peas, broccoli, natural yogurt, soured milk, peppers, fruits, guava, pineapple, strawberries, rosehips, salmon, tuna, trout, sunflower seeds, sprouts, carrots, grapes, ginger, horseradish, cayenne pepper, watercress, olive oil, raw cabbage, corn, nuts, onions, sardines, avocado, eggs	Lecithin, bioflavonoids, vitamin C, E, Beta-carotene, methionine, choline, inositol, St. Mary's Thistle (*Silybum marianum*), dandelion (*Taraxacum officinale*), golden seal (*Hydrastis canadensis*). Coenzyme Q-10, cranberry extract, Evening Primrose oil, B-complex, Omega3 fatty acids, zinc supplements, Lactobacillus acidophilus, Chlorella, Gingko biloba, Echinacea, garlic	Reduce food additives, colors and preservatives. Reduce excess alcohol, protein, salt, and dairy products. Avoid white flour and white sugar. Avoid smoky or smoggy environments. Deep breathing exercises and relaxation methods. Plenty of exercise Skin brushing Exposure to sunlight Drink plenty of water.

The Eye for an Eye Diet - Quick Reference Genetic Nutrition Table

Kidney Lymphatic

Main Common Complaints	Beneficial Foods	Beneficial Vitamins, Minerals, Herbs, Supplements	Other Advice
Weak kidneys and liver, bags under eyes, edema, bladder infections, kidney stones, nephritis, tonsillitis, bronchitis, infections, hay fever, skin problems, migraines, arthritis, heart and circulation problems, lymphatic congestion, fatigue, high blood pressure	Alfalfa sprouts, cranberries, blueberries, garlic, apricots, green leafy vegetables, bananas, asparagus, celery, parsley, artichokes, black currants, juice of watermelon, raw beet, cranberry and lemon, teas from parsley, dandelion, and raspberry, beans, egg yolk, lecithin, liver, wholegrains, yeast, berries, fruits, skins of fruits and vegetables, nuts, olive oil, wheat germ, walnuts, red peppers, salmon, tuna, sardines	Lecithin, bioflavonoids, vitamin C, E, Beta-carotene, St.Mary's thistle (*Silybum marianum*), dandelion (*Taraxacum officinale*), Glucosamine sulfate, Chondroitin sulfate, Omega 3 fatty acids, natural vitamin E	Drink plenty of water. Avoid excess protein consumption. Avoid excess sugar and salt. Avoid excess intake of oxalates such as rhubarb, spinach or black tea Avoid acid-forming foods such as meats, milk products, white sugar and refined grains. Never resist the need to urinate and don't avoid drinking water just so that you won't have to go so often.

The Eye for an Eye Diet- Quick Reference Genetic Nutrition Table

Neurolymphatic

Main Common Complaints	Beneficial Foods	Beneficial Vitamins, Minerals, Herbs, Supplements	Other Advice
Sensitivity to stress, weakness in the nerves, anxiety, neuroses, migraines, lymphatic congestion, allergies, nerve related asthma, stomach and skin problems, deficient in B vitamins, ulcers, weak adrenal glands, predisposition to breast cancer and female organs	Green leafy vegetables, eggs, legumes, pumpkin and sunflower seeds, sprouts, whole-grains, organ meats, chicken, fish, yeast, avocado, molasses, sardines, soybeans, Brewer's yeast, cashews, almonds, parsnips, apricots, oysters, wheat germ, fruits, berries, peppers, broccoli, parsley, ginger, natural yogurt, soured milk, lecithin	Lactobacillus acidophilus, Chlorella, Vitamin C, B-complex, lecithin, ginseng, licorice root extract (*Glycyrrhiza glabra*), Valerian (*Valeriana officinalis*), Gingko biloba	Avoid sugar and white flour products. Avoid coffee, tea and alcohol. Regular exercise, meditation, yoga Avoid refined sugars and grains, milk products and excess meats. Daily relaxation Drink plenty of water.

The Eye for an Eye Diet - Quick Reference Genetic Nutrition Table

Hydro-lymphatic

Main Common Complaints	Beneficial Foods	Beneficial Vitamins, Minerals, Herbs, Supplements	Other Advice
Chronic lymphatic congestion, persistent infections, asthma, bronchitis, colds, flu, heart weakness, high blood pressure, rheumatoid arthritis, fluid retention, angina pectoris, urinary infections, gallstones, kidney stones	Grape juice, cranberries, salmon, tuna, sardines, grape juice, blackberries, cherries, lecithin, yeast, beans, corn, onions, natural yogurt, soured milk, almonds, egg yolk, green leafy vegetables, soybeans, sesame seeds, parsley, dried figs, bananas, apricots, avocado, dates, cashews, pecans, raisins, sunflower seeds, wholegrains, molasses, spinach, beets, broccoli, celery, liver, olives, peas, oysters, apples, watermelon, lemon juice, pineapple, blueberries, grapes, garlic, cayenne pepper, horseradish, giner, peppers, black currants, guava, strawberries, rosehips, raw cabbage, brussel sprouts, cauliflower	Calcium, potassium, magnesium, sodium, iron, vitamin C, B-complex, E, Beta-carotene, Shiitake mushrooms (*Lentinus edodes*), Echinacea, Golden Seal (*Hydrastis canadensis*), Garlic, Bee pollen, Ginseng, zinc, Lactobacillus acidophilus, Chlorella, Lecithin, Slippery Elm (*Ulmus fulva*), liquorice root (*Glycyrrhiza glabra*), Glucosoamine sulfate, Chondroitin sulfate, Evening Primrose oil, Omega-3 fatty acids, coenzyme Q-10, vitamins C, E, bioflavonoids, garlic, ginkgo biloba, ginseng, hawthorn berry (*Crataegus monogyna*)	Avoid milk products, refined grains and white sugar. Avoid coffee, salt and alcohol. Regular exercise Regular lymphatic massage Avoid excess meats, saturated fats and citrus fruits. Avoid cough suppressants. Avoid smoky or smoggy environments. Practice deep-breathing exercises. Drink plenty of water.

The Eye for an Eye Diet- Quick Reference Genetic Nutrition Table

Hormonal

Main Common Complaints	Beneficial Foods	Beneficial Vitamins, Minerals, Herbs, Supplements	Other Advice
Hormonal disturbances, fluctuations in blood sugar, disturbances in mineral economy, painful menstruation, early menopause, prostate gland, thyroid gland problems, blood pressure fluctuations, fatigue, depression, constipation, poor digestion, pre-disposition to uterine and prostate cancer	Alfalfa, cucumber, cod, kelp, seaweed, oats, pumpkin seeds, oils from safflower, soybean and sunflower, corn, cashews, garlic, tuna, green leafy vegetables, eggs, legumes, nuts and seeds, sprouts, wholegrains, organ meats, chicken, fish, yeast, avocado, peppers, black currants, broccoli, parsley, guava, pineapple, strawberries, rosehips, raw cabbage, brussel sprouts, cauliflower, liver, carrots, apricots, fish liver oils, almonds, onions, dates, grape juice, asparagus, lobster, oysters, raisins, prunes, shrimp, sesames seeds, brown rice, ginger, bananas, sardines, clams, tomatoes, turnips	Lactobacillus acidophillus, Chlorella, Slippery Elm (*Ulmus Fulva*), Methionine, choline, inositol, Vitamin C, St. Mary's thistle (*Silybum marianum*), dandelion (*Taraxacum officinale*), vitamins A, E, B-complex, selenium, zinc, chromium picolinate, digestive enzymes, alfalfa, flaxseed oil, barberry (*Berberis vulgaris*), juniper berries (*Juniperus communis*), licorice (*Glycyrrhiza glabra*), ginko biloba, ginseng, black cohosh extract (*Cimifuga racemosa*). Wild Yam (*Dioscorea villosa*), Dong Quai extract (*Angelica sinensis*), Evening Primrose Oil, Kelp	Avoid white sugar and potatoes. Use whole fruits rather than juices. Eat smaller meals more often. Avoid stress and relax daily. Avoid refined foods and chemical additives. Include plenty of fiber. Avoid radiation from microwaves. Exercise regularly; yoga Deep breathing exercises and spend time in nature Drink plenty of water.

The Eye for an Eye Diet- Quick Reference Genetic Nutrition Table

Connective Tissue

Main Common Complaints	Beneficial Foods	Beneficial Vitamins, Minerals, Herbs, Supplements	Other Advice
Prolapse of abdominal organs, weak connective tissues and ligaments, frequent injuries, slow recovery and healing, poor posture, spinal problems, weakness in metabolism of vitamin C, heavy wrinkling in old age, circulation problems, infertility, heart complaints	Fruits, peppers, black currants, broccoli, guava, parsley, pineapple, strawberries, rosehips, raw cabbage, brussel sprouts, cauliflower, berries, skins of fruits and vegetables, oysters, veal, shrimp, herring, ginger, sunflower seeds, wholegrains, salmon, tuna, sardines, almonds, sesame seeds, cashews, molasses, soybeans, spinach, beets, legumes, eggs, juice from watermelon, raw beets, cranberries and lemon, teas from parsley, dandelion and raspberry, beans, lecithin, liver, yeast, sprouts, chicken, avocado, natural yogurt or soured milk	Vitamin C, E, B-complex, calcium, magnesium, bioflavonoids, acerola, Echinacea, bee pollen, Beta-carotene, Shiitake mushrooms (*Lentinus edodes*), Golden Seal (*Hydrastis canadensis*), Garlic, Ginseng, zinc, Lactobacillus acidophilus, Chlorella, Digestive enzymes, Slippery elm (*Ulmus fulva*). Omega-3 fatty acids, Glucosamine sulfate, lecithin, alfalfa	Regular endurance, flexibility and muscular strength exercise Avoid smoking, stress and smoggy environments. Eat plenty of raw fruits and vegetables. Ensure adequate sunlight. Avoid excess alcohol, fried foods, caffeine and sugar. Drink plenty of water.

The Eye for an Eye Diet- Quick Reference Genetic Nutrition Table

Hematogenic

Main Common Complaints	Beneficial Foods	Beneficial Vitamins, Minerals, Herbs, Supplements	Other Advice
Over-active nervous system, liver and gallbladder weakness, rapid circulation and viscous blood, asthma, thyroid problems, digestive problems, gallstones and kidney stones, skin disease, high cholesterol, arteriosclerosis, angina pectoris, varicose veins	Olive oil with lemon juice, apples, applesauce, beets, salmon, tuna, sardines, cabbage, kelp, avocado, chicken, liver, alfalfa, sprouts, legumes, green leafy vegetables, lettuce, natural yogurt and soured milk, onions, peppers, black currant, broccoli, guava, parsley, pineapple, strawberries, rosehips, raw cabbage, brussel sprouts, cauliflower, beans, eggs, lecithin, wholegrains, corn, oil rom safflower, soybean and sunflower, garlic, sunflower seeds, oysters, veal, shrimp, herring, ginger, berries, skins of fruits and vegetables	Methionine, choline, inositol, vitamin C, E, B-complex, lecithin, alfalfa, Omega-3 fatty acids, garlic, zinc, lysine, Coenzyme Q-10, gingko biloba, barberry (*Berberis vulgaris*), milk thistle (*Silybum marianum*), licorice (*Glycyrrhiza glabra*), peppermint (*Mentha piperita*), dandelion (*Taraxacum officinale*), bioflavonoids, Lactobacillus acidophilus, Chlorella, Slippery Elm (*Ulmus fulva*), Evening Primrose Oil, Omega-3 fatty acids, Valerian (*Valeriana officinalis*), chamomile, olive oil with lemon juice	Avoid milk products, refined carbohydrates, fried and spicy foods, saturated fats and margarines. Avoid excess coffee, alcohol, salt and sugar. Avoid ingestion of artificial additives. Stop smoking. Ensure regular exercise. Avoid negative emotions. Ensure adequate fiber. Skin brushing Drink plenty of water.

The Eye for an Eye Diet- Quick Reference Genetic Nutrition Table

Plethoric

Main Common Complaints	Beneficial Foods	Beneficial Vitamins, Minerals, Herbs, Supplements	Other Advice
Sluggish venous flow of blood, skin problems and red complexion, disturbances in bile flow, asthma, moody behavior, depression, fatigue, backaches, angina pectoris, thyroid gland problems, high blood cholesterol, arteriosclerosis, digestive problems	Almonds, oil from safflower, soybean and sunflower, shellfish, mushrooms, oysters, kelp, seaweed, salmon, tuna, sardines, bran, bananas, prunes, raw peas, alfalfa, cabbage, green leafy vegetables, lettuce, soybeans, spinach, sprouts, avocado, chicken, legumes, yeast, olive oil with lemon juice, apples, applesauce, beets, onions, natural yogurt or soured milk, garlic, corn, nuts, whole-grains, beans, lecithin, liver, brussel sprouts, cauliflower, raw cabbage, rosehips, strawberries, pineapple, parsley, guava, broccoli, black currant, peppers, sunflower seed, ginger, herring, oysters	Methionine, choline, inositol, vitamin C, E, B-complex, lecithin, digestive enzymes, zinc, alfalfa, Omega-3 fatty acids, garlic, lysine, coenzyme Q-10, gingko biloba, barberry (*Berberis vulgaris*), milk thistle (*Silybum marianum*), licorice (*Glycyrrhiza glabra*), peppermint (*Mentha piperita*), dandelion (*Taraxacum officinale*), bioflavonoids Lactobacillus acidophilus, Chlorella, Slippery Elm (*Ulmus fulva*), Evening Primrose Oil	Ensure regular exercise to improve venous blood flow. Avoid artificial additives. Avoid alcohol, coffee, saturated fats, fried foods, margarines, and excess refined carbohydrates and refined grains. Limit meat consumption and increase fiber to reduce constipation. Reduce milk products. Ensure adequate raw fruits and vegetables. Drink plenty of water.

The Eye for an Eye Diet- Quick Reference Genetic Nutrition Table

Mixed

Main Common Complaints	Beneficial Foods	Beneficial Vitamins, Minerals, Herbs, Supplements	Other Advice
Gastrointestinal problems, liver weakness, gallstones and gallbladder disease, fluctuating blood sugar levels, pancreatic problems, reduction of digestive enzymes, nerve weakness, acne, flatulence, constipation	Bran, dates, bananas, prunes, raw peas, grape juice, asparagus, lobster, oysters, raisins, shrimp, veal, herring, ginger, sunflower seeds, apples, applesauce, beets, olive oil with lemon juice, avocado, green leafy vegetables, sprouts, alfalfa, onions, sardines, natural yogurt or soured milk, sardines, garlic, corn, nuts, yeast, beans, lecithin, liver, wholegrains, eggs, cauliflower, strawberries, rosehips, raw cabbage, brussel sprouts, pineapple, broccoli, guava, parsley, peppers, black currants	Methionine, choline, inositol, vitamin C, E, B-complex, lecithin, digestive enzymes, Omega-3 fatty acids, garlic, barberry (*Berberis vulgaris*), milk thistle (*Silybum marianum*), licorice (*Glycyrrhiza glabra*), peppermint (*Mentha piperita*), dandelion (*Taraxacum officinale*), Lactobacillus acidophilus, Chlorella, Slippery Elm (*Ulmus fulva*), Evening Primrose Oil, Omega-3 fatty acids, zinc, Valerian (*Valeriana officinalis*), Chamomile, ginger, Chromium piccolinate, olive oil and lemon juice	Eat small regular meals five times a day. Avoid artificial additives. Avoid alcohol, coffee, saturated fats, fried foods, margarines, and excess refined carbohydrates and refined grains. Increase fiber to reduce constipation. Reduce milk products. Ensure adequate raw fruits and vegetables. Drink plenty of water.

Other books by Frank Navratil BSc. N.D.

If you have enjoyed this book and are interested in reading more about Iridology read:

"For Your Eyes Only"
also by Frank Navratil BSc. N.D.

This book has been translated into several languages and is one of the best books in the world on the art and science of Iridology.

The Eye for an Eye Diet Nutrition Courses on CD-ROM

Please contact us if you are interested in taking any of these exciting courses written by Frank Navratil BSc. N.D. about nutritional health and natural medicine.

Holistic Nutrition 1– Beginner Nutrition
Holistic Nutriton 2 – Intermediate Nutrition
Holistic Nutrition 3 – Advanced Nutrition

For Your Eyes Only Iridology Courses on CD-ROM

Iris 1 – Beginner Iridology
Iris 2 – Intermediate Iridology
Iris 3 – Advanced Iridology

Other available products

A variety of iridology and holistic nutrition charts, flashcards, CD-ROMs, magnifying lenses and other products are also available.

Contact

To order iridology and holistic nutrition books and products or for information on our CD-ROM home study courses contact us at:

irisproducts@irisdiagnosis.net

More information:

www.irisdiagnosis.net
The world's largest resource of iridology and nutrition education products

Return to Health Books

Index

Absorption 28
Acerola 149
Acne 238
Additives 108
Age-related times of stress 45
Aging 275
Alcohol 123
Allergies 240
Amino acids 59
Anorexia 234
Arthritis 242
Artificial sweeteners 116
Asthma 243
Avocado 130
Bioflavonoids 71, 149
Biotin 70
Bleaching agents 112
Blue eyes 171
Brown eyes 171
Calcium 75
Cancer 245
Carbohydrates 56
Cell 53
Chlorella 134
Chlorine 76
Chocolate 127
Cholesterol 140
Choline 72
Chromium 79
Chronic fatigue 247
Circulation 28
Coffee 121
Colors 110
Complex carbohydrates 56
Condiments 119
Connective Tissue constitution 175, 185, 199, 216, 226
Constipation 249
Constitution 19

Copper 78
Dates 131
Depression 250
Detoxification 29
Detoxification organs 30
Diabetes 252
Diarrhea 249
Digestion 27
Digestive disorders 255
Drugs 31, 36
Earthworms 51
Egg 130
Echinacea 147
Eczema 256
Endurance 158
Enzymes 137, 145
Eskimos 16
Essential fatty acids 73
Exercise 156
Fast foods 117
Fasting 154
Fat 62
Fatigue 247
Fats 62
Fertilizers 104
Fiber 88
Figs 131
Fish 132
Flavors 111
Flexibility 160
Folic Acid 70
Food contaminants 104
Food pyramid 94
Food storage 100
Gallbladder disease 264
Garlic 131
Genetic engineered foods 98
Genetic Eye constitution 19, 168, 173
Genotype 14

Gingko biloba 147
Ginseng 148
Grapes 134
Headache 268
Heart disease 257
Hematogenic constitution 175, 189, 200, 217, 227
Hesperidin 71
High blood pressure 259
Holistic health 33
Hormonal constitution 175, 184, 198, 213, 226
Hunza 16
Hydro-lymphatic constitution 175, 183, 197, 211, 225
Hypertension 259
Illusions 13
Infertility 260
Ingestion 26
Inositol 72
Instant foods 118
Iodine 78
Iridology 18
Iris 173
Iron 77
Kidney disease 263
Kidney Lymphatic constitution 174, 181, 195, 208, 224
Lactobacillus acidophilius 144
Lecithin 146
Liver disease 264
Living food 50
Lymphatic Hyper-active constitution 174, 179, 193, 203, 223
Lymphatic Hypo-active constitution 174, 180, 194, 205, 224
Magnesium 77
Margarine 118
Meat 119
Menopause 266
Menstruation 266
Microorganisms 105

Microwave cooking 103
Migraine 268
Milk 114
Minerals 74
Mixed constitution 176, 191, 201, 220, 228
Modifying agents 112
Muscular strength 159
Neurolymphatic constitution 175, 182, 196, 209, 225
Niacin 69
Non age-related times of stress 46
Nuts 131
Obesity 239
Olive oil 132
Omega-3 fatty acids 146
Oral contraceptive pill 261
Organic food 51
Osteoporosis 270
Overweight 230
Pantothenic Acid 69
Para-aminobenzoic acid 72
Pesticides 104
Phenotype 14
Phosphorus 75
Plethoric constitution 176, 190, 201, 218, 227
Polyunsaturated fatty acids 63
Potassium 76
Potatoes 118
Pregnancy 260
Preservatives 110
Propolis 148
Proteins 59
Psychological problems 47
Pupil 173
Pyramid 94
Pyridoxine 69
Regeneration 30
Riboflavin 68
Rutin 71
Saturated fat 126

Saturated fatty acids   63
Seeds   131
Selenium   79
Simple carbohydrates   58
Smoked food   117
Sodium   76
Soft drinks   116
Stress   271
Sugar   115, 124
Sulfur   75
Sweeteners   111
Tea   121
Thiamine   68
Tinnitis   273
Trans fatty acids   63
Underweight   231
Unsaturated fatty acids   63

Utilization   29
Vegeterian   149
Vitamin A   66
Vitamin B1   68
Vitamin B12   70
Vitamin B2   68
Vitamin B3   69
Vitamin B5   69
Vitamin B6   69
Vitamin C   71
Vitamin D   67
Vitamin E   67, 149
Vitamins   65
Water   80
White flour   115
Zinc   78